BELGIUM AND THE MONARCHY

From National Independence to National Disintegration

HERMAN VAN GOETHEM

BELGIUM AND THE MONARCHY

From National Independence to National Disintegration

Cover photo: Brussels, Royal Archives
Cover design: Stipontwerpt, Antwerp
Book design: Stipontwerpt, Antwerp
Printed in Belgium

–

Published by UPA
UPA is an imprint of ASP nv
(Academic and Scientific Publishers nv)
Ravensteingalerij 28
B-1000 Brussels
Tel. +0032 (0)2 289 26 50
Fax +0032 (0)2 289 26 59
e-mail: info@aspeditions.be
www.upa-editions.be

–

Translation of the Dutch text: Ian Connerty

–

ISBN 978 90 5487 698 4
NUR 698
Legal Deposit D/2010/11.161/015

–

All rights reserved. No parts of this book may be reproduced or transmitted in any form or by any means, electronic, mechanical, photocopying, recording, or otherwise, without the prior written permission of the publisher.

–

Illustrations:
- Brussels, Royal Archives: pp. 40, 88, 96, 101, 109, 110, 117, 118, 124, 125, 134, 206, 238, 239, 253
- Antwerp, Private Collection Janssens: pp. 23, 28, 30, 33, 42, 51, 52, 54, 56, 64, 72, 73, 78, 136, 143, 155, 162, 170, 172, 176, 180, 183, 190
- Antwerp, Private Collection Van Goethem: pp. 19, 91, 148, 196, 199, 259
- Antwerp, Private Collection Vanlangendonck: p. 81
- Jules Van Paesschen, photographer: p. 217
- *Boudewijn. Een koning en zijn tijd*, Tielt, Lannoo and Gemeentekrediet, 1998: pp. 228, 267
- Reiner Van Hove, photographer: p. 244
- Photo Reuters: p. 246

Introduction   9

- National administration and national language   11
- Dutch-speaking Flanders, French-speaking Wallonia and bilingual Brussels   12
- Belgium after 1893 – in search of a national concept   15
- Problems of terminology: nationalists, the Flemish Movement and federalism   16
- A focus on the monarchy   20

1 **Leopold I** (1831-1865)   25
- The influence of French language and culture in Flanders and the question of Belgian neutrality   27
- Leopold I and the 'true Belgians'   34
- Leopold I, advocate of the Flemish Movement   38

2 **Leopold II** (1865-1909) *The Situation Stagnates*   47
- An unknown king   48
- Crown Prince Boudewijn – a light in the darkness   50
- A concerned Leopold II   53

3 **The first cracks in the façade of national unity**   59
- The consolidation of a mass Flemish Movement   61
- New institutional problems   62
- In search of an answer: Belgium and bilingualism   67
- Monolingual Wallonia, bilingual Flanders   69
- The beginnings of a federal debate: the break-up of Belgium   71
- The social and economic agenda of the Flemish Movement   73
- Monolingualism for Flanders! … or not really?   75
- "Long live Wallonia, free and independent!"   80

4 **Albert I** (until 1918) *King and Commander-in-Chief* — **85**
- On the eve of the Great War — 87
- August 1914 – a 'foreign' war and an impossible domestic peace — 92
- Problems at the Belgian front — 95
- 1916: activist fireworks and a failed government declaration — 100
- Spring 1917 - towards and independent Flanders — 108
- The Open Letter to King Albert of 11 July 1917 — 113
- Summer 1917: General De Ceuninck acts and Albert makes himself heard — 115
- Nationalist discourse and holy wars — 120
- Summer 1917: King Albert's two-pronged policy — 122
- Spring 1918 – the government in panic — 123

5 **Albert I** (1918-1934) — **131**
- The Delacroix administration and the speech from the throne — 132
- Questions in parliament – May 1919 — 137
- King Albert and Frans Van Cauwelaert — 138
- Language legislation: 1921-1923 — 142
- 1921-1923: the first cracks in the Belgian national fabrics — 146
- Albert I and the Flemish question, 1925-1928 — 150
- The *coup de grâce* for bilingualism in Flanders, 1928-1932 — 153
- King Albert and the bilingualism of the central administration — 160

6 **Leopold III** (1934-1944/1950) *The Radical King* — **167**
- In continuation of King Albert, 1934-1940 — 169
- Belgium – on the road towards federalization, 1936-1940 — 173
- May 1940-September 1944 — 180

7 **Prince Charles** (1944-1950) *The Watchful Regent of Belgium* — **187**

8	**King Boudewijn** (1950-1993) *A Chronicle of Political Impotence*	**193**
•	The 'quiet' fifties	195
•	The Gilson language laws, 1962-1963	199
•	The state reforms of 1970	202
•	Belgium in the 1970s – lost in the mist. Region forming, Voeren and the 'rand' municipalities	210
•	Belgium in the 1970s – the monarchy under fire, Voeren and the amnesty question	213
•	King Boudewijn wants progress, part I: The Egmont Pact	216
•	King Boudewijn wants progress, part II: the constitutional reforms of 1980	222
•	King Boudwijn puts the breaks on: 1983-1988	224
•	1991-1993: state reform, confederalism and separatism	229
9	**Albert II** *A Land Adrift*	**235**
	Conclusion and diagnosis	**249**
•	Belgium 1831-1893	251
•	The power of institutional change: 1893 as a critical juncture	254
•	King Albert I and the Flemish Movement	258
•	The end of the "narrow-minded and egotistical minority": a balance	262
•	The power of an institutional choice: 1970	264
•	Belgium; an institutional perpetuum mobile	265
•	Belgium – a diagnosis	268
•	The end of Belgium? New critical junctures	276
	Endnotes	**281**
	Bibliography	**291**

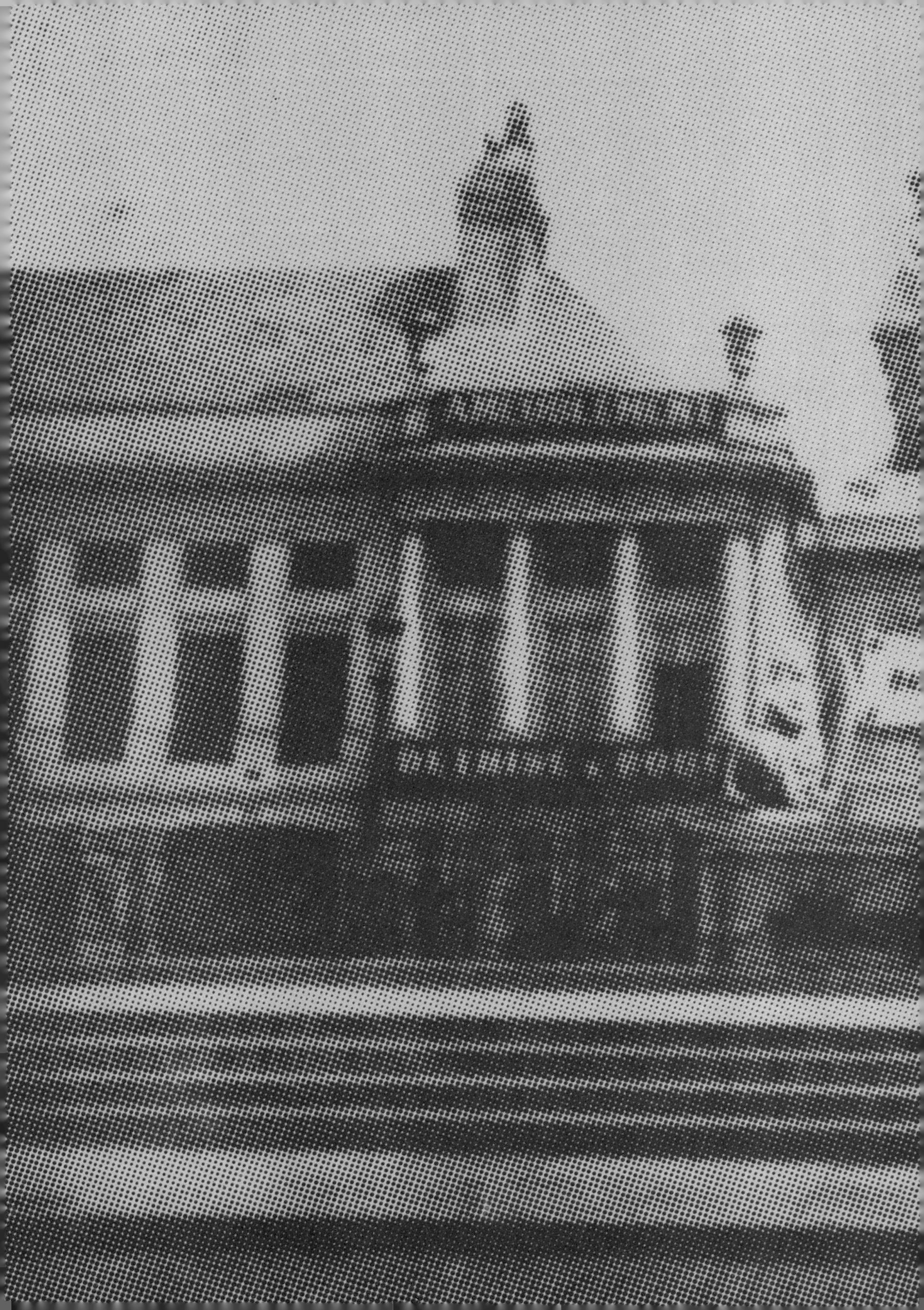

Introduction

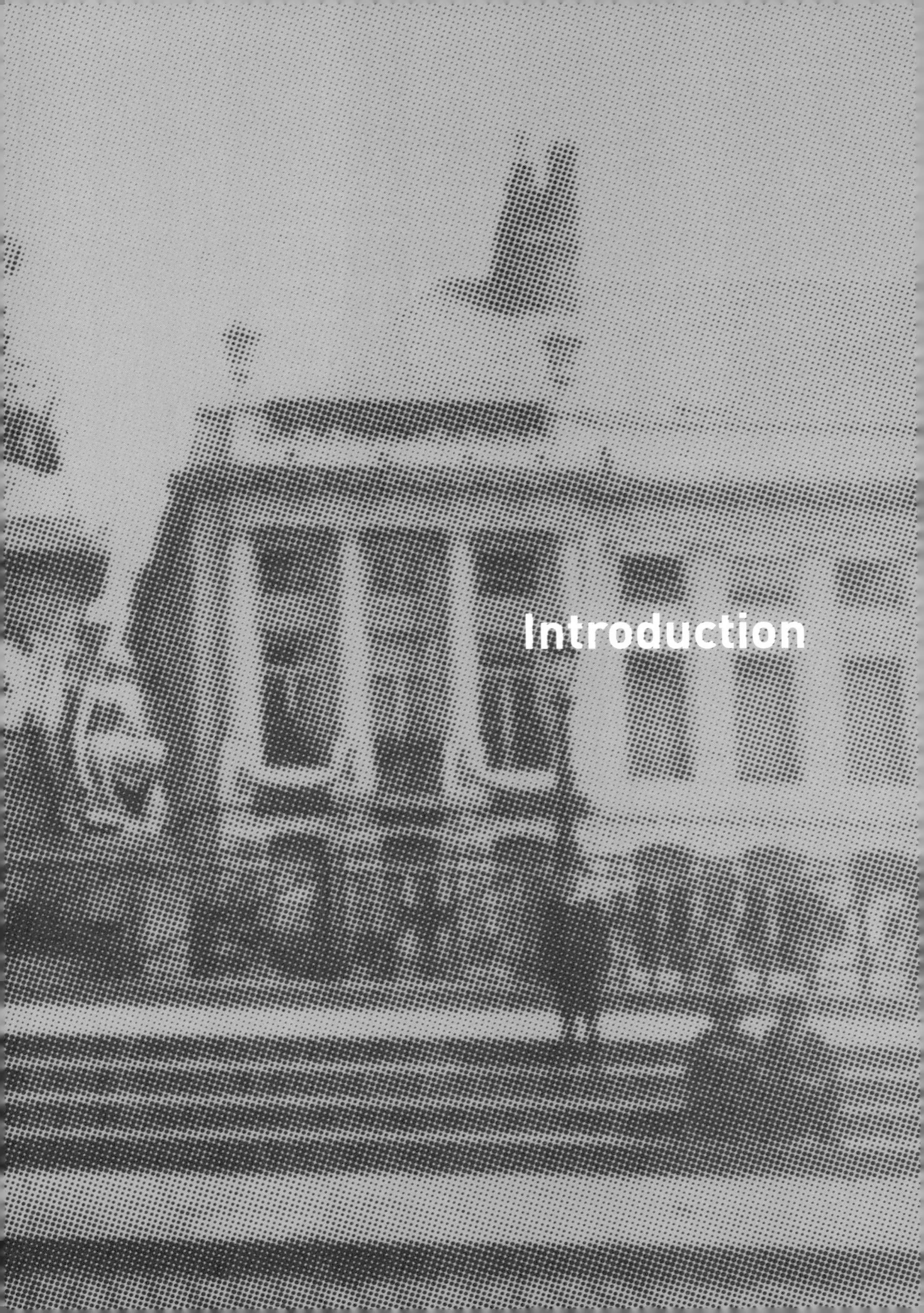

Belgium is standing at a crossroads. Since June 2007, the nation has been immersed in the deepest institutional crisis since its foundation in 1830-1831. At the time of writing (this book was completed in December 2010), this crisis seems no nearer solution, and Belgium continues to progress along the road towards national disintegration.

Both at home and abroad, the same question is being asked with increasing frequency. Is Belgium nearing the end of the road? Is this land, which lies at the very heart of Europe, about to disintegrate? And this at a time when many of the most important European institutions are based in Brussels, the capital of Belgium, but also the capital of Europe? Nobody, of course, can predict the future, but it is at least possible to make an analysis of the current situation. What exactly are the core issues? What are the most pressing problems? Such an analysis must ipso facto be an historical analysis. The story of Belgium and its particular difficulties is an old story, whose origins date back many centuries.

In order to understand this analysis, the reader will first need to understand some of the complex concepts relating to government, administration and the use of language in Belgium and in Europe.

National administration and national language

The history of language in Europe is a complex one. In the course of the centuries, a considerable number of 'traditional' linguistic minorities have disappeared. For example, in 1790 scarcely 2 million of the 12 million people living in France actually spoke French. The remaining 10 million spoke a variety of other languages, which often remained unwritten, such as Breton, Gascon or Béarnais. The majority of these now defunct languages were based on Latin, the language of the Roman Empire. Perhaps the most well known of them is the language of the Provencal, which was revived in a written form under the influence of Frédéric Mistral and the Romantic Movement in the 19th century, and which has since survived as a kind of popular folklore language.

Yet Provencal was the exception rather than the rule. Most unwritten languages had little chance of survival within the context of 19th century Europe, with its increasingly industrialised society and the growth of the modern liberal state. The state sought to promote industry by a policy of free trade, and it was evident that greater efficiency could be obtained if a country was governed in a single administrative language. As a result, the years following 1789 saw the gradual disappearance of one regional language after another. Even well-established written languages sometimes failed to survive. Consider the example of French-Flanders, an area of 'historic' Flanders which was annexed by France during the 17th century and never returned (this area is roughly bounded by the modern-day French cities of Dunkirk, Lille and St. Omer; see map at the beginning of this book). This region used to be exclusively Dutch-speaking, but following annexation under Louis XIV French was introduced as the single language for justice and administration. The local people continued to speak Dutch until the beginning of the 20th century, but this popular language was finally destined to disappear in the course of just three generations, its demise being hastened by the introduction of compulsory military service and compulsory education (both of which required a standardised language). In short, Dutch in French-Flanders has undergone a similar fate to the language of the Provencal: it only survives in the memories of the very old or as a relic of folklore.

Dutch-speaking Flanders, French-speaking Wallonia and bilingual Brussels

Belgium currently has a population of 10.6 million people, spread across a national territory which measures some 30,000 square kilometres. This small country has a federal political structure, as the result of a series of reforms introduced in the years after 1970. There are three officially designated 'regions': Flanders, Wallonia and Brussels. They each possess their own parliament, government and legislative powers, allied to a significant degree of administrative autonomy. Together, they controlled in the period 2000-2010 about 40% of Belgian national revenue.

Antwerp, Ghent and Bruges are the most important cities in Flanders. The main cities in Wallonia are Namur, Liege and Charleroi. The national capital is the city of Brussels. (For the following see map.)

In Flanders the official language is Dutch (also called Flemish). This means that Dutch is the language used in government, administration, education and the judiciary. In Wallonia, the official language for these same matters is French. In both regions, this official linguistic position is closely matched by linguistic reality: in Flanders the local population speaks Dutch and in Wallonia the local population speaks French. To this basic dichotomy should be added the fact that each region regards the language of the other region as a 'foreign' language, of which they often have little more than a passive knowledge. The situation is very different in Brussels. This region is officially bilingual, so that both Dutch and French are used.

There are approximately 6.1 million Flemings, 3.4 million Walloons, with a further 1.1 million people living in Brussels: commonly known as 'Brusselaars' or 'Bruxellois'.

As far as Wallonia is concerned, it should also be noted that it contains a small area near the German border – the so-called East Cantons – where German is both spoken and recognised as the official language. The population of these East Cantons is roughly 70,000 people.

However, the most striking thing about Belgium is the fact it is divided by a language frontier, which runs across the country in a roughly east-west direction. This frontier separates Dutch-speaking Flanders from French-speaking Wallonia, just as dramatically the River Rhine separates France from Germany. The frontier is sharply defined and its position has hardly changed during the past 1,000 years. Its origins date back to the fall of the Roman Empire and the subsequent 'invasion' of the German tribes, following which Europe was split into two distinct spheres of influence: the post-Roman world and the Germanic world. In the regions which remained essentially Roman, the indigenous language was usually replaced by a variant of Latin, the language spoken by the Romans. In regions where Roman influence largely disappeared or ceased to exist, the indigenous language was often replaced by a variant of one of the Germanic tongues. Viewed in linguistic terms, a 'mixed' Romano-Germanic language was not evident at all. This would be like trying to mix English and French. In other words, it was a question of one language or the other. As the centuries passed, a number of words were eventually swapped between these different languages, but the different linguistic basis of the languages remained essentially unaltered, as did the regions in which they were spoken.

The Roman-German linguistic frontier cuts across modern-day Belgium like a knife, with a Germanic language, Dutch, spoken in the North (Flanders) and a Latin language, French, spoken in the South (Wallonia). This was the traditionally accepted – but potentially divisive – linguistic situation which was inherited by the Belgian nation upon its foundation in 1830-1831.

This traditional language frontier was enshrined in law by the Belgian state reforms of 1962-1963. In view of the fact that one region wished to be governed in Dutch, while the other region wished to be governed in French, it was agreed by both sides that it was necessary to establish exactly where the boundary between the two linguistic communities should be drawn.

During the implementation of the 1962-1963 reforms, it was accepted that the language frontier could not always be 100% absolute. There were a limited number of small towns and villages, close to the linguistic border, where both Dutch-speakers and French-speakers were resident. To solve this problem, the politicians in Brussels decided to grant these villages what came to be known as 'language facilities'. This is an important concept for an understanding of the problems which followed, and which still exist today. Language facilities mean that the speakers of the minority language have the right, for themselves, to use that language in all matters relating to public administration, justice and the education of their children, at least as far as primary schooling (ages 6 to 12 years) is concerned. Similar language facilities were also granted to a small number of German-speakers, living in villages which bordered on the East Cantons. In these German-speaking East Cantons, language facilities are likewise granted to French-speakers.

It is worth emphasising that in the villages with language facilities, both languages do not enjoy an equal status. The majority language is the 'norm' for external matters and also the language for internal administration and communication. The minority language is only used as an exception, and its application is therefore much more restricted in comparison with the majority language. In short, language facilities are regarded as a kind of 'service' for the minority grouping.

To summarise, this situation means that Belgium has two distinct, official, *monolingual* regions: Dutch-speaking Flanders and French-speaking Wallonia. The only exceptions to this officially enshrined monolingualism are the villages along the language frontier, to which language facilities have been granted. However, these villages are so limited in number and size that they do very little to alter the overall picture of administrative homogeneity.

In addition to the two monolingual regions, there is also the large *bilingual* region of Brussels, with its 1.1 million inhabitants. Geographically, this linguistic island is located in Flanders, but close to the language frontier with Wallonia. The region is clearly defined in territorial terms, and is often referred to as the Brussels agglomeration. This agglomeration consists of 19 separate municipalities, including Brussels Capital City, and is collectively known as Brussels-19. Officially, the Dutch and French languages stand on an equal footing in Brussels-19. This means that public administration must be available in both languages, so that the local population are free to choose whichever language they prefer to speak. Yet while Brussels-19 is considered to be bilingual, it is estimated that only about 10% of these 1.1 million 'Brusselaars' are speaking Dutch. This means that while the Flemings form a majority in the nation as a whole, they actually represent only a small minority in the nation's capital.

In contrast to the situation in Flanders and Wallonia, the use of language in the Brussels region is constantly evolving. Brussels was once a predominantly Flemish city, in which just 15% of the population spoke French. However, the years following national independence in 1830-1831 saw a steadily increasing decline in the speaking of Dutch. The continuing 'Frenchification' of the national capital and its surrounding municipalities is a major political problem, which is as current today as it was in the 19th century. The bilingual Brussels region officially consists of 19 municipalities, but the growing influence of the French language is now spreading to the towns and villages which border Brussels-19, the so called 'rand' around Brussels. This is essentially the result of an influx of 'migrants' from French-speaking Wallonia or bilingual Brussels, who cross the language frontier in order to settle in areas which are traditionally Dutch-speaking. These 'migrants' are often well-to-do, so that they form a significant part of the socio-economic upper class. This process of 'gentrification' has gradually forced out the original – but poorer – (and largely Dutch-speaking) population, who are unable to afford the resultant increase in land and house prices.

This complex situation explains why the reformers of 1962-1963 also agreed that language facilities should be granted to six municipalities which are located in Flanders, but which share a common border with bilingual Brussels-19. These six municipalities form part of the Brussels 'rand' and have a population of some 60,000. Officially, the French-speakers represent a minority in these municipalities, but in reality they now form a majority in four of the six towns. This has naturally raised a number of questions about the political status of these communities. Are language facilities sufficient to meet the needs of the local population in practical terms? Or might it not be better to transfer the municipalities to the bilingual Brussels region? The Flemings and the Walloons have very different answers to these questions, and their failure to agree on such matters lies at the basis of many long-running Belgian political problems, which seem increasingly incapable of solution.

Belgium after 1893 – in search of a national concept

The question of the viability of Belgium as a geo-political construction will be a constantly recurring theme of this historical analysis. In the decades after 1830-1831 Belgium had a single administrative language – French – which was also used in Dutch-speaking Flanders. This was only made possible by the fact that the Flemish establishment at that time was predominantly bilingual. The Flemish elite's excellent knowledge of French was primarily a consequence of the period 1795-1814, when Belgium was formally annexed by revolutionary France, which imposed its own language as the sole language of government. This obviously had a profound effect on the Flemish ruling class: just as an official who is forced to work every day in English will eventually become Anglicised, so it was inevitable that the Flemish elite would gradually assume the manners, customs and language of their French overlords. However, the fact that during the census of 1846 just 3% of Flemings claimed to be able to speak French underlines the limited nature of bilingualism in Flanders. Even so, this French-speaking minority exerted an influence far beyond its numbers, since the census-based voting system ensured that this linguistic minority actually constituted a majority of the people entitled to vote in Flanders. In short, the bilingual Flemish elite held effective political power in its own hands.

A small group – initially, a very small group – of Flemings was increasingly unhappy with the further encroachment of French as the language of government and administration in Flanders. To begin with, this group was little more than a loose association of romantic dreamers. At this time, the language problem was not regarded as being a major political issue. One of the main arguments of this book is that such a situation was only possible under the census-based electoral system which existed until the end of the 19th century, i.e. during the period 1831 to 1893. The electoral reforms of 1893, which ensured that every man had at least one vote, led to the democratisation of Belgian society and acted as an important stimulus for the development of various 'social movements', including social democracy and Christian democracy. It also encouraged the foundation of what eventually came to be known as the Flemish Movement. This, in turn, provoked a reaction in Wallonia and inspired the creation of a Walloon Movement, which sought to 'protect' the French-speaking part of the country against Flemish demands. Just 20 years later, on the eve of the First World War, Flemings and Walloons were already discussing the possible institutional division of the nation along linguistic lines, and by the beginning of the 1930s federalism was firmly established on the national political agenda.

In this respect, the crucial question which needs to be answered is why the language legislation enacted between 1930 and 1938, and later perfected by a further series of reforms between 1962 and 1963, failed to provide a lasting solution to the nationality problem in Belgium. This legislation introduced administrative monolingualism in Flanders and removed from the bilingual Flemish elite their right to be governed, judged and educated in French. This should, in time, have led to a relaxation of linguistic tensions, but it did not. The reasons for this 'failure' must be sought in the subsequent programmes of state reform which were implemented in the years following 1970 and which resulted in the gradual institutional partition of the nation. What were the options chosen by successive governments during this process of federalisation? And why did these options fail to live up to people's expectations?

Because it now seems clear that they did indeed fail, and that the Belgian state continues to become increasingly divided along regional lines, in a manner which shows little sign of ending in the foreseeable future.

Problems of terminology: nationalists, the Flemish Movement and federalism

The Belgian nationality crisis has been dragging on for more than a century, prompted by the political activism of nationalist movements in Flanders (the Flemish Movement) and Wallonia (the Walloon Movement). Many other parts of Europe are also facing the revival of old issues relating to the rights of various national and ethnic groupings. However, in this respect, the Belgian nationality problem is atypical. There are no bullets flying through the streets of Antwerp and Liege. There is no need for UN peacekeepers in Brussels. On the contrary, the Flemings, the Walloons and the Brusselaars have been coexisting peacefully for several centuries. Having said this, both Flanders and Wallonia possess a strongly developed nationalist culture of their own, which is enhanced and passed down from one generation to the next. This process of cultural transference is not only characterised by the cold language of political reason, which argues in terms of own national power and own national gain, but also by a highly-charged emotional analysis, which often seems to owe little to rationality and much to the emotive power of ritual and symbolism.

The Flemish Movement, in particular, is strongly attached to its rituals, which range from the waving of its black-and-yellow Flemish Lion flags, right through to the famous IJzer Pilgrimage, an annual meeting of a thousand or so militant supporters of the Flemish cause, where an atmosphere of right-wing extremism is never very far away. The antics of these 'pilgrims' in the village of Diksmuide is by no means representative of wider public opinion in Flanders, yet they continue to attract the attention and (justifiable) incomprehension of the outside world. By contrast, the Walloon Movement places much less emphasis on ritual, but is just as strongly attached to its symbols as its Flemish counterpart. In this respect, the highly emotional quarrels about language facilities in some of the towns and villages along the language border – for example, in the Voer district of eastern Belgium during the period between the 1960s and the 1980s, and nowadays in the six municipalities of the 'rand' around Brussels – have a powerful symbolic value in both Wallonia and Flanders. Although they are almost insignificant in territorial terms, these areas serve as magnets which polarise all the irrational and emotional elements which characterise the nationality conflict between the Flemings and the Walloons. In this sense, they can be compared to the Protestant Orange Day marches in Northern Ireland: provocative displays of rivalry, which those who are not directly involved are wholly unable to understand.

Considerations of this kind lead to a further important question: what exactly does the term 'nationalism' mean within the Belgian context? An analysis of the Belgian situation first requires us to examine the origins of the Flemish and Walloon sub-nationalities. To do this, we can use the concept of *imagined community*, as developed by the historian Benedict Anderson. According to Anderson, nationalism can be seen as the mainspring of such an imagined community, in which people conceive an idealised notion of their own values, stories, myths and traditions, which they propagate and maintain from one generation to the next. In the minds of these people, their feeling of solidarity with other members of the same community is first and foremost based on their belief in shared common characteristics, which results in the minimising of differences within the community and the exaggeration of differences with 'others'. This eventually solidifies into a hardened 'us' and 'them' mentality, which is crucial to both the nature and the strength of the communal identity. This nationalist belief, this imagined community, is a fiction which can develop into a reality if it is given shape and form within a framework of concrete institutions, rituals and actions. Anderson has been rightly criticised for placing too heavy an emphasis on this 'subjectivist' construction. More objective criteria also play an important role in the development of a nationalist movement, such as a close identification with a specific geographical area. These criteria allow us to analyse the *ethnie*, in accordance with the theories developed by Anthony Smith. An ethnie is a group of people who believe in the existence of an own culture, who see themselves as a separate community with a separate identity and name, who share a common ethnic descent and who have a strong emotional attachment with the land occupied for successive generations by their forefathers.

Ethnies, as defined above, can also develop into nations, when they become associated with a modern state with clearly defined boundaries and its own economic identity. In multi-ethnic states, the judicial-political reality and the imagined ethnic fatherland seldom coincide. Belgium is just such a multi-ethnic state, with its clear split between Flemings and Walloons, and consequently is threatened with national disintegration as a result of the development of two internal and irreconcilable national movements.

Based on the analyses of Anderson and Smith, it is fair to characterise both the Flemish and the Walloon movements since their creation in the 19th century as 'nationalist'. However, this concept is not always useful for an analysis of the 'internal' Belgian situation. Questions such as 'who is a nationalist?' will therefore be approached from a more contemporary perspective, using the political criteria of the moment to form a meaningful assessment. The precise meaning of 'nationalism' within a Belgian framework needs to be interpreted in accordance with the changing contexts of the times. Some further explanation may serve to make this point clearer.

During the 19th century, a militant of the Flemish Movement – a *flamingant* or a *Vlaamsgezinde* – was someone who wished to find a place for the Dutch language *alongside* French in the public life of Flanders. This implied the use of Dutch in some shape or form in local government, the judiciary, the army, the education system and the press, but it did *not* imply the eradication of French throughout the region. In other words, during this period the militants were advocates of bilingualism in Flanders, based on a more widespread use of Dutch, but with extensive language facilities available for those who still wished to speak French. However, the years around 1900 witnessed a growing radicalisation of the political programme of the Flemish Movement. The more extreme militants now began to agitate in favour of a monolingual Flanders, with the abolition of all existing language facilities for the French-speakers (the large majority of whom were bilingual). At the same time, there were other more moderate militants, who continued to argue for the preservation of these facilities, particularly in the field of education. But as the mainstream gradually moved in the direction of the extremists, so it became increasingly difficult to describe the defenders of the language facilities as belonging to the Flemish Movement. In fact, after 1918 they were often disparagingly referred to as *Franskiljons*: a term of abuse roughly equivalents to the English 'frogs' or 'Frenchies'. Yesterday's militants had become today's reactionaries.

From 1912 onwards, yet another new radical trend emerged within the Flemish Movement. On this occasion the more militant elements began to call for the transformation of the unitary Belgian state into a more federal structure. They proposed to amend the constitution in order to allow a greater degree of self-government for both Flanders and Wallonia. It was the adherents of this new policy who were eventually described as being 'Flemish nationalists'. This is also the first meaning of the term 'Flemish nationalist' as used in this book: a person who sought to achieve greater political autonomy for Flanders, through a transfer of powers from the

A Flemish demonstration held on 11 July 1909, on the occasion of the commemoration of the legendary Battle of the Golden Spurs in 1302, when the citizens' army of Flanders defeated the might of feudal France. The protest banners demand the introduction of Dutch at the University of Ghent. The university was in the heart of Dutch-speaking Flanders, but the tuition was entirely in French.

central government to the regions, thereby creating a federal state structure. However, after the First World War the demands of the most radical militants in the Flemish Movement became still more extreme, so that some so-called Flemish nationalists now wished to move beyond mere federalism. This new breed of militants wanted nothing less than separatism, the creation of a fully independent Flemish state (with or without the possible addition of Flemish – i.e., Dutch-speaking – territories in Northern France). This is therefore the second meaning of the term 'Flemish nationalist', as used in this book. In contemporary Belgium the term is still used to refer to the separatists within the Flemish Movement: a small but powerful minority.

From the above explanations, it should already be apparent that within the Belgian political context the words 'federalism' and 'federalisation' also have a different meaning from what one might normally expect. In other countries, federalism usually implies a bringing together of disparate regional entities, whereas in Belgium – and therefore in this book – it means precisely the opposite: the greater separation of the component regions. Belgium has therefore been transformed from a state organised on a unitary basis into a state organised on a federal basis, whereas in most federal countries the reverse process is more usually the case. In this sense Belgium can perhaps best be compared with Canada, rather than with Germany or the United States.

A focus on the monarchy

The analysis in this book is based on a specific angle of approach; namely, the role of the monarchy. This theme has been chosen with care: the kings of Belgium occupy a central position in the long history of Belgian nationalism and national evolution.

The kings in question are Leopold I (1831-1865), who was succeeded by his son Leopold II (1865-1909), who in turn was succeeded by his nephew Albert I (1909-1934). Next to ascend the throne was Albert's son, Leopold III (1934-1950), whose perceived pro-German stance during the Second World War led him to be replaced by his brother, Prince Charles, who acted as regent between 1944 and 1950. This was the period of the so-called 'Royal Question'. In 1950, Leopold abdicated in favour of his son, Boudewijn (1950-1993). His death brought his brother Albert II (1993-) to the throne. Albert is still the reigning monarch, although his son, Crown Prince Philip, is being carefully groomed behind the scenes to eventually take his place. Given the current political situation in Belgium, this promises to be a difficult succession.

The kings of Belgium are the living personification of the continued existence of their nation. It is the king who appoints and dismisses his ministers (although always with the formal consent of a minister in function) and his constitutional position inevitably makes him a player in the history of inter-regional disputes. As a result, this has also made the position of the king a matter for nationalist debate. In this respect, one of the most persistent questions is whether or not the monarchs – as the ultimate symbol of the unified Belgian nation – could and should have done more to 'save' their country.

Yet this question is not always as straightforward as it seems. For example, in Flanders there has long been historical discussion about the attitude of King Albert I towards the Flemish Movement. However, the position of Albert I cannot be viewed in isolation. His policy was, at least in part, determined by the policy of his predecessors, Leopold I and Leopold II. Yet we know very little about the policy of this latter king, since he gave orders that large parts of his political archives should be destroyed towards the end of his life (presumably in order to conceal some of his shadier financial dealings and his often unsavoury activities in Congo). What we do know is that the eldest son of King Leopold II, Crown Prince Boudewijn, was popularly seen as some kind of Flemish 'messiah'. However, he died at the age of 21 in 1891, before he ever had the chance to come to the throne. The Flemings were devastated by this loss, and it naturally influenced the way in which they looked at Boudewijn's 'replacement' as heir to the throne. Moreover, this was one of the many periods in Belgian history when the future of the nation seemed uncertain. The electoral reforms of 1893 heralded in a new era of democratisation, which set in motion a process of transformation which was destined to dismantle the unitary state and reduce the role of the monarch to that of a pawn on the chessboard of inter-regional dispute. This has been made abundantly plain during the reign of the current king, Albert II, although it was less apparent under his predecessor, Boudewijn I.

If we undertake an analysis of Belgian history from the perspective of the monarchy, we need first to answer a crucial question: just how powerful is the king in Belgium? In 1830-1831 the Kingdom of Belgium was established as a 'modern', constitutional and parliamentary monarchy. This constitution was intended to reconcile the traditional rights of the monarch with the democratic rights of the people. But it was the Nation, represented in a democratically elected parliament, which was sovereign. The king was not granted any executive powers of his own, but was obliged to work in collaboration with his ministers. Together, they formed the government. It was, however, agreed that the position of the king should be inviolable, in order to ensure the hereditary succession of the monarchy.

In reality, the king of Belgium is essentially a privileged counsellor for his ministers. It is his task to encourage, warn and advise. This means that a shrewd king can sometimes exert considerable influence. Even so, it is the ministers who have the final word, since they are free to accept or reject the counsel of the king, as they see fit.

Traditionally, the monarch exercises his advisory role with great discretion. In principle, his opinions are only communicated directly to his ministers in private. This implies that the outside world should learn little or nothing of the 'secrets of Laken' (where the royal residence is situated). Should this not be the case, the king might find himself open to public criticism, in which case his position might become 'violable', with all that this entails for the constitutional nature of his function. In addition to this discretion, the king is also protected by a constitutional exemption from responsibility. This means that ministers remain at all times fully responsible for decisions taken by the government, even if they have followed the king's advice. In short, the ministers agree to cover for the king. After 1831, it soon became apparent that this ministerial cover would also need to apply to the public appearances of the monarch. Royal speeches and royal attendance at particular functions could often have political connotations. For this reason, the competent minister was usually required to give his approval in advance. But if problems arose, it was agreed that everything must be done to keep the king out of the firing line. Or as a principle of British constitutional law succinctly puts it: "The king can do no wrong".

On the negative side of the coin, this fiction of royal inviolability ensures that the king is highly dependent upon his ministers. He can take no political decision or action without their prior knowledge and consent. And a wise minister will only grant this consent if he is confident that a majority in parliament would be likely to support him: otherwise he might find himself under attack for opinions actually formulated and uttered by the king, who would remain 'untouchable'.

Yet it would be wrong to assume that the king is little more than a puppet. There are always ways for him to exert influence and pressure. And during the process of government formation he possesses very real powers, albeit within strict constitutional limitations. The results of the election are obviously indicative, but it is the right of the king to invite a *formateur* to form the new government. Nevertheless, it is self-evident that the king can only appoint a *formateur* who is likely to command a parliamentary majority. Nor can the wishes of the political parties be wholly ignored. In particular, this last factor has significantly altered the balance of power in the government-forming process. The grip of the king on ministerial appointments has declined in proportion to the growth in the power of the political parties.

Once the government has taken office, the king has much less scope to influence policy. This influence has been gradually eroded, from the time of King Leopold I until the present day, particularly as a result of the following developments: the growth of political parties since the 19th century (with a corresponding growth in pressure for the appointment of 'their' ministers); the democratisation of the franchise in 1893 (which significantly increased the power of parliament); the growth of coalition government after 1918 (with its delicate internal balances, in sharp contrast to the previous system of single-party dominance); and finally the so-called Royal Question under King Leopold III. The growing importance of the media has also made its effects felt. The monarchy has always been a popular subject for the popular press, and the growth in newspaper circulation since the end of the 19th century has allowed them to mobilise and shape public opinion, either for or against the king. This has encouraged the monarchs (particularly the more recent incumbents) to act with greater caution.

All these factors mean that Leopold I was able to have a more direct impact on the political life of the nation than King Boudewijn or Albert II. Yet having said this, all Belgium's monarchs have ultimately been required to work within the same formal constitutional limitations: they must back down when ministers make clear their intention to resign if royal 'pressure' is not withdrawn. Some kings, notably King Leopold II, have sometimes ignored this unwritten rule, but it has usually rebounded against them in the long run. In this sense, Belgium is like most other constitutional monarchies: parliamentary sovereignty and ministerial responsibility will ultimately triumph over royal obstinacy.

Introduction

Brussels, the *Place des Martyrs*, monument dedicated to the Belgians who died in their 'fight for freedom' in 1830.

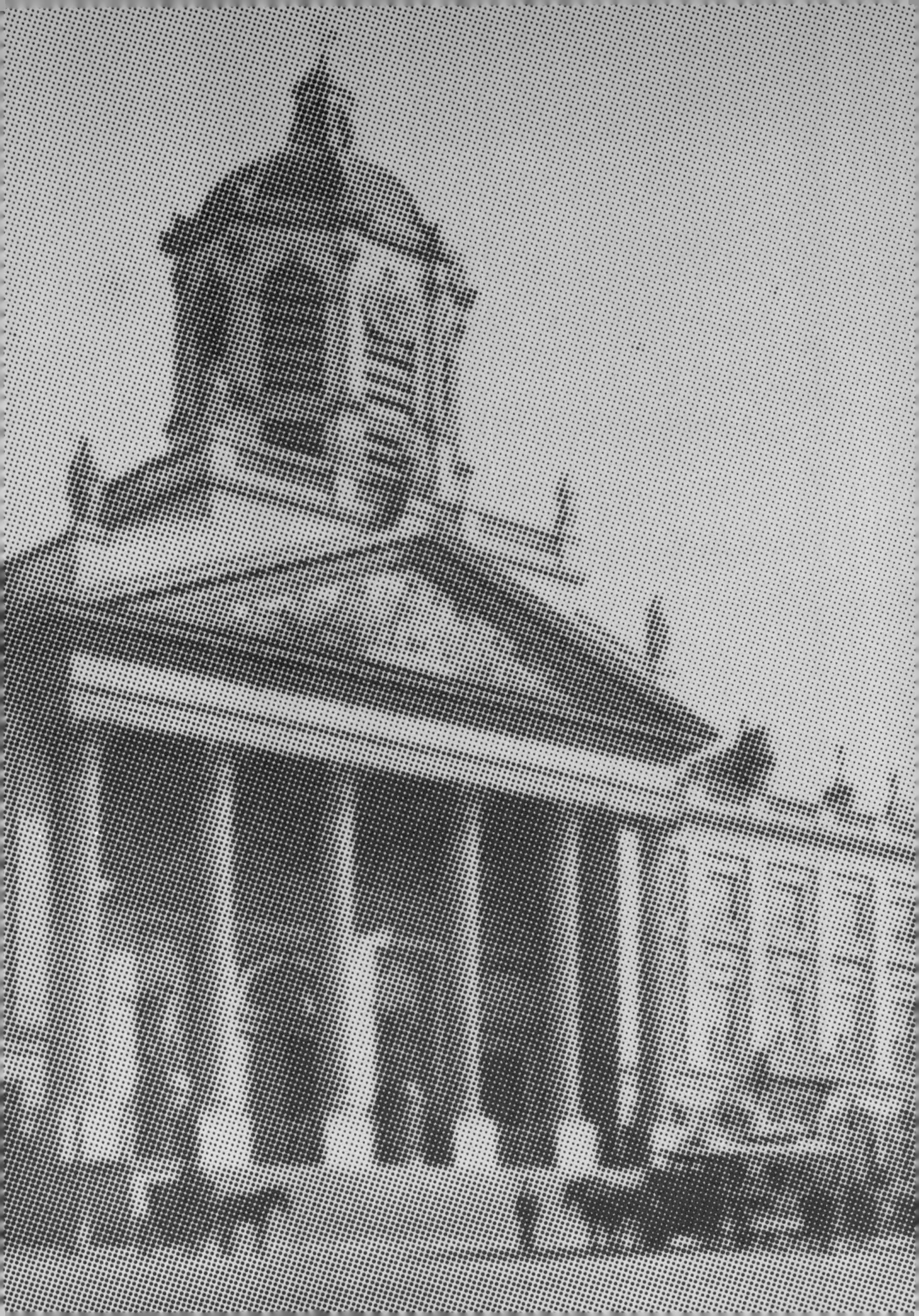

1

Leopold I

(1831-1865)

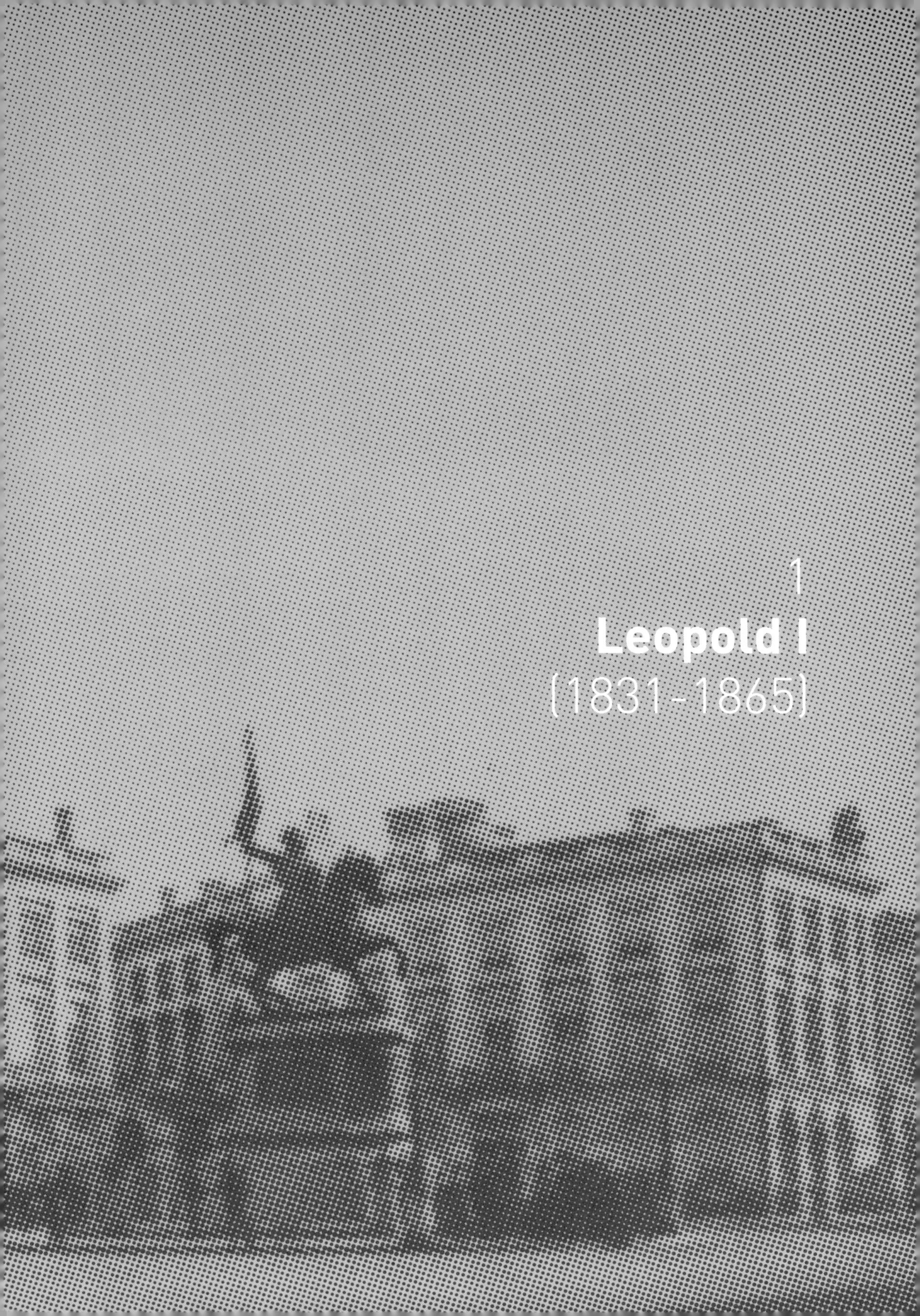

The influence of French language and culture in Flanders and the question of Belgian neutrality

What was the position of the Dutch language in Belgium when King Leopold ascended the throne in 1831?

During the 18th century – when the region was still referred to as the Southern Netherlands – Dutch was used as the language of justice and administration throughout Flanders. Dutch was also the language of the people – as it had been for centuries. True, French had become fashionable with the elite in Flanders, as it was in many other cities throughout Europe at this time, but this was little more than a fad. It was only possible to speak of a significant degree of 'Frenchification' in Brussels, influenced to a certain extent by the habits of the royal court and by a small 'immigration' from Wallonia. Yet even here Dutch remained the dominant tongue.

The Dutch spoken in Flanders was fundamentally the same Dutch spoken in the Dutch Republic (the present day Netherlands, at the northern frontier of Belgium). It was true that the languages in these two geo-political entities had grown somewhat apart after the cession of the republican provinces from the Southern Netherlands in 1585, and many people referred to the language of the south as 'Flemish' and the language of the north as 'Hollands'. Even so, these two 'languages' were in essence nothing more than minor variants of a common Dutch language: spelling and pronunciation might differ from place to place, but the origins and basic grammatical rules were the same everywhere.

The development of the language in the northern provinces was able to benefit from a flourishing period of literary growth in the years after 1585. This led to a certain consensus about matters of spelling. However, this was not the case in the south. Here the 'purity' of the language was diluted by a multiplicity of dialects and different forms of spelling. There was no question of any consistent level of literary achievement. Rather the reverse. If the Dutch of Flanders survived in written form during the 18th century, this was largely due to the fact that it was still used as the language of civil administration.

Between 1795 and 1814 Belgium was effectively a part of France, having been annexed by the revolutionary French republic and later by the French empire of Napoleon Bonaparte. These new political masters governed the province of Flanders almost exclusively in French. This applied to both the administration and to the justice system – and represented a radical break with the situation which had existed prior to 1795. After the fall of Napoleon, the Belgian provinces were united in 1815 with their old northern neighbours to create a unified Kingdom of the Netherlands. This was a so-called 'enlightened monarchy' and its new king was the Hollander, King William I of the House of Orange-Nassau.

Belgium and the Monarchy. From National Independence to National Disintegration.

Brussels, the *Place Royale*, where King Leopold I ascended to the throne on 21 July 1831

   In 1819, William took the decision to abolish the Napoleonic obligation to govern Flanders in the French tongue. This was followed by a brief period in which civil officials in Flanders were free to use their own language of preference, but it was expected that from 1823 onwards every official would use Dutch. However, after 25 years during which French was the sole language of government, the Flemish establishment found it no easy matter to once again address the common people in their own tongue. They had become used to working in French – and that was the way they wanted to keep it. Nevertheless, on 1 January 1823 the official use of Dutch as the language of administration was introduced throughout Flanders, including Brussels. This led to a number of problems in the latter city, where a significant minority of the elite was unable to speak Dutch. This meant that these officials were forced to move to the French-speaking province of Wallonia, in order to further pursue their careers. Elsewhere in Flanders the introduction of Dutch was less problematical, since the French-speaking officials often spoke Dutch at home. William's measures were also disturbing for the French-speakers in Wallonia, since there were indications that in the long term he planned to introduce Dutch as the official language in their province as well. This would have been highly contentious, since the Wallonian elite spoke only French – and nothing else. However, things never progressed that far. In September 1830 revolution broke out, and modern-day Belgium declared its independence from what is now modern day Holland (or The Netherlands).

The Belgian revolutionaries repealed the legislation which made the use of Dutch compulsory as the language of government in Flanders. Instead, the new Belgian constitution enshrined the principle of 'freedom of language'. In the spirit of the times, this meant that the country's officials were once again at liberty to choose their own language of preference. In Brussels, this more or less implied an automatic choice for French, since the city administration wanted to be able to attract members of the Wallonian elite. The Flemish elite knew French, but the Wallonia elite knew no Dutch. If you wanted to 'fish in both pools' – a desire which was natural in the new nation's capital city – then French was the obvious choice.

Elsewhere in Flanders there was a more gradually reintroduction of French into local government and the judicial system. Viewed from a contemporary perspective, the use of French seemed to offer a number of political and administrative advantages. The 19th century was the century of the great nation states and it was widely believed that the best manner to ensure the continued unity of these states was the introduction of a single language of government.

By extension, this principle was not only applied in Flanders to government, but also to the education of the country's children. Here the introduction of French was even more far-reaching, since it was important that the next generation of the national elite should be groomed for careers in public administration – and this meant, essentially, for careers in French. Dutch was only taught to children in primary education, between the ages of 6 and 12 years. Even then, these primary schools were expected to 'prepare' their better pupils for the transition to secondary education (12-18 years), where the lessons were given in French. This was a process which accelerated dramatically after 1830.

There were other groups of Flemish Belgians who opted for French for more specific reasons. Belgium was a Catholic country, and the anti-clerical liberals regarded the Flemish language with suspicion, since the Catholic Church had traditionally supported this 'language of the people'. In turn, the clerics regarded French as the language of the modernists, whose new philosophy was harmful to the peaceful development of society. The Church believed in individuals who were essentially unfree and unequal, locked in the structure of a hierarchical society, where authority and obedience were the greatest virtues. The French Revolution – with its emphasis on the free and autonomous individual – seriously challenged this view. As a result, the Church regarded the French Revolution – and, by extension, the French language – as a modern form of heresy, which found expression not only in a new form of government, but also in the pages of a licentious press, disreputable novels and immoral plays.

In this sense, French was indeed the language of modernity and free-thinking. Consequently, many of the new ideas and new social developments simply passed the Flemish people by, trapped as they were in their illiteracy and their ignorance of the French language. Little wonder that the majority of the liberals came to see Flemish as a symbol for social ossification and obscurantism of the worst kind.

Leopold I of Saxe-Coburg-Gotha (1790-1865), King of the Belgians from 1831 onwards. A photograph from 1856 by court photographer Louis Ghémar.

As each year passed, so the use and influence of French in the machinery of state in Flanders became ever greater. This progress was as insidious as it was far-reaching, often being aided by the social conventions of the time. As soon as one person used French in a particular matter, the other professionals involved in the same matter felt inclined to follow – otherwise they might risk being seen as 'backward' or 'old-fashioned'. And once one matter had been dealt with in French, it was not always easy to switch back to Dutch for the next one. The combined effect of these mechanisms was considerable – and rapid. By 1840, most courts and local administrative bodies in Flanders were using French as the sole language for their written records, particular in the cities or at arrondissement level and above. It was still possible to use Dutch in these institutions, but only as a spoken language, principally when dealing with the non-French-speaking masses. When statements were being taken, the secretary or clerk of the court would immediately translate the spoken Flemish into written French.

1 Leopold I (1831-1865)

Whilst indifference and social conventions were important factors in helping to spread the use of French, they were by no means the only ones. In reality, it was becoming more and more difficult in practical terms to continue using Dutch as a language for written administration in Flanders. In contrast to the days of the Ancien Régime, there was no longer any clear consensus with regard to the meanings of technical and legal terminology in Dutch. During the period 1819-1830 the 'Hollands' of the Northern Dutch served as a universally accepted guideline, even in Flanders, since it contained many elements of a strongly-developed, uniform language. All this changed with the Revolution of 1830. From September 1830 onwards, it was no longer the North Hollanders who were penning the legal texts and the administrative guidelines. And with very few exceptions, the Dutch-speaking intelligentsia in Flanders was unable to fill the resulting void. The imprecision of Flemish made it less suitable as an administrative language, where clarity and accuracy of meaning are paramount. Official texts are binding – and must therefore not be capable of misinterpretation. In these circumstances, it will come as no surprise that after the Revolution of 1830 the translation of new laws and decrees into Dutch became a major difficulty. If we read the modest efforts of the Flemish literati of the 1830s, or if we peruse the even more modest efforts of the Flemish journalists of the same period, it soon becomes clear that the Dutch language was facing a serious crisis in Belgium.

That the language did not disappear completely from Flanders is largely attributable to two specific factors. Firstly, there was the influence of the Romantic Movement, which placed a new emphasis on 'popular' customs and dialects. Secondly, there was the special position which Belgium occupied on the political stage of Europe – and this brings us neatly to the role of the Belgian monarchy.

When Leopold of Saksen-Coburg-Gotha came to the throne in 1831, the Flemish part of his kingdom was already in the grip of an increasing spread in the use of French in its institutional life. As a native German and the widower of the British crown-princess, Charlotte, he had little time or sympathy for these complex social, cultural and political issues. He was certainly not a Francophile per se. In his correspondence, he used German, French and English, depending upon the nationality of his correspondent. This same linguistic flexibility was also evident in his conversation. When the Dutch ambassador Falck arrived to present his credentials in October 1839, he had a long and detailed conversation with Leopold, during which the king switched between French and High-German, "to discuss certain matters in greater confidence" (as Falck later commented).[1] This was just one of many occasions when Leopold seemed keen to highlight the similarities between Dutch and his native tongue.

Nor did the king feel any strong affinity towards the new philosophy of the post-revolutionary world. Born in 1790 – a year after the French Revolution began – he belonged to a transitional generation. He accepted the new modern forms of state in a formal sense (he had little choice), but in most matters his inclinations were those of the Ancien Régime. He had no time for anti-clerical or – even worse – anti-religious liberals. Although born a Protestant, he not only respected but also actively supported the Catholic Church. For him, religion was the best basis for the development of a viable social and political system. He regarded the Catholic faith as one of the most important elements for promoting unity within his kingdom: the cement of the nation. It was with good reason that he referred to the Catholic religion on more than one occasion as being the nationalism of Belgium.

For this reason, if for no other, the king would have been prepared to support the use of the popular language of the people in Flanders. After all, this was the language used by the Church for the propagation of the Faith. But there were other reasons too: much weightier political reasons. The most important of these was the geographical position of Belgium and its role in the European balance of power. Belgium was a small country sandwiched between two giants: Germany and France. Both of them would have been delighted to annex their pocket-sized neighbour, since it would have significantly improved their own strategic and economic position. The truth of this assertion had been demonstrated repeatedly throughout history, as this tiny patch of land had been fought over time after time, often with the mastery of Europe at stake. In fact, it was often referred to as *le boulevard de l'Europe* and as recently as 1815 had been the scene of the last big showdown between the European Great Powers.

Following Napoleon's final defeat at Waterloo, these Great Powers (Prussia, Austria, England, France and Russia) devised a neat geo-political solution which they hoped would secure peace for generations to come. At the Congress of Vienna, they agreed to set up a large neutral buffer between France and the vulnerable principalities of Germany. This buffer was the Kingdom of the Netherlands. However, in 1830 this buffer was split in two, following the Belgian Revolution. The Great Powers were unwilling or unable to intervene militarily, and so the existence of the new nation was quickly recognised and accepted. This meant that Belgium also inherited the key role as buffer between France and Germany, and therefore meant that the country had a vital part to play in maintaining the European balance of power. However, this role could only be played if Belgium agreed to accept permanent neutrality – and if it could persuade its more powerful neighbours not to infringe this neutrality. This was the key task of the Belgian monarchy: to watch over the position of Belgium in Europe. It was a task for which the first Belgian king was ideally suited. His birth, marriage and career made him a model European prince: it was almost as if he was a mandatory of the Great Powers. This 'European mandate' would also influence the policy of his successors, particularly Albert I (1909-1934) and Leopold III (1934-1944/1950).

Flanders and the use of the Dutch language in Belgium were important pawns in the delicate but dangerous chess game of neutrality. The largest – and most obvious – problem was France. It is possible to give numerous examples of the manner

Officers in the Belgian army, circa 1860. During this period (and for many years to come), the officer corps conversed exclusively in French.

in which the French exerted their influence over their northern neighbour. The Belgian state universities were packed with French lecturers and professors. The Belgian army was similarly staffed with a number of French officers (as a consequence of the absence of a national officer training corps for home-grown talent). The government contained a number of French-born ministers (who had become naturalised Belgians). The development of Belgian civil law closely followed the French model. The press was dominated by French newspaper barons who employed French editors. In the first years following independence, some Belgian newspapers even included news from France on the pages for 'domestic affairs'! At the same time, newspapers in France were writing that there was no such thing as "*une nationalité belge*" (a Belgian nationality), in a clear attempt to whip up pro-annexation sentiments.

If Belgian neutrality was to be taken seriously, it was clear that some kind of reaction to this French infiltration was necessary. It was not long in coming. Between 1831 and 1833 Leopold appointed 2,407 new officers to the army, of whom 104 were of French nationality. But there were also 34 Poles and 10 Germans – a matter of great irritation in Paris. An important role was also allocated to the Flemings, with their 'Germanic' language. King Leopold was not the only person to appreciate the potential of this popular regional culture. After 1830 – albeit to a very limited degree – a number of the better educated Flemings began to show some first fleeting signs of resistance to the growing influence of French language and customs. These 'language lovers' formed the nucleus of a nascent Flemish Movement, which in later years would make political as well as cultural demands. These Flemish 'nationalists' were strongly influenced by the Romantic Movement, with its devotion to irrationality and the emotions, its emphasis on local customs and its love of the past. They first came to prominence in the 1830s with their defence of the Flemish language, and they were quick to make use of the international context to support their claims. They argued that Flemish acted as a political buffer between Belgium and France, and that it was the Flemish people who gave Belgium its own specifically national – i.e. non-French – character. The members of the Flemish Movement regarded themselves as being 'true Belgians', in contrast to their French-speaking fellow citizens in Wallonia. The importance of Belgian neutrality gave these first Flemish nationalists an importance which their limited numbers and their equally limited achievements might not immediately suggest. It also explains why the Dutch language was guaranteed to receive the support of King Leopold I.

One of the earliest instances of this support dates from 1833. After the Revolution, the new Belgian government was impressed by the need to develop its own national army as quickly as possible. In the new Belgian state French replaced Dutch as the language of command, but this led to problems with the large numbers of Flemish non-commissioned officers who had no knowledge of French. In 1833, the Minister of War – the French-born, Belgian naturalised General Évain – wrote out new training and exercise manuals for both the cavalry and the infantry. In his letter which accompanied the distribution of the manuals, he pointed out that the new guidelines were not being issued in both languages, but that it was nonetheless expected that officers would show due patience for their subordinates who had difficulty in comprehending the new instructions. He added that it was "the express wish of the King" that the officers should remain courteous towards their men and that there could be no question of punishment for any lack of understanding.[2] Pronouncements by ministers with regard to the formal wishes of the king were a rare occurrence, since even at this early stage in the development of the Belgian monarchy it was already recognised that the inviolability of the king's position was not compatible with the expression of personal opinions. That Leopold chose on this occasion to ignore this important piece of royal protocol shows how strongly he felt about the matter.

Leopold I and the 'true Belgians'

During these years the king also made it very clear that he favoured the preservation of Dutch, both as a spoken language and as a language of culture. It was equally clear that the king saw this preference as a means of counterbalancing the growing influence of French language, manners and customs. In this sense, he was on the same wave length as the first adherents of the Flemish Movement. When Leopold visited the Flemish region of the Kempen in 1834, he enquired from the mayor of Geel about the town's education system. He impressed upon the mayor the importance of giving Dutch a proper place in schools and not allowing it to become neglected. "We must preserve everything that is national," said Leopold.[3] In the early decades of his reign the king frequently showed awareness of and sympathy for the nascent Flemish Movement, even though in the eyes of the French-speaking Belgians this movement was associated with the politics of King William I of The Netherlands. For example, Leopold gave financial support to a number of Flemish authors writing in Dutch. In 1837 he granted an audience to Hendrik Conscience, in which he advised the writer to cut out all French and all other 'bastard' foreign words from the Dutch language. Conscience later recorded the king's words (spoken in French) as follows: "It gives me pleasure to see that people are using the Flemish language, the language of a significant part of our kingdom. As Belgium has more than one national language, it is important that people use them both. This leads to a more civilised population and helps to develop a national sentiment."[4] It seems as if Leopold was keen to encourage bilingualism amongst all his subjects, which was also one of the aims of the Flemish Movement in its early years. Leopold certainly set the Belgians a good example: in the winter of 1842-1843 he appointed a Dutch teacher for his own children.

The middle years of his reign also confirmed the extent to which Leopold saw the Flemish Movement as a bulwark against growing French influence – perhaps even against a growing French threat. In his conversation with Ambassador Falck in October 1839, the king warned of the dangers of French expansionism, suggesting that Paris first wanted to annex Belgium, before moving on to The Netherlands. Leopold stressed the need for both countries to present a united front to counteract this possibility.

It is against this background that the agreement of unified spelling rules for Flemish and Dutch in 1844 should be seen. The spelling issue was an important one. Primary education throughout Flanders was usually taught in Dutch, certainly in the countryside, but the question was: which Dutch? Similar problems arose in connection with the unofficial Dutch translations of the French documents in the *Bulletin officiel*, the state gazette in which all new legislation was published. In 1837, members of parliament protested formally about the poor quality of these translations. At the request of the Brussels branch of the Flemish-minded *Maatschappij tot bevordering der Nederduitse Taal en Letterkunde* (Society for the Furtherance of Flemish Language and Literature), with branches in the Flemish cities of Antwerp, Leuven, Ghent and Bruges, the king issued a royal decree which set up a national competition to find the best way to unify Flemish spelling. This decree was signed by Leopold himself and by the Minister of the Interior, Count de Theux. In this way, the king and de Theux demonstrated that they had not only made a clear and unequivocal choice for the preservation of the Dutch language in Belgium, but that they also wished to strengthen its position within the country by linking it to the spelling rules prevailing across the border in The

Netherlands. The first steps towards Dutch linguistic unity were taken in July 1837, when a spelling commission was appointed. The commission was packed with scholars who favoured an adjustment of 'Flemish' Dutch to reflect the spelling rules of 'Hollands' Dutch, and their recommendations reflected this preference. It was also no coincidence that the commission completed its work in August 1839, just months after the final peace settlement between Belgium and The Netherlands in respect of the revolutionary war of 1830. Even so, the commission's recommendations led to serious and heated discussions in Flanders, with people dividing along the now traditional lines of 'old-fashioned, Catholic Flemish' against 'progressive, Protestant Hollands'. However, a new royal decree dated 1 January 1844 announced that henceforth the new spelling rules would be used for the semi-official Dutch translations of the *Bulletin officiel* .

On 19 January 1844, Leo De Foere – a member of parliament and a priest – entered a formal protest in the lower chamber against the new royal decree, claiming that this 'adoption' of 'Hollands' spelling was an affront to the Catholic soul of the Flemish people. The resulting debate was fierce – both inside and outside parliament – and lasted for several weeks. Many of the literary societies joined in the discussions (the majority were against De Foere) and several published pamphlets. One of the pro-De Foere publications was significantly (if rather long-windedly) entitled: *Some Flemish and Belgian dialogues, from which can be seen what intrigues are being perpetrated in my free and beloved fatherland, with the express purpose of blinding rich and poor, clergy and laity, king and ministers to the insidious plans to have the Hollands language accepted under the guise of the so-called Flemish Commission!!! By a true Belgian!* This shows that the members of the Flemish Movement once again wished to portray themselves as the 'true Belgians', but also makes clear that this not only implied resistance to French influence but also (at least sometimes) to Dutch influence as well. This was at variance with the position of the king and his government, who were in favour of closer ties between Flanders and The Netherlands. Be that as it may, there is little doubt that the royal decrees of 1836 and 1844 were instrumental in preventing the disappearance of Dutch as a mainstream language in Flanders. This was certainly the opinion of a group of 300 leading Flemish sympathisers in Brussels, who came together on 11 February 1844 to celebrate the passing of the new spelling laws. At the end of their deliberations, they sent a delegation to see the king, specifically to thank him for his role in helping to secure the enactment of these two crucial decrees.

Yet soon there were other battles to fight. At the beginning of the 1840s, the Flemish Movement organised its first political protest – a petition campaign – against the growing spread of French influences within the government. As far as the use of language in the civil administration and the justice system were concerned, some of the petitioners demanded bilingualism in Flanders, others wanted full Dutch monolingualism, while yet others were content with the use of Dutch as a matter of principle, but with possibility to request the use of French if practice required it (what is known today as 'language facilities'). Running parallel with these developments, there were similar demands that the use of Dutch in Flemish secondary schools and at the State University of Ghent should enjoy the same status as the use of French. The petition only managed to gather some 13,000 signatures, so that it can hardly be described as a success. However, it did ensure that the reclaiming of Flanders for the Dutch language and Dutch culture was now firmly on the political agenda. Reporting to his superiors in The Hague in 1840, Ambassador Falck commented that in addition to the continuing struggle between Catholics and liberals, there was also "another form of internal division, which is not necessarily visible day by day, but which is nonetheless very real and has deep roots (...). I mean the growing distrust between the Flemings and the Walloons."[5] Writing from Coburg in 1841, Freiherr von Stockmar told King Leopold that the Franco-Belgian customs treaty (which was being prepared at that time) would only serve to widen the rift between Flanders and Wallonia.[6] This was an astute analysis, since at that time very few people made the connection between the language question and the Flemish and Walloon economies.

The foreign press followed all these matters closely. In 1847, the king appointed Hendrik Conscience as the new teacher of Dutch for the two royal princes. This was largely an honorary appointment, but it had considerable symbolic significance. The king had announced his decision on 21 July – the anniversary of his ascent to the throne – and had made it public at Neuilly, on the outskirts of the French capital (where his wife's family held property). The German press – not exactly pro-French at the best of times – took this opportunity to lavish praise on the Flemish Movement and to stress the 'Germanic' nature of the Flemish people. The *Kölnische Zeitung* even went so far as to describe the appointment as "sensational"[7], while the Parisian *Journal des Débats* commented sardonically: "It is no longer necessary to hide the fact that the Prussian government has been working for some time to include Belgium within its sphere of influence."[8]

In Belgium itself, things did not necessarily seem so black and white. The situation was further complicated by party political considerations. The year 1847 marked the beginning of a long period of liberal governments with sizeable majorities. This did not work in favour of the Flemish Movement and liberal opinion soon hardened against 'nationalist' sympathies. In part this was a result of the majority voting system which was in operation at the time. Under this system, the party which obtained most votes in a given electoral district won all the seats attached to that district. Rather like the modern-day British and American voting systems, this Belgian system resulted in the development of a two party structure: the two parties being the Catholics and the liberals. This led to a polarisation of views across the political spectrum and meant that the language question was increasingly interpreted in light of the wider conflict between the church and the free-thinkers. The clergy needed the Flemish language for their communion – and communication – with the common people. As a result, the Catholics defended Flemish almost as a matter of faith.

This traditionalist, conservative approach was strengthened still further after the liberal victory in the elections of 1847. The Catholics now saw the popular language of the people as the only way of 'protecting' the masses from the worst excesses of modern ideology. In these circumstances, it is hardly surprising that the liberals became less interested in the Flemish tongue, since they could justifiably claim that it was being (mis)used against them by their political opponents. As we have seen, this was not a position shared by King Leopold.

In the final analysis, Leopold's children grew up knowing very little about the Dutch language. The king wished to give the outside world the impression that his children were learning Dutch, but in reality they made very little effort – or progress. This was already clear in 1849, when the 14 year-old Duke of Brabant – the future King Leopold II – addressed a delegation from Flemish theatrical societies in French. The duke apologised to the delegation for his inability to speak to them in their own language, but claimed that he understood most of what they said. This is doubtful, since there were numerous other instances when the young prince showed an almost complete lack of understanding for one of his own native tongues. In its New Year's wishes for the Belgian people, published on 31 December 1849, the *Handelsblad* newspaper wished the Duke of Brabant more success in his efforts to learn Dutch. Yet the future king never acquired anything more than a passive knowledge, which was largely based (as had been the case with his father) on his much better understanding of German. He certainly never spoke the language. Nor, for that matter, did his siblings, Prince Philip and Princess Charlotte. And they all failed to understand the irritation which this caused to their Flemish subjects: a protest in 1856 openly blamed the king for his children's failure to master Dutch.

Leopold I, advocate of the Flemish Movement

In February 1848, a new revolution broke out in France, the neighbouring country with which Belgium was so closely linked. King Louis-Philippe – Leopold's father-in-law – was toppled from his throne and a series of similar revolts soon broke out across Europe. Conservative regimes fell in several countries and it seemed as if only Belgium was immune. Most observers ascribed this 'success' to the deep and traditional Catholicism of the Flemish people, which had given them greater respect for authority and a greater willingness to accept their lot in life. In his correspondence, King Leopold was certainly full of praise for the common people of his kingdom. Writing to his niece, Queen Victoria of England, on 19 February 1848, he noted (somewhat ironically) that full adult suffrage in Belgium would produce 'good' (i.e. conservative) results, "our people of the lower orders being in fact *ce que nous avons de mieux.*" In a new letter to Victoria on 4 March – when the troubles in France were at their height – he commented, "Our poor people behave <u>beautifully</u>." He went on to praise their desire for "national union and [their] devotion to the national existence of the country."[9] In short, the king saw the Flemish people – and the Flemish Movement – as being traditional, conservative and pro-Belgian. As such, they were guaranteed to receive his support.

The destabilisation of France in 1848 simply served to strengthen this conviction. Events in Paris seemed to presage a general European war – a war in which Belgium could only be a loser. Nor did the situation improve when Louis-Napoleon – a grandson of the great Bonaparte – seized power in December 1848. The new president (later emperor) was well-known for his expansionist views, so that Leopold now feared France more than ever. And with good reason: the annexation plans of the new French republic were scarcely concealed. Between 1848 and 1853 the French newspapers were full of articles which detailed the advantages of incorporating Belgium into *la patrie*. It is also worth noting that these articles were keen to portray Belgium as an exclusively French-speaking country. Not surprisingly, this provoked a counter-reaction in Belgium, both in the press and in a series of privately published pamphlets. Keeping the French at arm's length was now the nation's most important priority. In these circumstances, the Flemish Movement could be a useful tool for Leopold, notwithstanding (or perhaps because of) the Movement's own desire for closer links with Germany, where the press was full of laudatory comment about *die Flämische Bewegung*.

From 1848 onwards, King Leopold's speeches repeatedly and explicitly showed his support for the Flemish Movement and their political demands. The first such speech dates from March 1848, when the revolution in France was still in full swing. During the 19th century, it was the custom in times of peril for loyal subjects and loyal associations to send declarations of support to the royal palace, pledging their continued allegiance. Yet within the context of this 'nationalistic' ritual, the Flemish associations were keen to stress their many years of 'national struggle' to achieve Belgian independence. And this message did not go unheard. Leopold often made time to receive Flemish delegations in person. On one such occasion he expressed his wish that the Flemish people would 'obtain their just desserts' (or words to that effect). With this political 'statement' the king seemed to be adopting a position directly opposed to his own liberal ministers.

This soon became evident in a number of different issues. In June 1849, parliament discussed new proposals relating to the two Belgian state universities, in Ghent (in Flanders) and Liege (in Wallonia).[10] Minister Rogier declared that the government had first thought of including a good working knowledge of Dutch as part of the general entrance examination, but had finally decided against this, since it was contrary to the constitutional principle of freedom of language. In other words, it was not constitutionally possible to force the French-speaking Walloons to learn Dutch. This infuriated the Flemish deputies, who submitted a number of amendments, demanding

Pierre De Decker (1812-1891), Member of Parliament for the town of Dendermonde and minister of the crown from 1855 to 1857. The photograph was taken around 1860 and was part of the collection of Prince Philip (1837-1905), the second son of Leopold I. The photograph has been inscribed by the prince.

that the original intention should be honoured. But this inevitably meant that the (generally) monolingual Walloons would be placed at a considerable disadvantage in comparison with the (generally) bilingual Flemish students. The debate went around in circles for some time, but it eventually became clear that the Flemish amendments would be rejected. At this point, the Flemish Catholic politician Pierre De Decker stood to address his parliamentary colleagues: "What are we facing in Belgium? We are facing a deep division of the population into two very different races. No one is more anxious than I for a true union between all Belgian citizens. But I am forced to recognise an incontestable fact: in Belgium there are two distinct races, speaking two different languages and belonging to two different orders of civilisation. It is no longer possible to ignore this fact." De Decker also made reference to the European revolutions of 1848. He saw these revolutions as an expression of the common people's desire for self-determination, the first principle of which is a respect for one's own language.

Yet his eloquence was all to no avail: the most important language amendments were defeated by 53 votes to 37.

Even so, this parliamentary defeat did lead to a greater awareness and understanding of the issues involved – as was demonstrated in the spring of 1850, when attention was turned to the plans of the liberal government to reorganise secondary education. In the Flemish secondary schools Dutch would henceforth be taught as a compulsory language subject. For some study programmes a 'thorough' knowledge was required. For other programmes an 'adequate' knowledge was sufficient. The Flemish Movement found this unacceptable and turned to its favoured political weapon: the petition. In Brussels a kind of central committee was set up, which in future would coordinate the various petition actions emanating from Flanders. The petition text issued on this occasion by the Brussels committee demanded that the required level of knowledge should always be 'thorough' (they regarded the word 'adequate' as degrading for their language and insufficient in practical terms) and that this standard should be applied in Brussels and throughout Flanders. But they went even further. Not only did they insist that lessons in English and German should also be taught in Dutch, but they also revived some of the demands contained in the very first Flemish petition of 1840. In particular, they wanted the popular language of the province to be used exclusively for teaching in primary schools; they wanted Dutch to be accorded the same status as French at the state university in Ghent; and they requested that a separate Flemish Royal Academy of Letters should be set up, or at least that there should be a distinct Dutch-language section within the existing Royal Academy.

While the government's education proposals were being debated in the Senate, the king received a delegation of pro-Flemish sympathisers, who handed him the petition based on the text of the Brussels committee. The delegation leader impressed upon the king that his Flemish subjects were expecting him to intervene personally in this matter. Leopold's reply is significant (my italics): *"I accept that your demands are just and reasonable.* I have always loved the good, old Flemish language. It is the language of a large part of our country. I would like to see this language flourish, since our country has always been in part Flemish. *I admit that since the events of 1830 we have perhaps overlooked the needs of that good, old Flemish language. This must be said, because it is the truth.* Our national motto of 'L'Union fait la force' [Strength through Union] has not always been applicable (...). This union did not exist in reality. There were just two years when we were really united, to create our nation and our nationality (...). *To sum up, gentlemen, for all these reasons it is my fond wish that the Flemish language should be treated kindly.*"[11]

With this speech, the king made public his own personal feelings on the language question. But on this occasion it was all of no consequence. Minister Rogier refused to change his plans (as the subsequent parliamentary debates made clear) and as a constitutional monarch it was Leopold who was forced to give way.

Belgium and the Monarchy. From National Independence to National Disintegration.

Yet it had not all been a waste of time. The education debate of 1850 marked a further step forward in the political organisation of the Flemish Movement. The creation of the central committee in Brussels was an important first step along the road to coordinated action. This was evident, for example, in the spring of 1853, when Crown Prince Leopold, the Duke of Brabant, celebrated his eighteenth birthday and his coming of age. The Central Committee (by now with capital letters) launched an action "to persuade every Fleming to send a message of congratulations to His Royal Highness, the Duke of Brabant." The response of the various Flemish societies and associations was overwhelming, and on 9 April the young duke's birthday was

Marie-Henriette of Austria (1836-1902), circa 1860.

celebrated with great verve. That same evening, the king sent his sons – Leopold and Philip – to attend a Dutch play in Brussels. There they were addressed by the social-liberal Jacob Kats, also in Dutch. To the delight of the public, he thanked them "in the name of all Flemish-speaking Belgians" and expressed the hope that the royal princes would come to understand even more than before the importance of the people's language.[12]

On 1 May, the Central Committee organised a meeting for all "Flemish militants", at which the Antwerp writer Lode Gerrits defended the establishment of a separate pro-Flemish political party. King Leopold even met a delegation from the Central Committee and a short time later he invited a number of leading parliamentarians to the palace to discuss ideas about the political situation in Belgium. One of the members of parliament – there is evidence to suggest that it might have been Pierre De Decker – spoke to the king about the Flemish question. The Antwerp *Handelsblad* wrote on 7 May that Leopold had confirmed his "attachment to the basic Flemish principles. His Majesty again declared – as he had done during the audience granted to the members of the Flemish commission [Central Committee] – that he was convinced of the justice of the Flemish demands and said that even though these demands had not yet been fully recognised in law, the Flemish people had remained faithful to the constitution of 1830." In its editorial comment the *Handelsblad* also emphasised that Flanders did not want to break away from Wallonia, but simply wished to ensure that its people were treated equally before the law, as the constitution required. On 16 May, the social-liberal newspaper *De Broedermin* added its own contribution to the debate, reporting a comment of Leopold's that he was surprised that "Dutch was not spoken during the meetings of the city council in Ghent". It seemed that the king was gradually finding more and more in common with the Flemish Movement.

Yet Leopold was also occupied by other, perhaps even weightier, matters. In 1853, he was able to secure the engagement of the Duke of Brabant to the 16 year-old Marie-Henriette from Austria. This marriage brought a life of misery to the young German princess, but it was a brilliant diplomatic coup for Belgium, allowing Leopold to parry Louis-Napoleon's latest annexation plans. Louis-Napoleon (by now he had had himself crowned as Emperor Napoleon III) was furious and spoke of a "German-Belgian alliance".[13] It is perhaps no coincidence that Leopold made his pro-Flemish comments to the leading parliamentarians shortly before he set off with his son to Vienna and Berlin to negotiate this match, which would help to cement his kingdom's position in Europe.

In this context, it is also interesting to note what happened during the ceremonial visit of the new royal couple to Antwerp in September 1853. The royal party sat patiently through the speeches of one welcoming committee after another. But in a dramatic breach of protocol, the chairman of the Flemish societies addressed the duke and his bride in Dutch (traditionally, the establishment always addressed members of the royal family in French). The content of his speech was no less controversial – and pro-Flemish: "Most royal princess, as Lower-German [i.e. Flemish] Belgians, we are doubly pleased with your happy entrance into our royal family. In addition to the virtues with which you are graced by nature, we welcome you as the daughter of a people to whom we are related through blood. We are blessed with the certainty that Your Majesty will understand the true character of your humble Flemish subjects."[14]

In March 1855, Leopold was able to create a new government under the leadership of Pierre De Decker – the politician who had defended the 1840 petition movement in parliament. In the intervening years he had often championed Flemish national identity as a bulwark against the possible threat of French annexation. On 27 June 1856, the king and Minister of the Interior De Decker signed a royal decree which established the so-called Grievance Commission. This commission was designed to take measures which would help to promote the development of Flemish literature and would create a legal framework for the use of Dutch in government matters. Little is known about Leopold's role in helping to set up the Grievance Commission, but it seems likely (in view of the matters that we have previously discussed) that his contribution was a significant one. It seems even more likely if one considers the words which the king addressed to a meeting of Flemish societies in Ghent on 31 August 1856 (my italics): "I could speak to you in Flemish, but I would find it impossible to express myself with the accuracy of your secretary. I love the Flemish language. I love it very much, just as I love the Flemish people. I read and write in Flemish. In other words, the Flemish language is also my language. After all, Flemish and German have the same common origins. I appreciate the efforts which have been made to develop Flemish literature and drama. *I will do all in my power to ensure that all Belgians enjoy the same rights, irrespective of their language of preference.*"[15]

King Leopold I died in December 1865. The Flemish press reviewed his reign with a feeling of nostalgia and wrote (with justification) that the king had taken their side in the Flemish question, but that he had been let down by a lack of support from the politicians. Unfortunately, things did not seem likely to improve under his son...

2
Leopold II
(1865-1909)

The Situation Stagnates

An unknown king

Amidst all the unrest surrounding the work of the Grievance Commission, in September 1856 the 21 year-old Prince Leopold received several resounding letters of praise from various Flemish literary societies. The young prince asked a senior member of the palace staff, Baron Goffinet, whether or not he should reply in Flemish. In the margin of Leopold's written question the baron pencilled a firm '*Non*'. Puzzled by the answer, the prince asked the question again. This time, the baron's reply was more extensive. "Viscount Conway has told me that he has never replied on behalf of the king in the Flemish language – not to anyone... There is still much to be said on this delicate issue of French and Flemish. It is a matter which requires much thought! Prudence suggests that it is [illegible] better to remain at a safe distance from this struggle, which has threatened on more than one occasion to erupt and to upset the delicate balance for us all."[16]

This is an isolated but nonetheless interesting anecdote on the language question – one of the few that is available to the historians of Belgium's second king. Nevertheless, it is very clear that after 1865 King Leopold II quickly became much less popular with the adherents of the Flemish Movement than his father had been. By now the Movement was working in the direction of specific language laws, a series of which were passed in the years after 1873. These laws enshrined the basic principle that Dutch should be the administrative and judicial language of Flanders. There were still numerous exceptions to this basic principle and everyone still had the right to request that matters relating to his or her own person should be conducted in French. This effectively meant that French-speakers and bilingual citizens were granted language facilities throughout the Flemish provinces. As a partial counterbalance, in 1883 there was a slight improvement in the status of Dutch within the secondary education system in Flanders (for boys between the ages of 12 and 18 years), which was organised by the state. One of these improvements was that lessons in the Dutch language should henceforth be given in... Dutch! Previously, such lessons had often been taught in French, which effectively reduced Dutch to the status of a foreign language.

Leopold II never made a single statement which would allow the Flemish radicals to believe that the king was sympathetic in principle to their political objectives. As a result, the press was reduced to drawing its own conclusions based on the king's own use and understanding of Dutch. Did he understand Dutch? (He almost certainly did.) Did he speak it? (Almost never.) It was clear that French was still his preferred tongue, as was also the case with his brother, Prince Philip. In stark contrast, Queen Marie-Henriette did make an effort to speak Dutch. This was particularly awkward at state functions at which the royal couple were both present, since the queen babbled away in one national language, while the king continued to talk exclusively in the other! This inability (or unwillingness) of the king and his brother to speak Dutch was occasionally a source of criticism in the Flemish press. Nevertheless, at the express wish of the king, Prince Philip's children were given lessens in Dutch by their tutor Jules Bosmans, as a result of which they acquired an active working knowledge of the language.

Given this background, what did the king think about the new language laws in legal matters (1873), in administrative matters (1878) and in educational matters (1883)? Sadly, we have no idea. The surviving documents relating to the king make no mention of this legislation. Not that this is unusual. The more copious archives of other senior politicians and ministers also contain few references to the language laws. For example, the surviving correspondence between the Frère-Orban cabinet (1878-1884) and the king contains not a single word over the law of 1883. It is almost as if the language question was unimportant. This is reflected in the way in which the Flemish politicians were only able to get language-related proposals onto the parliamentary agenda during the volatile pre-election periods: the periods when deals were struck in order to attract the votes of undecided electors.

Crown Prince Boudewijn – a light in the darkness

Suddenly, it seemed that things might be about to change – thanks to the oldest son of Prince Philip: the young Crown Prince Boudewijn. On 15 August 1887, the royal family assembled in Bruges to take part in the festivities to celebrate the unveiling of statues to two great Flemish heroes: Jan Breydel and Pieter De Coninck. Some 685 years earlier – on 11 July 1302 – they had been the leaders of a 'people's' army which had defeated the might of feudal France at the Battle of the Golden Spurs near the Flemish city of Kortrijk. Under the influence of the writings of Hendrik Conscience this battle had acquired an almost mythical status, which strengthened the nationalist sentiments of the more romantic Flemings. The fact that Jan Breydel probably never existed and that the 'people's' army was cut to pieces by the French in 1305 was no longer deemed important. From 1840 onwards, 11 July was observed as a day of Flemish celebration, which also served to further enhance Flemish 'national' identity (11 July is now a public holiday within the Flemish region).

The festivities in Bruges were attended by people from across the length and breadth of Flanders. The Flemish societies had started the ball rolling on the day prior to the arrival of the royal party and their activities – as might be expected – were conducted exclusively in Dutch. However, the king's speech the next day was given entirely in French – to which a loyal public replied with *Vive le roi!* (French for 'Long live the king!). It was a display of loyalty which left the important Bruges newspaper *Het Volksbelang* with a slightly sour taste in the mouth: "Ever since 1830, it seems as if the Flemish people have had little choice but to welcome their king in this manner. But they do it instinctively, because they sense that the king is not a Flemish king."[17] The palace

2 Leopold II (1865-1909)

Ghemar Frères, Photographes du Roi, Bruxelles

Déposé.

Leopold II (1835-1909), King of the Belgians from December 1865 onwards. A photograph by Louis Ghémar; on the next page, a portrait by the Parisian photographer Nadar. Both date from the years around 1864. Photographs in the form of a 'carte de visite' (visiting card) were all the rage in the 1860s. Pictures of the royal families of Europe were particularly popular with the public and were big earners for the photographers. The kings and princes were happy to be photographed, since the spreading of their image in this manner strengthened the bond of their dynasties with the people.

Belgium and the Monarchy. From National Independence to National Disintegration.

was further criticised because of the very poor Dutch translation of the speech which was circulated amongst the crowd. It was perhaps in reaction to this criticism that the king and his advisers decided to play their trump card: the 18 year-old Prince Boudewijn, heir to the throne. The following day he spoke in his uncle's stead and addressed the people perfectly – in Dutch. The thousands of enthusiastic spectators responded by singing the *Flemish Lion*, a romanticised nationalist song which was closely linked to the cult surrounding the Battle of the Golden Spurs. The young prince stood in honour of this song – which was regarded as a kind of unofficial Flemish national anthem – and thereby won the hearts of all those present. It is difficult to imagine in these modern times just how significant this gesture was – and how greatly it was appreciated by the massed crowds gathered in Bruges. The prince's triumph (and the people's reaction to it) was reported in lyrical terms in newspapers at home and abroad. Even the French-speaking press seemed to be impressed by what everyone perceived as the collective rebirth of a true Flemish national sentiment.

Viewed from their 'oppressed' perspective, the Flemish people soon came to see Prince Boudewijn as some kind of mythical, almost Messianic saviour. It was believed that once "our Flemish prince" became king, he would settle the language question once and for all. Perhaps the prince believed it, too. He often attended ceremonies in Flanders and always spoke in Dutch. This not only delighted his audiences, but also delighted the prince himself, who was visibly moved by the enthusiastic reaction of his Flemish subjects. But the dream came to an end in January 1891, when Boudewijn died at the tragically young age of 21. The news came as a huge shock to the nation, since the palace had kept news of his illness a secret. The collective grief in Flanders was immense, and can be compared to the outpouring of popular feeling in Great Britain for the death of Princess Diana in 1997. As part of the state funeral, the Flemish societies were asked by King Leopold to carry a mourning wreath on a Flemish flag. Thanks to the Flemish Movement, the Flemish people did now indeed have their own flag: a black Flemish lion on a field of gold - the symbol of the warriors of 1302.

A concerned Leopold II

It was impossible for King Leopold to behave as though the events which took place in Bruges in August 1887 had never happened. After Boudewijn had set the example, it was clear that some kind of response from the monarch was also necessary. On 13 October 1887, he visited the new Dutch-speaking theatre in Brussels. Burgomaster Charles Buls also addressed his sovereign in Dutch and Leopold replied in the same language – albeit with a heavy German accent. In September 1890, the king gave another speech in Dutch and he continued to do so – sporadically – for the remainder of his reign. Even so, the importance of these brief forays into the Dutch language should not be underestimated. The *Journal de Bruxelles* described them in 1890 as being "the

Belgium and the Monarchy. From National Independence to National Disintegration.

Bruges at the end of the 19th century. At the bottom stands the statue of Jan Breydel and Pieter De Coninck, which was inaugurated in 1887.

solemn and constitutional adherence to the principle of fundamental equality between the languages of our country."[18] The language question had long been focussed on the issue of whether the Walloons should try to learn Dutch, in the same manner as the Flemings had always been required to learn French. Now the king was setting an example – even if it was an infrequent one.

Nevertheless, the whole question of the Walloons and Dutch continued to be difficult, particularly since the language laws required senior officials in Flanders to use the Dutch language. The problem was that a considerable number of these officials actually came from Wallonia – and therefore had no knowledge of Dutch whatsoever! This anomaly was exploited by the Flemish Movement, but also provoked a backlash from the French-speaking bureaucrats. From 1884 onwards the first stirrings were felt in Flemish cities such as Ghent and Antwerp of what later came to be known as the Walloon Movement.

Leopold II was aware of these developments – he could hardly be otherwise. For example, on 25 February 1892 he received a delegation from the Flemish Catholic Union (Vlaamse Katholieke Landsbond), who presented him with a petition containing a curious mixture of demands. Firstly, they urged the sovereign to ensure that the new heir to the royal throne, Prince Albert, should be properly instructed in "their dear Flemish mother tongue". The Union also asked that greater attention should be paid to the use of Dutch in the Belgian colony of Congo, and pointed out that all official notices in the Belgian navy were still issued exclusively in French. According to the press reports of the meeting, the king replied that there were only Flemish-speakers in the navy (a strange comment in the circumstances). He also said that there was no official language in Congo but added that if the Flemish people were more numerous in the colony, then their language rights might be better respected there. He was, however, able to ensure the delegation that the language tuition of Prince Albert would be properly taken care of. One Flemish newspaper reported that during an informal conversation after the meeting the king told the Flemings that, no matter how just their struggle, they should "avoid all feelings of bitterness toward their Walloon brothers, since this could only lead to great difficulties."[19] It is the only important comment made by Leopold on the language question which has survived. In a note dated 27 February 1892 – probably in response to a ministerial request for information – the king gave his own summary of this meeting: "I received the Flemings. I told them that Flemish is spoken on our ships, that nigger language is spoken in Congo and that my nephew, who is receiving the education of his parents, speaks Flemish."[20] The tone seems anything but friendly.

Perhaps more important was Leopold's attitude towards the dispute which raged between 1896 and 1898 surrounding the so-called Equality Law. Since 1830 the laws of Belgium had been promulgated exclusively in French. This new law was designed to ensure that in future all legislation would be discussed, voted and enacted

Belgium and the Monarchy. From National Independence to National Disintegration.

The Royal Palace in Brussels at the end of the 19th century. The entrance on the right leads to the royal park, on the other side of which stands the Belgian Parliament.

in both Dutch and French. Was the king perhaps responsible for the reluctant attitude of the Senate towards this proposal? It will never be possible to know this with any degree of certainty, but it is worth noting that on 5 February 1898 – at the height of the debate – the king's brother, Philippe, wrote in a letter to the tutor of his son Albert: "My enthusiasm for Flemish is under zero."[21] In 1899, Prince Albert would actually describe his father as being in the anti-Flemish camp; he too wasn't at that time in favour of the Equality Law.[22]

The archive at the Royal Palace in Brussels still contains a file with details of the petitions which were received by the king during the period 1890-1910. These documents reveal something about King Leopold II and his approach to the language question. For example, during a ministerial council held in April 1894 the government, following the king's lead, refused to allow a petition which requested that the speeches of Leopold and the Organising Committee at the opening of the World Exhibition in Antwerp should be given in Dutch, because of the international character of the event. As a compromise, it was agreed that one of the Flemish dignitaries would address the king in Dutch when he visited the separate tourist section of the exhibition, known as 'Old Antwerp', following which the king would also reply in Dutch – in a 'speech' which was just four sentences long! This was typical of Leopold's attitude, which was based on the premise that if he ignored the problem, it might eventually go away. Most of the petitions sent to him were noted in the margin "no reply necessary" or "HM [His Majesty] chooses not to follow up this matter". On a 1908 petition from the National Flemish Union (Nationaal Vlaams Verbond), which asked that government ministers should henceforth be expected to speak both national languages, the ageing king simply wrote "to be filed away".[23]

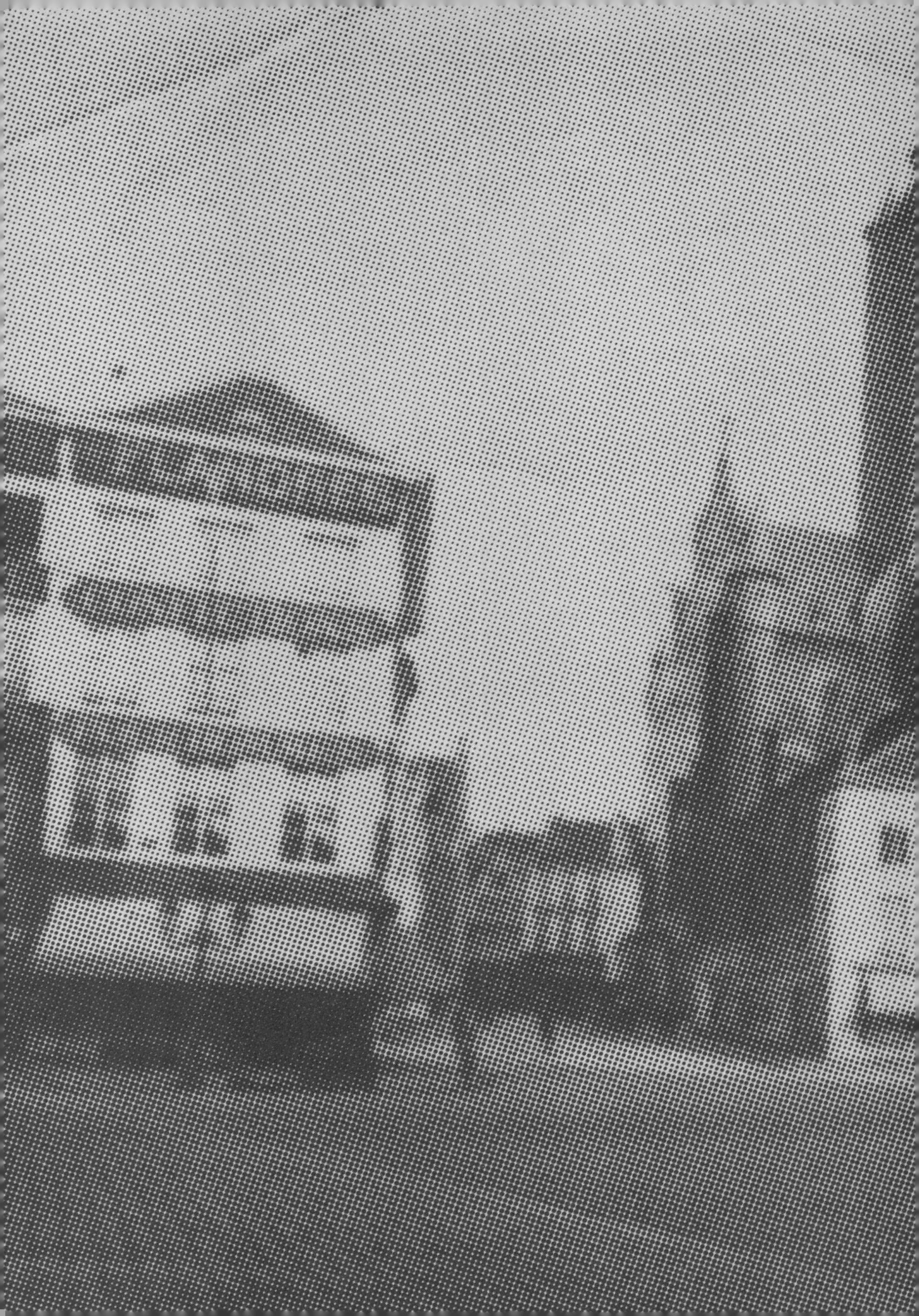

3
The first cracks in the façade of national unity

The consolidation of a mass Flemish Movement

Since its foundation in 1831, the Belgian state had operated a tax-based voting system of male suffrage, which meant that only the rich were able to vote. In the period 1831-1893 this meant that there were between 40,000 and 80,000 voters. In Flanders this small group also included the small bilingual elite. However, by 1893 this position was no longer tenable and a form of universal male suffrage was introduced: with three votes per person for the rich, two votes for the well-to-do middle class and a single vote for the ordinary man-in-the-street. One of the first effects of this democratisation was that the language question achieved a political significance it had never enjoyed before. It soon became clear that it was impossible to satisfy the aspirations of both Flemings and Walloons within the same unitary Belgian state structure. In this sense, the break in Belgian national solidarity can be said to date from 1893. The structure had only survived intact this long, because of a suffrage system which effectively denied political rights to non-French speakers. The census of 1890 recorded that 3.5 million Belgians spoke Dutch, out of a total population of some 6 million. In view of the fact that some 800,000 Belgians (including the Brussels region) qualified as being 'bilingual', this meant that 2.7 million Belgians were non-French speakers, equivalent to 45% of the population. These were nearly all 'ordinary' people who did not have the vote before 1893. The introduction of universal male suffrage at last gave this underprivileged mass a say in the political life of the nation. As a result, a key element in Flemish national awareness was able to grow even more rapidly: the conviction that in Flanders there lived a race of people who, irrespective of class and creed, formed an integrated whole, a Flemish people living on Flemish soil, who were somehow different from 'the others'.

This spreading of a true national sentiment across all layers of society is what distinguishes the modern nation state from the proto-nations of the Ancien Régime. In this sense, nationalism is a product of the 19th century. It is certainly true that during the last decades of the century the Flemish Movement gained increasing support from every social group, a development which was intensified by the parallel growth of a cheap and politically opinionated press. This growing awareness and radicalisation was reflected in the language laws of 1873 and 1889, which were applicable to legal matters and which gave ordinary Flemings a greater right of choice with regard to the language in which criminal trials were conducted. When the judge asked the defendant in which language he wished to be defended, prior to 1875 the vast majority answered that they had no preference. By 1890, this same majority was now answering: 'in Flemish'.[24] This shift was a significant one, particularly if one remembers that criminal cases usually involved persons for the lower end of the social-economic spectrum. Sometimes these 'national' feelings found expression in a different form. In 1897, a group of agricultural labourers threw bricks through the windows of the castle belonging to Count Vilain XIIII in the small Flemish village of Bazel. What had the count done to incite the fury of the mob? He had simply dared to vote against the Equality Law in the Senate.

This transformation of the Flemish Movement into a mass movement was now underpinned by the democratisation of the suffrage system. In Belgium after 1893, there were 223,000 voters with three votes, 293,000 voters with two votes and 853,000 voters who had to be satisfied with a single vote. This made up a total of 2,108,000 votes in all. It is reasonable to assume that most of the single vote holders in Flanders could not speak French, and that the two and three vote groups also contained a considerable number of non-French-speaking Flemings. The precise linguistic division within the three groupings is unknown, but, as has already been mentioned, 45% of the population as a whole were not French-speakers. This means that between 600,000 and 800,000 votes were in the hands of people who knew very little or no French. This electoral emancipation ensured that the Flemish question would become a prominent issue in the new parliament. Moreover, it would be linked in a specific manner to a number of specific subjects. As a result, the unique bilingualism of Belgium was destined to lead to a series of new *institutional* problems which would prove impossible to solve. These problems would therefore continue to fester in the body politic, infecting it ever more deeply, particularly when *socio-economic* problems also were superimposed on the language question, as was soon to happen.

New institutional problems

What were these new institutional problems? In the years before the electoral reform of 1893, the Flemish press had emphasised that democratisation "would open the way for workers and farmers, who will be able at the very least to influence those who represent the established interests in the Lower House, which will require them to speak their own Flemish language."[25] In Wallonia there was also a growing appreciation that the reform of the franchise would have an explosive effect on the language question and that, as a result, the Walloons might find themselves backed increasingly into a corner. As early as 1890, leftist newspapers such as *La Réforme* and *La Chronique* were predicting that these developments would make the 'federalisation' (see p.19 for the meaning of this term) of the state system inevitable. This was perhaps looking a little too far ahead, but the election of non-French speakers to parliament did indeed raise some difficult questions. Simultaneous translation facilities for a formal gathering of that size simply did not exist (in fact, it would not be until 1936, following the invention of microphones and headphones, that such facilities were finally introduced in the Belgian parliament). So what to do? The matter was complicated still further by the fact that the problem was not confined to Flemings who could not speak French. It now transpired that some of the Flemings who were able to speak French were no longer willing to do so – as a matter of principle. In 1892-1893, the bilingual members of the

'Neder-Duitse Bond' (Nether-German Union) in Antwerp (one of the most important pro-Flemish political organisations at that time) committed themselves to speak only Dutch in parliament, if they were elected. Similar declarations were made in Bruges and Brussels. This was a new phenomenon – bilingual Flemings who were no longer prepared to speak French in the presence of monolingual Walloons. It was typical of a growing radicalisation, which reflected the expectation that the new electoral system would at last allow the Flemish people to secure the rights which they believed their language had long deserved. After 1894 a small number of bilingual Flemish members of parliament did indeed keep their promise to speak only Dutch during parliamentary debates. Even so, the number of speeches in Dutch remained relatively small: just 17 out of a total of 635 in 1899 – but they always created a stir. The Walloons just could not understand what was happening – both literally and figuratively! To make matters even worse, the first completely non-French speaking (i.e. non-bilingual) Flemish member of parliament was elected to the Lower House in 1898.

After 1893 there were also a number of other language-related difficulties. For example, what to do about the translation of proposed pieces of legislation? It was no longer possible to discuss and pass laws exclusively in French, as had been the case in the past. Now everything would need to be dealt with in both languages. (In this respect, it is interesting to note that the 'rights' of the small German-speaking minority were quietly swept under the carpet.) In 1895, the Flemish members of parliament submitted a draft bill which would bring this about. The bill was easily passed in the Lower House, but in February 1896 it was rejected by the more conservative Senate. Outraged, the Flemish Movement rapidly mobilised public opinion to support what now became known as the Equality Law. Not surprisingly, there was an equally heated response from the more flamboyant Wallonian liberals. In this sense, the struggle surrounding the Equality Law made a significant contribution towards the development of the so-called Walloon Movement. This Movement would continue to survive until after the end of the Second World War, throughout which time it remained essentially a small, elitist 'top-down' grouping, supported by French-speaking officials in Flanders and the establishment in Wallonia, particularly in the provinces of Liege and Hainaut – in short, the groups who until the electoral reforms of 1893 had held power in their hands.

The mass of ordinary Flemings interpreted the issues at stake in an emotional manner. They insisted that parliament should declare the two languages to be equal, so that Flemish could be seen to be as 'good' as French, and the Flemings as 'worthy' as the Walloons. Of course, there were also more practical, political issues involved. The Equality Law implied that all ministers would have to be bilingual, since it was expected that they could discuss proposed legislation in both languages. The same was true of the chairman of both the Lower House and the Senate. It was even anticipated that in some circumstances officials and magistrates in Wallonia itself would be required to use Dutch: there was a controversial 'interpretation' clause in the law, which stated

Belgium and the Monarchy. From National Independence to National Disintegration.

Leopold II, circa 1890

that if the text of the legislation was unclear in one language, the text in the other language would first be consulted to clarify the matter. This again implied that Walloon officials, wherever they worked, would need to learn Dutch as a matter of principle. In short, the Equality Law effectively put a Flemish pistol to the head of the Wallonian establishment: learn our language – or else!

The democratisation of the franchise in 1893 turned the Belgian ship of state onto a new course: a course which would eventually lead to national disintegration on the rocks of linguistic division. According to the political scientist Paul Pierson, in every complex and unpredictable political situation there are 'critical junctures', points which are reached when new institutional choices can irreversibly push a particular issue in a certain direction, so that new long-term structural patterns are generated.[26] This analysis is sometimes criticised from a historical perspective as being too determinist.[27] However, it cannot be denied that some political decisions do have fundamental and irreversible long-term consequences which go far beyond their immediate importance. The electoral reform of 1893 was precisely such a decision. In no time at all, it created a series of institutional crises which forced both Flemings and Walloons to face up to the realities of a completely new political situation.

But were these problems really so unsolvable? Consider the question of bilingualism for ministers and officials in Wallonia. The evidence of the 20th century suggests that this need not have been such a problem after all. In the past hundred years Belgium has had numerous administrations in which the ministers – and even the prime minister – were unable to speak Dutch. As for the famous 'interpretation' clause, this was much more a question of theoretical principle than practical application. And what of multi-lingual parliamentary debates? Until well into the 1960s and 1970s the vast majority of Flemish politicians still spoke fluent French. The 'success' of this pragmatic approach would seem to suggest that the introduction of the Dutch language into the Belgian parliamentary system was essentially a nationalist, political act, in which the politicians concerned played on the emotions of a malleable electorate.

Indeed, it is difficult to avoid the conclusion that after 1893 political agitation took priority over pragmatism and *bonhomie*. The Flemish Movement had by now reached full maturity, with its emotional demands for respect and equality. It had first sprung from a sentimental and romantic attachment to the Flemish language, which after 1830 led to a growing reaction against the attempts to further spread the use of French in the judicial and administrative systems. During the early years of its struggle the movement had received support from King Leopold I, because he felt that Flemish helped to define his nation's identity in a manner which made a clear distinction with neighbouring France. As time passed, the movement also found its way increasingly into the hearts and minds of ordinary Flemish people, but their aspirations were blocked by the elitist electoral tax-based voting system. This meant that effective power remained in the hands of the French-speakers and a smaller number of bilingual Flemings, who were slow to respond to the emotional *crie de cœur* of Flanders.

It was perhaps symptomatic of this situation that the first of the language laws – passed in 1873 – dealt with criminal trials. During the 1860s, the Flemish press had gone to great lengths to support Jan Coucke and Pieter Goethals, who (it was believed) had been unfairly condemned to death and executed, simply because as Flemings they were unable to conduct a proper defence in a trial which was held exclusively in French. This incident quickly mobilised strong feelings in Flanders, even amongst those entitled to vote under the tax-based system. In reality, these 'martyrs' were not innocent, but that was no longer the point. The radical Flemings made the cause their own, using it to make propaganda to support their political aims, whilst at the same time raising Coucke and Goethals (who by lucky coincidence had the same first names as that other heroic Flemish duo from 1302 – Jan Breydel and Pieter De Coninck) to the status of legendary heroes. The Walloons could not really understand what all the fuss was about. Jules Bara – one of the more intelligent members of the Wallonian elite – was correct when he said in parliament that the new language law was unnecessary, since there had been no serious complaints since 1830. And indeed, a trial can be held quite satisfactorily with the use of translators (as is still often the case today). But for the Flemings, this was not the real issue. The use of the popular Flemish language in criminal trials was more a question of national dignity than judicial necessity. Much the same was true of the language laws dealing with administrative matters, passed in 1878. In the past, it had always proved possible to find ways to translate documents which the Flemings had been unable to understand. This was doubly necessary, since the majority of the ordinary Flemings were unable to read, even in their own language. Yet once again, this was beside the point: it was the principle of the matter that counted. In this manner, the radicals were able to use extra-parliamentary incidents to whip up sufficient popular feeling, so that even the tax-based parliament was forced to act.

After the electoral reforms of 1893, 'the Flemish people' decided that it was time to make their weight felt. The breakthrough into the political arena of a mass Flemish movement meant that the Flemish political leaders no longer needed to be as pragmatic as they had been in the past when dealing with the language issue. In years gone by, they had needed to persuade and were often forced to compromise. Now they were in a position to confront – and this confrontational attitude quickly began to raise fundamental questions about the institutional organisation of the Belgian nation. The result was a self-perpetuating cascade of Flemish and Walloon reactions and counter-reactions, a raging torrent of mutual incomprehension which still threatens to swamp the delicate balance of inter-community relations. For Belgium, the electoral reforms of 1893 were the political equivalent of opening Pandora's box.

In search of an answer: Belgium and bilingualism

After 1893, successive governments were faced with a new political situation, namely that the language question could no longer be limited to the granting of language facilities to the French-speakers in Flanders. From now on, the state would be obliged to take account of non-French speakers at every institutional level. It did not require much foresight to see that in the medium to long term this would inevitably lead to serious 'nationality' problems, which could easily disturb the fragile equilibrium of the Belgian model. It was for this reason that the government decided to adopt a fundamentally different approach, which first took shape in the Equality Law of 1898: an approach based on institutional bilingualism throughout the country. Ministers, magistrates and officials would all be encouraged to learn both languages. This was to be the 'national' answer to the problem of Flemish-Walloon relations. Full bilingualism had been a demand of the politicised Flemings ever since 1830. By 1891 the socialist newspaper *Vooruit* (Progress) was writing that the Walloons should be "obliged to learn the basic principles of the Flemish language (...) This is the only solution to the language conflict: that all Belgians should be capable of understanding each other."[28] The Catholic governments which dominated the period 1884-1914 repeatedly showed themselves to be in favour of this bilingual solution, even in Wallonia (although they were thinking largely in terms of bilingualism for well-educated 'citizens' rather than the unlettered 'masses'). During these years, leading scientists and academics also attempted to find a theoretical basis to support the bilingual nature of Belgian society. For example, the jurist and literary commentator Edmond Picard (who was also a notorious anti-Semite) used various ethnic and cultural-historical premises as the basis for his theory of 'the Belgian soul', meaning those fundamental national characteristics which transcended the language divide. The historian Henri Pirenne – writing in his great national history, compiled during this period – thought that the origins of Belgian unity should be sought in the Burgundian period and in the further development of what he described as the historical bilingualism of Flanders.

During the parliamentary debates of November 1896, the Equality Law not only received support from the Flemish members, but also from a number of bilingually-minded Walloons. In particular, the Wallonian socialists grouped around Jules Destrée had a good deal of sympathy with the Flemish demands. Equally important were the signals of support coming from government quarters. A month earlier, the Minister of Justice – the Ghent barrister Victor Begerem – had required potential candidates for a position as justice of the peace in a Walloon district to sit a Dutch entrance examination (this district was close to the language frontier and also contained a number of Flemish-speaking communities). There were also growing demands – in both parliament and press – that courts in Wallonia should be compelled, if requested, to conduct their cases on the basis of the Flemish texts of the relevant laws. Even opposition politicians, such as the Walloon socialist Georges Lorand, were prepared to support the principle that legal institutions throughout the land must be familiar with both national languages. It is worth noting that Lorand's comments were made in the report of the parliamentary committee charged with drafting the text of the Equality Law. In this respect, it is certainly true that the preparation of legislative texts in Dutch paved the way for the greater introduction of Dutch into the daily processes of civil administration in Belgium. The Antwerp politician Edward Coremans even argued that cases before the Court of Cassation should also be heard in Dutch. This was a logical demand: the court was responsible for the final interpretation of legislative texts – and since these texts were henceforth also to be written in Dutch, it followed that its judges must be able to understand that language. At a meeting of the Flemish Catholic Union on 13 September 1896, Coremans declared: "We should be able to speak our Flemish in Wallonia, just like they speak their French here in Flanders."[29]

The prospect of a whole series of measures designed to spread the use of Dutch provoked a sharp reaction in Wallonia, particularly from the French-speaking liberals. But some elements of the Flemish press – such as the conservative-Catholic *Le Bien Public* in Ghent – also opposed the language laws. In fact, in the autumn of 1896 general resistance to the new Equality Law began to harden considerably. This was the atmosphere in which the Senate in January 1897 considered the proposals which had been forwarded by the Lower House. The Flemish senator Charles Van Vreckem emphasised in his committee report that Flemish would only be used in Wallonia in exceptional circumstances. He hoped that this would calm the fears of the French-speakers, but it had precisely the opposite effect – largely because he wrote in the same report that the new law implied "incontestably" that the holders of senior functions in the magistracy would henceforth need to understand both languages.[30] To add fuel to the fire, at the end of the month Minister Begerem made a number of other comments (many of them far from clear) from which it was possible to infer that the government was indeed seeking to introduce bilingualism throughout the entire country.[31] These well-meaning but injudicious statements helped to solidify the opposition of the French-speaking elite towards the new legislation. Writing in an important French magazine in April 1897, the Liege poet Albert Mockel gave a realistic – if somewhat cynical – analysis of the situation. He thought that the division of the country into separate federal units was unavoidable – but that nobody had the courage to say it: "Wallonia for the Walloons, Flanders for the Flemings – and Brussels for the Belgians!"[32] It was a slogan which seemed to capture the spirit of the moment. The Senate rejected the Equality Law and sent it back to the Lower House in a much watered-down form. The government backed down and was suddenly at pains to emphasise that it had never intended to 'bilingualise' Wallonia. But this was not true – and was simply postponing the inevitable. The government *did* still intend to press on with its favoured policy, as later events would prove: in 1898 the Equality Law was passed in its original form.

Monolingual Wallonia, bilingual Flanders

This policy option – the introduction of bilingualism throughout the country – reflected a lack of insight into the true feelings of Wallonian public opinion. There was a widespread, unspoken (but nonetheless clear) unwillingness in Wallonia to learn the Dutch language. This dislike had deep historical roots. During the period 1815-1830, the Walloons regarded themselves (probably with some justification) as second-class citizens, because they did not understand the language of the state – which at this time, under the Kingdom of the Netherlands, was Dutch. The depth of this inferiority complex can be judged by the fact that the pro-Walloon movements at the end of the 19th century still referred back to the rule of King William I, almost 70 years before. Moreover, the Walloons also had a strong mistrust of Flemish as a language per se. The spelling rules had only recently been fixed and Flemish literature – at least, at this stage – was hardly of encouraging quality. Even more importantly, a reliable technical vocabulary was lacking in almost every field of endeavour. This was a particular problem in the administrative field, since state officials needed a precise language with a clear and unchanging terminology, which everybody understood to mean the same. All this led to a natural reluctance on the part of the Walloons to treat Dutch seriously. Their reluctance was further strengthened by the fact that the government gave the impression that the introduction of bilingualism for practising officials would be complete and immediate, whereas in reality the 'bilingualising' of Wallonia could only be achieved gradually through long-term changes in teaching practices at secondary level.

This cocktail of objections served to strengthen the pre-existing Walloon unwillingness to learn Flemish. Moreover, in the context of the period following 1890 it was possible to link this standpoint to a number of simplistic political arguments: the Flemish Movement was undermining the foundations of the nation; the Flemish Movement was nothing more than a means for the Catholic coalition to keep hold of power; or (after 1918) the Flemish radicals were pro-German traitors. As a result of arguments such as these, Dutch is still seen as a second-rank language in Wallonia, even today. And it was little different in the years before the Equality Law. The Catholic governments of the day introduced bilingual coins, stamps, banknotes, train timetables, etc. This provoked an irritated reaction from the Walloons, who felt that the government was introducing official Dutch language inscriptions into their region via the backdoor.[33]

The Flemish politicians had clearly misjudged the strength of public opinion in Wallonia – but how could this happen? The Catholic governments which imposed their language policy on the country between 1894 and 1914 depended to a large extent on Flanders for their parliamentary majority. Their empathy with Wallonia was therefore that much less. This was reflected in the fact that nearly all the government's ministers came from Flanders or Dutch-speaking Brussels. Between 1884 and 1890 there was not a single minister from a Walloon electoral district. Between 1890 and 1902 there was just one! In addition, the Flemings felt strengthened in their enthusiasm for bilingualism by the realisation that Wallonia was not as uniformly French-speaking as was often claimed. In the industrial cities there were significant enclaves of 'imported' Flemish workers. There was also the example of the small bilingual establishment in Flanders, which was portrayed to the Walloons as a norm to be followed.

This Flemish bilingualism – as it existed at the end of the 19th century – requires some further explanation. Based on a well-founded criticism of the fundamentally asocial nature of the existing system of linguistic apartheid, Flemings argued along nationalist-ideological lines that there was no such thing as good bilingual French-speakers, but only parvenu Flemish-speakers who had bastardised an alien language. This was incorrect. It is certainly beyond dispute that many bilingual Flemings had made the French language their own by the end of the 19th century. It was a language which they used with great ease and considerable talent. The thorough 'Frenchification' of secondary education, with its broad emphasis on the importance of languages in general, was an excellent training ground for the mastery of French. The bilingual Flemings often used Dutch at home for every day, domestic matters, but in more formal contexts – school, profession, official matters – the language of Molière was the norm. Social and public life in the large and medium-sized Flemish towns was largely conducted in French and this was reflected in the way the towns looked. Street names and tram notices had traditionally been in both languages, but after 1895 a new element arrived on the scene: street advertising – and this was largely in French. A similar picture is painted by an examination of sources such as family archives: letters, photographs and other documents all show that the bilingual Flemings were very bilingual indeed.

This predominance of French was confined to the upper layers of society. The number of bilingual speakers in Flanders (outside Brussels) probably amounted to about 3% of the population in 1846 and had only risen to around 5% by 1930. But the seeming smallness of these figures should not disguise the importance of bilingualism within the Flemish community. In the larger cities and in university centres, such as Leuven, the number of bilingual speakers was higher. Moreover, cities are centres of culture – and the pre-eminence of French in the upper socio-economic levels of society led to the development of a high-quality French-language stream of culture in Flanders, which was much superior to its Dutch-language equivalent. And it was precisely from this cultured, bilingual environment that the government recruited most of its officials and magistrates, including almost all the most radical pro-Flemish politicians.

The beginnings of a federal debate: the break-up of Belgium

The Equality Law therefore encountered strong resistance in Wallonia, largely because Dutch had been introduced as an administrative language on a matter of principle. The nascent Walloon Movement made much progress during these years – and caused a great deal of public uproar. As with their Flemish equivalent, the Movement did not shrink from using blatantly 'ethnic' arguments. Jobs in Wallonia should go to their 'own people', people of their 'own blood', who were therefore 'different' from the Flemings. This type of ethnic doctrine (which was not uncommon for the period) was scarcely disguised in the Movement's literature and would continue to form a part of its thinking until the Second World War, following which it was replaced by the myth of a 'civil' Walloon Movement, which honoured the principles of freedom and solidarity. Faced with the strength of the Walloon reaction to the Equality Law, the Wallonian socialists who had supported the principles of bilingualism between 1896 and 1898 were now forced to make a rapid about turn, or else run the risk of being branded as traitors to 'la race wallonne'. The Walloon Movement now proclaimed the right of monolingualism throughout Wallonia, whilst at the same time defending the need for administrative bilingualism in Flanders. In a move that was equally paradoxical, the Walloon socialists adopted a similar stance, thereby allying themselves to the ruling class in Flanders!

During the furious debates surrounding the Equality Law, it was possible to hear for the first time in Wallonia a very clear anti-Belgian note. If Flanders chose to use its electoral supremacy to force bilingualism on Wallonia, then the Walloons would respond by demanding the 'administrative partition' of the country. Precisely what this meant was far from clear, even to the Walloons themselves, but it seemed at the very least to imply a strictly French-speaking Wallonia, with some form of political self-government. This was more or less what the Liege politician Julien Delaite was suggesting in December 1898, when he proposed a Walloon parliament with its own government and tax-raising powers.[34] To some extent, these were 'knee-jerk' reactions, and the Walloon Movement soon came to realise that the maintenance of the Belgian state offered the best prospects for the future development of Wallonia as a whole. Their demands were therefore confined to the introduction of a single vote system; the blocking of further Flemish demands; the preservation of the bilingual system in Flanders; and greater provincial autonomy. To this extent, the Walloon Movement remained a 'negative' movement, aimed against the Flemish progressives and radicals. It failed for the moment to attract mass support but, more importantly, it had considerable influence with the Walloon establishment of the day (it was largely organised and run by French-speaking government officials). This influence reached a new high-water mark in 1905, the year in which the Walloon National Congress held its annual meeting in the auditorium of Liege University during the World Exhibition

Leuven, circa 1875: a bilingual townscape.
A *maison de confiance* stands next to a *fabrique de cols* in true Parisian style, where everything is sold *à prix fixe* (fixed price). At the bottom left, a bilingual street sign for the Mechelsestraat.

(which, ironically, was designed to celebrate the 75th anniversary of the Belgian state). No fewer than 558 delegates were in attendance, many of them important industrialists or businessmen.

On the other side of the linguistic divide, the debates surrounding the Equality Law also led some of the leading members of the Flemish Movement to think more seriously about administrative partition. On 14 February 1896, Juliaan De Vriendt wrote to Max Rooses: "Under no circumstances must there be any mention from our side of administrative partition. But if the Walloons want it, we should accept it. We have everything to gain by it!"[35] This may have been a commonly held view and perhaps explains why Destrée accused the Flemish Catholics in the Lower House of working towards the political division of the country. In a similar vein, a few days later another Walloon member criticised the Catholics for using the Equality Law as a means to provoke administrative partition, as a prelude to full political separation.[36] Was this a case of the pot calling the kettle black? Probably not. In reality, there was no serious interest in federalism within the Flemish Movement before circa 1900.

Even so, the first cracks in the Belgian national fabric had begun to appear. This was not simply the result of the continuing impossibility of reconciling the

Ghent in the 1890s: a bilingual townscape.
On the left, there is a clothing store, bearing the proud name of *Aux FLANDRES*. Near the old St. Nicolas Church stood one of the few bookstores of the day selling Dutch-language works. This store was run by the Ghent liberal, Émile Van Goethem.

principle of universal suffrage with a new state organisation which would treat both Flemings and Walloons fairly. In Flanders, there was now also a growing trend in favour of institutional monolingualism, which implied the termination of language facilities for French-speakers. Basing their arguments on the principle of equality, the Flemish radicals argued that they were justified in rejecting administrative bilingualism in Flanders, since this was precisely what the Walloon radicals had done in Wallonia. In this respect, the Equality Law marked the start of a new political era and a new direction for both the Flemish Movement and the Belgian nation.

The social and economic agenda of the Flemish Movement

The premise that the year 1893 represents a critical juncture in Belgian history has been supported by the Dutch political scientist Jan Erk.[37] He, too, believes that the democratisation of the electoral system was a landmark decision which was ultimately destined to split the Belgian nation down the middle. In this respect, he has placed great emphasis on the results of the national elections, which after 1894 were dominated by a right-wing, Catholic population in Flanders and a left-wing, socialist population in Wallonia. In this sense, universal suffrage highlighted the fundamental differences between the working masses in the nation's two component regions. Largely as a result of the electoral reforms, the Catholic parties enjoyed an unbroken absolute majority in parliament until after the First World War. This meant that a largely leftist Wallonia was governed by a series of largely rightist, Catholic governments, whose centre of gravity was firmly in Flanders. In these circumstances, it was hardly surprising that Walloon radicalism grew. The Walloon Movement flourished and moved further to the left, while the Flemish Movement continued to position itself to the right of centre.

Erk therefore sees a clear link between the defining events of 1893 and the growth of popular labour movements in both regions, which produced a series of electoral results calculated to divide, rather than unite the nation. However, it is also possible to put a broader interpretation on these events. 1893 also saw the introduction of a Flemish and a Walloon socio-economic agenda into Belgian political life. By seeking to achieve monolingualism in Flanders, it would be possible to create a well-defined, pure geographical area, in which the new Flemish intelligentsia could develop new themes and new analyses. This was particularly true in the complex and crucial socio-economic field. The democratisation of the franchise inevitably placed such matters high on the political agenda but (with almost equal inevitability) they quickly became entangled in the language question. In some respects, this was not new. In the past, the Flemish question had occasionally been defined in social and economic terms. After 1830, it quickly became apparent that there was a correlation between the language frontier and various social frontiers, but it was not possible to analyse this phenomenon, because of a lack of reliable analytic models. However, the development of the science of sociology, together with the growth of a new school of political economy based on Marx's theories of class struggle, counterbalanced by the Catholic doctrines contained in the papal encyclical *Rerum Novarum*, resulted at the end of the 19th century in a broad consensus within Flanders that the language question was also a social question and a question of economic power.

During the debates on the Equality Law in the Lower House, the Christian-democrat politician Juliaan De Vriendt emphasised that linguistic equality would help significantly to reduce social deprivation in Flanders. This explains why at this point the Walloon socialists were also willing to support the principle of general bilingualism, at least for senior officials. The discovery of coal in the Kempen region in 1901, in Flanders, gave a new impulse to the Flemish socio-economic agenda. The dismayed Walloon Movement looked on enviously – and with alarm. These were the years in which the Flemish politician Lodewijk De Raet developed his own political message, a message which he broadcast with great brio and much to the irritation of his Wallonian counterparts. From where would the specialist staff necessary for the Kempen mines be recruited, he asked? Surely not from Wallonia? No, a thousand times no! The coal reserves of the Kempen must be entrusted to Flemish hands, just like the harbour in Antwerp should also be reclaimed for the Flemish economy. For this reason De Raet stressed the importance of Dutch not only at university level, but also in the region's business colleges. This would allow the schooling of a Flemish financial elite, who would manage new Flemish banks directing Flemish resources to Flemish projects. He also argued for the greater use of Dutch in technical schools and for the training of Flemish consuls.

In his study of the economic agenda of the Flemish Movement the historian Olivier Boehme was correct in his assessment that De Raet was not attempting to be deliberately anti-Belgian, but that he nonetheless laid the foundations for the Flemish-nationalist approach to social and economic matters.[38] This was an approach in which the idea of Flanders as a separate entity stood central. Boehme's investigation revealed another important fact: "The decision to view relations – and therefore also socio-economic relations - within the Belgian state from the perspective of a French-Dutch or Flanders-Wallonia fault line was actually taken before the necessary data had been collected and assessed. This data came later, and simply served to confirm a position which had already been taken." In reality, before the institutional changes of the 1970s, Flanders and Wallonia had never been clearly defined as recognisable economic units. In contrast, the Belgian national state came very close to becoming a territorially integrated unit in the years around 1950, with the emergence of the Flemish Walloon economic pole based on the axis Antwerp-Brussels-Charleroi. This all fits very neatly within the context of the current trend for research into 'nationalist' origins, where the emphasis is placed on 'invented' traditions as constituent elements of a national identity. The nation can be defined as an 'imagined community', in which people develop a concept of their own perceived values, stories, myths and traditions. This concept is thereafter acknowledged and maintained, but only within very strictly defined territorial boundaries. As a result of this process, mythical 'Belgian' heroes, such as Geoffrey of Bouillon, were doomed to anonymity, to be replaced by semi-fictitious Flemish champions, such as Jan Breydel. In this manner, Flanders has grown to become a 'nation'. The fact that the foundations of this nation are largely 'imagined' does nothing to detract from the reality of the nation's existence, once the 'invention of a community' has taken place.

Monolingualism for Flanders! ... or not really?

In the context of the time, the new orientation towards monolingualism in Flanders was characterised by its radicalism. In this respect, it remained a minority viewpoint in the years before the First World War, certainly as far as the establishment was concerned. During this period, most of the politicians still tended to see the solution to the language question in terms of full bilingualism throughout Belgium, which implied that bilingualism in Flanders would also be maintained. This was reflected in the measures of successive Catholic governments. For example, the law of 15 June 1899, relating to the new military penal code, allowed Flemish soldiers court-martialled in Wallonia to be defended in their own language. Judges who did not speak Dutch would automatically receive a deputy who did. Measures such as these ensured that the use of Dutch in Wallonia increased around the turn of the century. In April 1906, the government decided to take things a step further, by proposing legislation which would require pupils leaving secondary education to sit a bilingual national exam. This effectively meant that students would be required to speak a second language (Dutch in Wallonia or German in the cantons around Arlon and Verviers) before they would be admitted to university. Not surprisingly, there was a storm of protest in Wallonia, whereas the Flemish radicals saw it as another attempt to delay the advance of monolingualism in their region. The plan was quietly shelved, but was replaced by a new and equally contentious issue in March-April 1907. Parliament was discussing proposals relating to the coal mines. The Flemish Catholics wanted to amend these proposals, so that candidates would have to speak Dutch before being eligible for a position in the Flemish mine administration or for a function in the national mine administration. In response, the Minister of Labour (a Walloon) put forward an even more far-reaching amendment, which would have introduced bilingualism in Wallonia for various jobs in the mining industry, including engineers (basing his case on the large number of Flemings working in the Walloon pits). Once again, nothing came of these proposal but they were symptomatic of the spirit of the times. Even little things could lead to irritation and dispute, such as the compulsory introduction of bilingual street signs in Wallonia in the years around 1910. As Jules Destrée later wrote: "The translations were useless for the Flemings and annoying for the Walloons, since they were a permanent reminder of their conquest."[39]

And so it went on. In 1909-1910, the question of national bilingualism once again came to the fore with regard to new legislation dealing with the labour councils (the forerunners of the modern-day labour courts). Surely the chairmen of these councils would need to speak both national languages? In the Lower House the rights of the 120,000 Flemings working in Wallonia were fiercely defended by the Ghent socialist Edward Anseele, following which a furious discussion broke out between the Walloon and Flemish socialist factions (in contrast to the period 1896-1898, the socialist supporters of bilingualism were now to be found exclusively in the Flemish camp). The Walloon politician Aurèle Maroille shouted out that parliament would soon be demanding that all judges in Wallonia should learn Dutch, to which Anseele replied: "Why not?" It was certainly true that many migratory Flemish workers were required to appear before these councils in Wallonia, but Anseele's comment was more provocative than serious. A much milder government amendment was finally approved which required the clerks of the councils to be bilingual. Yet even this watered-down proposal was the cause of much heated debate when it finally reached the Senate in March 1910. The highpoint was reached when the otherwise moderate Liege senator Emile Dupont cried out: "Long live administrative partition!"[40] That such a respected politician should make such a statement in the Senate says much about the atmosphere of the time and made a strong impression on contemporary society.

Gradually, the Flemish Movement began to change its thinking, a move which the historian Harry Van Velthoven has rightly described as "a historical decision with far-reaching consequences".[41] Increasingly, the Flemish progressives were prepared to tone down their agitation for bilingualism in Wallonia, providing that in return the Walloon members of parliament were prepared to support proposals which would reduce the level of administrative bilingualism in Flanders. In this manner, for example, a compromise was reached whereby the Flemings agreed that the language provisions in the labour council legislation should only be applicable in Flanders, while the Walloons were prepared to approve a new language law for the further introduction of Dutch in parts of the Flemish secondary education system. It was not foreseen at this stage that this gradual limitation of bilingualism might eventually result in administrative monolingualism in Flanders. This was unfamiliar territory for the Flemish Movement and nobody really knew where the new policy would lead.

Government policy was also inconsistent and on occasions even helped to undermine its own doctrine of general administrative bilingualism for the country as a whole. In fact, government policy was beginning to change and was moving gradually in the direction favoured by the Walloon Movement: protection of the non-Dutch speakers in Wallonia and the preservation of bilingualism in Flanders. This was actually a return to the old policy from the days of the tax-based electoral system. Prior to the 1893 reforms, the effectiveness of administrative bilingualism, particularly in Flanders, had often been sabotaged by clever political manoeuvring. Consider, for example, the administrative law of 1878, which stipulated that in the future officials who came into contact with the public must learn Dutch. Notwithstanding this provision, there were still two types of language examinations for new entrants: a monolingual test in French and a bilingual test in French and Dutch. An equal number of vacancies were allocated to the successful candidates of both tests. For the French-speakers, the monolingual test was relatively easy, requiring little more than a level of knowledge which they had already learned at primary school. Such entrants often declined to sit the second bilingual test, choosing to confine their careers to Wallonia or to positions which did not involve contact with the public. For the Flemish speakers it was different. There was no monolingual test in Dutch, and so they had to take the bilingual text. But for them the level of knowledge required for French was equivalent to what they had learned in secondary school. In other words, for the Flemings the test was relatively harder – and therefore more of them failed. So much so, that there were insufficient successful candidates to fill the number of vacancies allocated to the bilingual test. And so these

Belgium and the Monarchy. From National Independence to National Disintegration.

Leopold II, circa 1908

surplus vacancies were filled by... candidates from a reserve list, made up of those who had passed the monolingual French test in Wallonia! This meant that relatively unschooled Flemings were unable to find their way into the civil service because of their poor French, whereas Walloon candidates with absolutely no knowledge of Dutch were appointed all over Flanders.

Such manipulation bordered on the grotesque, but was ultimately doomed to failure. Tactics of this kind could not survive the enfranchisement of the Flemish masses in 1893, nor the growing personnel demands of an expanding administrative system. From 1907 onwards, a series of 37 articles appeared in the Dutch-language De Standaard newspaper, which highlighted this problem. In 1908, the conservative minister Helleputte granted civil servants a limited right of association, following which the Flemish-speaking administrators began to organise themselves around the language question. From 1910 onwards, the Flemish Public Servants Union held an annual conference, attended by hundreds of delegates, who protested loudly against the language discrimination resulting from the government's pro-Walloon appointments policy.

In terms of the Flemish Movement, these developments led to increasing radicalisation, under the motto: "Down with bilingualism!" This went hand in hand with a broadening of the ideological base of the Movement, since their language-related protests were now organised more and more along cross-party lines (in part as a result of the Movement's electoral breakthrough in the years following 1894). There was a growing belief that a 'Flemish struggle' could achieve almost anything. And why not? The Flemings were now clearly in the majority, both in the country and in parliament. What could stand in the way of administrative monolingualism in Flanders?

Only the Flemings themselves. Consider the campaign to transform the university in Ghent into a Dutch-speaking university. After 1910, this campaign gathered pace under the impulse of three leading Flemish politicians: the Catholic Frans Van Cauwelaert, the liberal Louis Franck and the socialist Camille Huysmans. The ordinary man in the street – the vast majority of whom could not speak French – had no difficulty in supporting the radical option for the education of Flanders' intellectual elite exclusively in Dutch. The 'battle' for the University of Ghent could therefore rely on the support of the Flemish masses. However, it was another matter with the Flemish establishment. It soon became apparent that they were less happy with the course being steered with such enthusiasm by their radical political leaders. The years between 1910 and 1914 were destined to reveal just how weak support for monolingualism amongst the ruling elite in Flanders really was. The pattern was repeated during and after the First World War, when the country's ruling class again demonstrated its reluctance to have its sons educated in Dutch alone. Surely there must always be a place – and an important place – for the French language in a 'cultured' upbringing? Was it now really necessary to abandon this intellectually sophisticated language just for the sake of 'the Flemish people'? And in an era when Belgian representatives were still sent to all the corners of the world, particularly Egypt and Congo, would the country's diplomats not be better served with a French diploma?

In short, the growth of mass support for the Flemish Movement was paralleled by an increasing reluctance among the Flemish middle and upper classes to accept more drastic Flemish monolingualism, particularly if it affected their own little world. It is certainly true that the division along linguistic lines, which in the past had reflected the workings of the tax-based voting system, continued to operate for many years with regard to proposals to introduce more Dutch within the education system. It was far easier to radicalise the masses than the establishment. In this respect, many Belgian historians overestimate the level of consensus within 'the' Flemish Movement on the issue of monolingualism in university education. True, the movement was very active, and the archives for this period are full of Flemish publications, Flemish pamphlets, Flemish letters, Flemish posters, Flemish reports, etc. But a vociferous minority does not necessarily reflect the opinions of the majority, and publicity does not equate to power. The most noticeable feature of these documents was their radicalism – and this radicalism did not appeal to key sections of the Flemish community. These more moderate nationalists seldom made their voices heard – they risked being branded as traitors – but they were still a political force to be reckoned with.

Yet even bearing this qualification in mind, it is nevertheless true that in general terms the Flemish Movement became increasingly radical in the years around 1900, partly because of the impact of mass participation and partly because the question of monolingualism in Flanders – albeit with many caveats – was now firmly on the political agenda.

"Long live Wallonia, free and independent!"

A similar radicalisation was also apparent in Wallonia. Since the liberal defeat in the election of 1884, the centre of gravity for government policy had switched to Flanders. As a consequence of this shift, and given the political conservatism of the majority in Flanders, the Walloon progressives had to tolerate the shelving of many of their most cherished plans: compulsory education for children, greater union freedom, better social provisions, etc. The government was even accused to seeking to disadvantage Wallonia by manipulation of the national budget. From this Walloon point of view, there was a simple remedy to put all these matters right: the introduction of the single vote electoral system. But how could they ever persuade the Catholic majority to accept such a thing? The position of the Belgian liberals and socialists seemed hopeless. Or was it? The Catholic majority was gradually whittled away and by 1910 had been reduced to just six seats in the Lower House. In 1912, the socialists and the liberals

3 The first cracks in the façade of national unity

Albert I (1875-1934), King of the Belgians from 1909 onwards. His son – who would later become King Leopold III (born 1901) – sits on his lap.

formed an electoral alliance. This remarkable development opened up the possibility of bringing to an end the Catholic dominance which had persisted since 1884. The electoral campaign was also marked by a very clear divide along regional lines. The leftists in Wallonia identified the Flemish Movement not just with Catholicism but with Flanders as a whole, so that the campaign became polarised on the differences between the two regions, in a manner which divided the national political parties deeply. But it was all to no avail. In the election of July 1912, the Catholic block increased its majority to 16 seats, provoking a series of strikes and riots in Brussels and Wallonia, in which a number of protesters were killed. This intense reaction was a mixture of anti-clerical and anti-Flemish feeling, and gave new impulsion to the Walloon Movement. On the evening the results were announced, Jules Destrée gave a firebrand speech in which he demanded immediate administrative partition, as the only way to free Wallonia from the yoke of Flemish-Catholic oppression. He elaborated on his ideas a few days later in a newspaper article in *Le Journal de Charleroi*. The article ended with the emotive declaration: "Long live Wallonia, free and independent".[42] During the days which followed, the provincial councils in Liege and Hainaut both passed resolutions in favour of administrative partition, and the French-speaking liberal and socialist press was packed with editorials supporting this standpoint. On 7 July, a volatile Walloon Congress in Liege passed a similar resolution and at the end of August, Destrée published a controversial open letter to the king: *Lettre au Roi sur la Séparation de la Wallonie et de la Flandre*.

Destrée presented King Albert I (1909-1934) with a very ethnic analysis of the Flanders-Wallonia dispute: "Let me tell you the truth, Sire, the great and terrible truth: there are no such things as Belgians." A farmer from the Kempen and a steelworker from Charleroi were two different types of beings. They represented two distinct races of people, the Flemings and the Walloons, each with their own unique 'nature'. Something which interested one race might be a matter of complete indifference to the other race. The Walloons (anno 1912) were excitable, inconstant and inclined to revolt against authority, whereas the Flemings were seen as slow, stubborn, patient and disciplined. Then, of course, there was also the Brussels type - but Destrée thought that they were uninteresting: "They seem to combine the bad qualities of both races, but without any of the compensating advantages."

Destrée argued at some length that the Flemish – by virtue of their language, their struggle for self-expression and their numerical superiority – represented a serious threat to the Walloons. For this reason, he defended the concept of a far-reaching federalism along the lines of the Swiss or American models, both of which allowed considerable autonomy in domestic affairs. According to Destrée, this was the most important issue confronting the Belgian nation – and it would not be solved by ministers or political parties. Only a free and independent spirit – such as the king himself – could show the people the way.

Destrée's letter created something of a stir, both by its direct appeal to the person of the king and by the strident tone in which it was written. The reaction in Flanders bordered on disbelief. Moreover, Destrée had let the genie out of the bottle. Since the Walloons were now arguing for administrative separation, a number of Flemings decided to jump on the same bandwagon. This was perhaps most evident within the Catholic and free-thinking youth movements in Antwerp and in the increasing number of articles on the subject in the Flemish press.[43]

In a similar manner, a marginal youth group in Ghent published a magazine at the start of 1914 with the provocative title *Bestuurlijke Scheiding* (Administrative Partition – the title was, in fact, the most important thing about this otherwise irrelevant publication). However, in the months immediately before the outbreak of war there was also a significant radicalisation amongst the Catholic mainstream in Flanders. In February 1914 Emiel Wildiers, a leading Christian-democrat, made a speech openly in favour of partition. At roughly the same time the magazine *Hooger Leven* – a well-respected publication linked to a Catholic group of Flemish progressives led by Professor Emiel Vliebergh – printed an anonymous article under the initials D.T., which was severely critical of the Catholic majority's current approach to the partition issue.[44] "There is only one way which we can follow, if we wish to bring to an end these annoying and intolerable abuses: we need to discover an effective remedy which will allow the personal interests of the Belgian citizen, in the Flemish region of our country, to be reconciled with the wider social interests of the Flemish people. This remedy is already known to us. It has been much talked about in recent times (...) The unjustified fear which the mere mention of its name arouses in some quarters is evidence in itself that the application of this method is feasible. All right-minded, clear-thinking people, out of respect for justice, out of concern for the internal peace and welfare of the Belgian nation, must give their approval for its immediate introduction." A few sentences later, D.T. reveals the nature of this remedy, which had been the subject of so much heated debate in recent years: "Administrative separation". The diffidence with which the magazine 'dared' to mention these words suggests that the author had a good insight into the power of simple slogans within a nationalist culture. Be that as it may, in July 1914 the influential Flemish Catholic Union formulated its most pointed motion during the pre-war period, asking whether the Flemings first had to threaten administrative separation before they would be given a fair hearing.

Taken together, these incidents form a significant body of opinion, particularly if we keep in mind that it is not only myths and stories, but also ideas and projects, which give shape to a nation.

ANTWERPEN - Hoboken

4
Albert I
(until 1918)

King and Commander-in-Chief

The future King Albert I probably had few difficulties with the policy pursued by the 'Flemish' governments after 1894, namely, bilingualism throughout the country. Albert can certainly be seen as a kindred spirit of Picard, with his concept of the 'Belgian soul', and the prince was an interested reader of Pirenne's monumental works on Belgian history. With the prospect of one day becoming king, from 1891 onwards he had undertaken the study of Dutch. In 1900, Albert married a German princess, Elisabeth, Duchess in Beieren. A few days before the death of King Leopold II in December 1909, the French military attaché in Brussels, Colonel Dury, wrote: "The new court will have strong pro-German tendencies. In reality, everything is run by the Duchess of Flanders [Albert's mother, who had been born as the Princess of Hohenzollern-Sigmaringen], who is completely German. The new king is also German by education and, in contrast to King Leopold and Prince Boudewijn, has retained none of his affinity for France."[45] The new king would indeed be suspicious of his powerful neighbour to the south – a fact which would once again have implications for the international impact of the Flemish Movement.

On the eve of the Great War

Immediately following the death of King Leopold, the Flemish Movement launched a well-organised campaign to persuade the new king to swear his constitutional oath in both Dutch and French; previously it had always been in French alone. At the suggestion of Minister Schollaert the king agreed and the oath was heard in Dutch for the first time on 23 December 1909. (The subsequent speech from the throne was exclusively in French, but the Flemish activists were still prepared to accept this.) Moreover, right from the very beginning of his reign Albert addressed his people in Dutch at official functions in Flanders (albeit using a pre-written text) and he ensured that his children also learned the language. Even so, during the period before the Second World War Dutch remained essentially a 'foreign' tongue for the Belgian royal family. It is only from the generation of Boudewijn I and Albert II that it is possible to speak of truly bilingual kings.

It was understandable that King Albert should be worried about the unity of his country and he did all he could to cement the cracks in the national fabric. During a special celebratory congress held in March 1910, the Flemish societies decided – to loud applause – to send a message of thanks to the king for his willingness to swear the royal oath in both languages. In a letter of reply dated 23 March 1910, the cabinet of the king let it be known that His Majesty had accepted their "loyal address" with thanks, adding that in his heart the "Flemish people" could never be separated from the rest of the Belgians.[46]

After the contentious elections of 1912, an anxious king wrote to Minister de Broqueville to express his concern about the internal divisions of the country, which were becoming polarised "in a most regrettable manner; that is to say, in a manner

Belgium and the Monarchy. From National Independence to National Disintegration.

A photograph of the wedding in 1900 of the then Prince Albert (1875-1934) with Elisabeth, Duchess in Beieren (1876-1965). The photograph has been signed by Albert.

which opposes beliefs, races and classes."[47] But how did the king propose to solve it? On 15 August 1912, King Albert and Queen Elisabeth visited Antwerp, to take part in celebrations to be held the next day in honour of the memory of the Flemish writer, Hendrik Conscience, and the Walloon diplomat, August Lambermont. In his Dutch speech to the people of Antwerp, the king said that this double celebration underlined the truth of the Belgian national motto: *Eendracht maakt Macht* (Union is Strength) and he appealed for greater national unity, based on the shared common history of both Flemings and Walloons.[48] This appeal received much publicity and made a strong impression on both sides of the linguistic divide. Jules Destrée even referred to it in his *Open Letter to the King*. Writing to his secretary Jules Ingenbleek about this letter, the king commented: "I have read Destrée's letter, and he is, without doubt, a great literary talent. Everything which he says is true, but it is no less true that administrative partition would be a bad thing, involving many more dangers and inconveniences than the current situation."[49]

The king had alternative solutions in mind. His ideas on education were expressed by Ingenbleek in April 1910 as follows: "An immediate decision is required. The solution would be: in Wallonia, education exclusively in French; in Flanders, two different systems, one exclusively in French and the other exclusively in Flemish. This, of course, to apply to secondary and further education. The city to be selected for the university would be Antwerp. One or two faculties could be set up, according to local preference."[50] This system had the advantage of flexibility. It would have been possible in Flanders, for example, to follow secondary education in Flemish before moving on to a French-speaking university. Or vice versa. The radicals could opt for a Flemish secondary education *and* a Flemish university, while the same option also existed in French. Ingenbleek's comments suggest that the king was unwilling to undermine the principle of monolingualism in Wallonia, but at the same time was sensitive towards Flemish demands for the development of their own Dutch-language culture and elite. This explains his support for the creation of a full Dutch-language education network from secondary level onwards. However, he was equally anxious to stimulate bilingualism, particularly for those students in Flanders who were planning to progress to further education. Nevertheless, his idea for two separate monolingual systems in Flanders was not in keeping with the thinking of the more militant Flemish activists, whose aim was to create a single Dutch-speaking state university in Flanders, located in Ghent. Even so, the very least that one can say is that the king had his own original views on the subject.

During the immediate pre-war period there was growing resistance in Flanders to the granting of language facilities in both administration and justice. This resistance came primarily from the civil servants themselves. It is not known what King Albert thought about this development, but no doubt his thinking was as original as it was in other fields. Take, for example, the question of language reform in the army. Between 1909 and 1913 the Flemish militants were pressing for fairer arrangements for Flemish-speakers, and the king probably had some sympathy with their demands. This was evident from a much later comment, made to the ministerial council held in De Panne on 1 February 1918. In a discussion about language problems in the army, the king declared: "I was already in favour of regional units in 1913."[51] Regional recruiting was one of the pre-war objectives of the Flemish radicals and also found sympathy among the Walloon socialists. Since language differences were linked to specific regions, regional recruiting would allow Flemish soldiers to serve in quasi monolingual units, which would also be the case in Wallonia. However, the ministers in the de Broqueville government – unlike the king – were not persuaded by the logic of this argument. They listened instead to the prophets of doom who believed that 'separate' regional armies would bring the Belgian state a step closer to disintegration. The king clearly thought differently – but why? The fact that regional recruiting would please both the Flemish Movement and the Walloon socialists was an added bonus, but his main considerations were probably military. Regional recruiting would help to strengthen *esprit de corps* and troops would be more inclined to show initiative when surrounded by officers and comrades who spoke their own language. Being based closer to home – instead of on the other side of the country – would also be good for morale. This was certainly the case in France and Austria-Hungary, where regional recruiting had been introduced with success. However, because the parliamentary majority seemed to be scared of its separatist implications, the Flemish radicals abandoned their demands for regional units, and pressed instead for single language units which could be posted throughout the country. In other words, Dutch-speaking regiments could be stationed in Wallonia, and French-speaking regiments in Flanders. This, they believed, would overcome the fears of separatism (although they failed to reckon with the Walloon militants, who were opposed to Flemish soldiers on Walloon soil in any way, shape or form).

Yet it all made no difference. The Catholic majority was not prepared to countenance either regional recruiting or single language units. Instead, they came up with an alternative language proposal which was much less far-reaching. French remained the language of command: according to Prime Minister de Broqueville, this would not cause any difficulties, since the Flemish soldiers would be taught the French commands in the course of their training. However, it was also decided that the general organisation of the army should be made bilingual, to ensure that any likelihood of future language difficulties would disappear over time. The law of 2 July 1913 was therefore the first army law to contain language provisions and decreed that the military authorities must also acquire a knowledge of Dutch. This was to be introduced gradually, on a year-by-year basis. Pupils at the military training college were required to learn Dutch from 1917 onwards. Candidate military doctors were required to sit a Dutch examination with effect from 1915. General training of the rank-and-file was also

King Albert I and Queen Elisabeth leaving a ceremony at the statue of Baron Lambermont, Antwerp, 15 August 1912.

to be given in both Dutch and French, a measure introduced on 1 January 1914. From the same date there was also an obligation to issue all written notices and instructions in both languages. These were all positive steps in the right direction, but it would be a generation before their effects were fully felt. This was perhaps inevitable: the lack of training facilities in Dutch was bound to cause problems, particularly since no real transitional period was foreseen.

In January 1914, the Lower House also began debating new proposals for primary education. There were still many exclusively French-speaking primary schools (ages 6 to 12 years) in Flanders, particularly in the larger cities, and this while the Dutch-language schools were required to prepare their pupils for a transition to French at secondary level. The Flemish radicals wanted full Dutch-language primary education throughout Flanders, with the second national language only being taught from the fifth year onwards. However, an amendment to this effect was torpedoed by Minister Prosper Poullet, a pro-Flemish Catholic from Leuven. Instead, the government devised a new arrangement whereby it was still possible to set up French classes in Flanders for groups of more than 20 children, which was the case in almost every Flemish city. The Flemish press claimed that the king had had a hand in this strategy, because he was afraid of the separatist movement in Wallonia and therefore did not want to be seen to be giving too many concessions to the Flemings. The government newspaper

Le XXe Siècle published a denial, probably at Albert's request. And it does indeed seem more likely that responsibility for the preservation of these language facilities in primary education rested with the Catholic ministers. In this they were supported by a large number of elitist Flemish-Catholic members of the Lower House, who were still not convinced of the need for Dutch-language primary education in Flanders.

August 1914 – a 'foreign' war and an impossible domestic peace

The First World War began on 4 August 1914. Germany wished to attack its arch-enemy France, but this was only possible if the German armies were allowed to pass through neutral Belgian territory. Not surprisingly, the Belgian government was not prepared to sanction this hostile act and so a German invasion became unavoidable. The Belgian Army rushed to defend its borders, under the personal command of King Albert. In this capacity as commander-in-chief of the army, the king was operating without ministerial responsibility (an anomaly which would be repeated in 1940 during the reign of his son, Leopold III).

The German advance in 1914 was finally brought to a halt along the banks of the IJzer, a small river in the extreme west of the country, close to the border with France (see map at the beginning of this book). Just 50 of Belgium's 2,630 towns and villages remained unoccupied. Throughout the war, the king was determined to stay within this small parcel of 'free' national territory and he met regularly with his ministers at the seaside resort of De Panne. The government itself had withdrawn to France, where a small village near Le Havre had also been given the temporary diplomatic status of Belgian territory. This government ruled by ministerial decree, since it was no longer possible to convene the parliament. However, in a gesture of national unity, this essentially Catholic government (under the leadership of Charles de Broqueville) allowed two liberal and one socialist minister to sit in its cabinet for the duration of the war: initially as ministers without portfolio, but later in positions of effective responsibility and power. It was the first coalition government in Belgian political history.

In a special session of parliament held on 4 August 1914, King Albert had appealed to all Belgians to put their communal differences to one side, in the interests of the greater good of the nation. In a proclamation issued to his army a day later, he quoted no less a person than the great Julius Caesar, who had referred to the Belgians as "the bravest of all the Gauls" (*horum omnium fortissimi sunt Belgae*). He further reminded the Flemish people of their heroic victory over the French at the Battle of the Golden Spurs in 1302 (the battle which had acquired mythical status during the 1840s, thanks to the writings of Hendrik Conscience, who conveniently forgot that many Walloons had also fought on the Flemish side). He similarly reminded the Walloon people of the sacrifice of the 600 warriors of Franchimont, who in 1468 had died in a desperate attempt to repel 'foreign' invaders from the city of Liege (an event which since 1912 onwards had acquired a similar mythical status, as the Walloons went in search of their own 'invented traditions'). In the jingoistic atmosphere of 1914, it seemed to make little difference that the Flemish had been fighting against the French (who were now allies) or that the Franchimontese had actually been rebelling against the lawful authority of the Duke of Burgundy. Everyone understood that the king was appealing to *national* sentiment, to the patriotic heart of his people. And it was in this spirit that his people reacted: the Flemings and the Walloons buried their regional differences in a united effort to free the country from enemy occupation.

This, however, was easier said than done. During the early phases of the campaign, the German Army seemed unstoppable, leaving a trail of destruction and mass executions in its wake as it pressed forwards across the Belgian countryside. This conscious German strategy had clear disadvantages. At an international level, it lost the Germans all support for their actions which they might otherwise have secured. Within the conquered territory, it also lost them the political sympathy of the local population, which they had hoped to receive in some areas of the country. As early as September 1914, the German chancellor had given instructions that the Flemish language question should be exploited to German advantage. However, the reaction of the Flemings to these overtures was lukewarm in the extreme. The only response came from a small group of extreme Flemish nationalists in Ghent: the same circles which had published the magazine *Bestuurlijke Scheiding* (Administrative Separation) immediately before the outbreak of the war. This group was now calling itself 'Jong Vlaanderen' (Young Flanders), and its dominant force was Jan Domela Nieuwenhuis, a fanatical Protestant priest from neighbouring Holland, who had been living and preaching in Ghent since 1903.

This Flemish collaboration with the Germans – which would later be referred to as 'activism' – had little immediate impact or support. But as the war dragged on, so this offered the possibility of a gradual change in public opinion. Surely Germany was more than just an inhuman military machine? Was it not a centre of European culture? The land of Beethoven, Goethe and Dürer? Did it really have nothing to offer the people of Flanders, whose language shared the same roots? And what if they eventually won the war? If the German Empire held its ground – and that is precisely what it looked like doing – this would inevitably mean a redrawing of the political map of Europe which had been established after 1815. If some kind of compromise peace was agreed, would this really be such a bad thing for Flanders? The war was one thing, but the peace might be something completely different. If Europe was about to be re-divided in accordance with the wishes of the Great Powers, it might be wise to be sitting next to the Germans at the conference table... This geo-political background slowly persuaded the more pragmatic (village) intellectuals in Flanders to move in the direction of the German camp. This created a climate in which it became possible for the occupying authorities to gradually split the Flemish nationalists away from the Belgian national resistance movement, which could tolerate no compromise with the enemy. The Germans exploited this *Flamenpolitik* with considerable subtlety. They released Flemish prisoners-of-war more quickly than their French-speaking counterparts. They imposed a strict and Flemish-friendly interpretation of the language laws, which no Belgian government of the day could ever have accepted. This was the politics of 'divide and rule' – and it gradually seemed to be working. This first became noticeable from February 1915 onwards, particularly in the city of Antwerp. As the historian Sophie De Schaepdrijver has pointed out, in the first instance this was little more than a gradual shift from unconditional loyalty towards a more conditional support for Belgium's war aims.[52]

In this respect, the press in occupied Belgium played a key role. However naïve it might now sound, few people at the time realised that this press was controlled and often financed by the German authorities. Not surprisingly, these newspapers painted a very different picture of the war in comparison with the Belgian journals which were still being published in the unoccupied territory, in France and in The Netherlands (which, in contrast to the Second World War, was a neutral country). This confusing situation inevitably led to a kind of 'press war', which (with equal inevitability) had a strong Flanders/Wallonia – Flemish/French character. The first problems had already arisen at the end of 1914, but the conflict burst well and truly into life in May-June 1915, when the Belgian press-in-exile in The Netherlands published a series of provocative articles arguing for the expansion of Belgium's national frontiers as a *sine qua non* for any post-war peace settlement. This was a theme which was closely related to the language question, and further fuel was added to the fire at the end of June 1915, when Alberic Deswarte – another Flemish exile in The Netherlands, writing in *De Vlaamsche Stem* (The Voice of Flanders) – openly demanded full administrative separation. This would have caused uproar in any circumstances, but matters were made worse when the Flemish Catholic politician Frans Van Cauwelaert found evidence that *De Vlaamsche Stem* – notwithstanding its publication in neutral Holland – had been infiltrated by the Germans. Realising that they were the victim of a German propaganda trap and under growing public pressure, most of the editorial team felt that they had little option but to resign. The only 'survivors' were Antoon Jacob and the poet René De Clercq, who now became the editor-in-chief. But the general tone of the paper remained much the same. It was De Clercq, acting on behalf of a Flemish society, who on 11 July 1915 sent a telegram from the Dutch town of Bussum to the king in De Panne. The subject of this telegram was nothing less than the future of Flanders and, in particular, the importance of granting the region the required degree of autonomy within the Belgian state framework. In other words, De Clercq and his friends were suggesting a type of federalism. When the Flemish telegram received no answer, the society decided to send a French version. Secretary Ingenbleek this time forwarded a reply from the unhappy king (a reply which had been approved in advance by Prime Minister de Broqueville). The telegrams had caused considerable outrage, but the king's reply was dry and formal: the matter would be referred to the post-war government, which would take appropriate steps in the interest of the Belgian people. However, the king could not resist adding the following comment: "Until such time as this is possible, the king makes an urgent appeal to all Belgians that they should strive in the face of the enemy for nothing other than the liberation of our national territory".[53]

Nevertheless, it was inevitable that the government would be required to take a more immediate official position on the disturbing rise of activism. So it was that in October 1915 King Albert signed a royal decree, proposed by Minister Poullet, to the effect that René De Clercq should be relieved of his pre-war status as a civil servant. Similar measures were taken against Antoon Jacob. Their position had become untenable, given their refusal to resign from *De Vlaamsche Stem*. These measures were only retaliatory pinpricks, but this is almost beside the point. The fragile domestic peace had been well and truly broken – and once again it had been broken on the rocks of the language question. The way was now open for the activists to claim the status of martyrs – and there is nothing more calculated to boost the confidence of a nascent national movement than a few willing martyrs. The Germans were also rubbing their hands with glee, and quickly let it be known that they were prepared to consider far-reaching political concessions in Flanders. The German *Flamenpolitik* was assuming greater proportions – and it seemed to be working.

Problems at the Belgian front

Running parallel with these developments in occupied Belgium, the language question was also causing difficulties at the front. The line of trenches now stretched unbroken from the Belgian coast at the mouth of the River IJzer, through France, to the borders of Switzerland. It seemed impossible for either side to break through this line, and from 1915 onwards the military deadlock led to a growing feeling of unrest and defeatism in all the warring armies. This unrest often displayed a strong social dimension. In particular, the ordinary rank-and-file, who were living and dying in the mud by their thousands, came into increasing conflict with the elitist officer class, who seemed to show little concern for their sufferings.

Amongst the Flemish soldiers on the IJzer front, this discontent crystallised around the language question. The language barrier also created a social barrier. If you were unable to speak French, you were unlikely to win promotion, since French was the language used for most technical matters in military circles and was also the language of preference of the officer corps. For this reason, the language barrier had a certain stigma attached to it: in the army, it was almost like a badge of inferiority. Flemish

Belgium and the Monarchy. From National Independence to National Disintegration.

De Panne in April 1915. King Albert, Prince Leopold and Princess Marie-José, in a photograph taken by Queen Elisabeth. During the war, the royal family lived in a modest house in De Panne. The artistically-minded queen took snapshots of their daily life and also photographed the many foreign dignitaries who came to visit them.

was the language spoken by the junior ranks, the socially inferior. French was the language of the senior ranks, who were both socially and militarily superior. In short, the higher echelons of the army tended to look down on the lower echelons – and the focus for this condescension was language. This asocial attitude exhibited by the army high command was strongly contested by a number of language-conscious Flemish intellectuals, many of whom served as ordinary soldiers. Compulsory national service had only been introduced at the end of 1913 and the officer corps was still not used to dealing with a free-speaking soldiery. Moreover, the limited language provisions which had been included in the Army Act of 1913 were being flagrantly ignored by the general staff – a point which was made very clear in the angry letters from front line soldiers which the Catholic politician Frans Van Cauwelaert began to receive in the summer of 1915. And as the months passed, so the problem escalated. Walloon officers became more and more irritated at the tentative protests of their Flemish troops against the military use of language. Minister Alois Van de Vyvere wrote to Van Cauwelaert on this subject in 1916: "The officers are either Walloons or French-speaking Flemings. They are intellectually anti-Flemish, without even realising it. *J'aime les Flamands mais les flamingants ont à compter avec moi!* [I love the Flemings, but the Flemish militants will have to answer to me!]. These words were written to me by a brave and well-meaning colonel. And what is he saying? He is saying that he – a Fleming from Leuven – is always prepared to use his own terrible Dutch to speak to Flemish troops who understand no French, but that he regards the young Flemish students in his regiment who address him directly in Dutch as 'nationalists' or 'hot-heads'. What does this mean? That it is not the mass of unschooled Flemings who are suffering, but rather their more educated countrymen. And what can be done about it? There is never anything precise that you can put your finger on, that you can formally complain about. The colonel in question is highly regarded by his Flemish troops. 'He's a good chap', say most of them, but he is much hated – and with good reason – by a handful of his Flemish students." [54]

If we analyse this quotation in more detail, it seems to confirm that the language question in the trenches was concentrated on the fundamental, 'nationalist' issues which had scandalised the traditional 'Belgicists' since the 1890s. The Flemish students were all bilingual by virtue of their secondary education and further studies. In other words, the matter revolved around bilingual Flemings who were refusing as a matter of principle to speak French to someone whose knowledge of Dutch was poor. In short, it reflected the new orientation of the Flemish Movement in the direction of a radical monolingualism for Flanders.

Another aspect of the same problem was the fact that the Flemings formed a substantial majority of the rank-and-file, whereas nearly all the officers – and certainly the senior officers – seemed to be French-speaking. This created the impression that the youth of Flanders was little more than cannon-fodder for the francophone elite. Perhaps this was not all that far from the truth. The census of 1910 showed that 55% of the national population was living in Flanders, whereas the casualty statistics for the period 1915-1918 reveal that almost 69% of the fatalities during that period originated from that region. This 'over-representation' was largely the result of the recruiting system used in 1914. The class of 1914 was only eligible for call-up in September of that year, but by this time the Germans had already overrun almost all of Wallonia. This meant that the new recruits came largely from the unoccupied west of the country – which was predominantly Flemish-speaking. Much the same applied to the soldiers who were recruited from amongst the refugees who had fled abroad during the early months of the war. On the other hand, only 49% of the non-commissioned officers killed in action were from Flanders – which reflects their language-restricted representation in the more senior ranks. The lower general standard of education in Flanders also meant that fewer Flemings were to be found on the army staff or in the technical arms, such as the engineers or the artillery, which traditionally occupied 'safer' positions behind the front lines.

After 1916, there was a persistent rumour that 80% of the soldiers fighting in the trenches were Flemish. This was to be a powerful lever in the debates which followed. In retrospect, it is clear that this was an exaggeration of the truth. As we have seen, the actual casualty rate was 69%, but this still means that a quarter more Flemings than Walloons died during the heroic defence of the Belgian Army along the River IJzer. This social reality was shocking to many of those who were forced to live through it, day after day. At the same time, we must be careful not to move too far in the opposite direction. There were indeed serious language problems in the Belgian Army during the First World War, but their effect must be kept in a proper perspective. It was not the case – as many people in Flanders still claim – that Flemish soldiers were sent needlessly to their death because of their inability to understand the orders which had been issued to them in French. The military training of the day gave most foot-soldiers a basic understanding of French military terms, while the education of the French-speaking officer class was of a sufficient quality to ensure that most of them could speak a few sentences of Dutch. It was certainly irritating that most of the army communiqués – including those of King Albert – were written in French (and seldom translated), but this was hardly a matter of military life and death. Crucial orders were always made clear to the men, most frequently through the intervention of bilingual sergeants, who served as a kind of unofficial liaison service between the officers and the rank-and-file. More serious were the problems in the military hospitals, where the doctors (as might be expected) often had little understanding of Dutch and where the individual – and often illiterate – Flemish soldiers were left largely to their own devices.

In October 1915, two Flemish members of parliament – Frans Van Cauwelaert and Alfons Van de Perre – hoped to pour oil on the troubled waters of Flemish national sentiment, both at the front and in the occupied territories. In a letter to King Albert, they asked the sovereign to offer the people "some wise council and benevolent words" on these difficult issues. The king simply referred them to the government and pointed out that Minister Poullet had taken up residence in unoccupied Holland, from where he hoped to be better able to defend the interests of the Flemish community at home and abroad.[55]

Van de Perre made direct contact with Poullet and with the government in Le Havre. He obtained some minor concessions. In a circular issued by Minister of War de Broqueville on 13 January, the army was reminded that the provisions of the Army Act of 1913 – which foresaw the issuing of commands and other communications in both national languages – still applied, even in time of war. He 'ordered' that the officers should henceforth do all in their power to communicate with their Flemish soldiers in Dutch and 'insisted' that all candidate-officers should be convinced of the importance of the Dutch language as a means of ensuring good and effective leadership.

Yet in reality, these were little more than suggestions and recommendations. The introduction of Dutch into the officer corps could only take place gradually, year by year (as had also been foreseen in the 1913 Army Act). This was a process which would take decades, and neither the king nor de Broqueville was prepared to do what an adjutant at the front, Jozef Rombouts, had suggested in a letter to Van de Perre: "Instead of encouraging the officers to do it [i.e., comply with the terms of the Army Act], they should force them to do it."[56] As time would show, it was destined to be a similar story with regard to the introduction of Dutch into the judiciary and the state administration in Flanders. It was simply unrealistic to expect the dominance of the French language to disappear overnight: this would only happen little by little, as more and more students graduated with a greater knowledge of the Flemish tongue. The key in all three cases – army, law and administration – was the development of high-quality Dutch language education at secondary and university levels in Flanders. To think otherwise was simply putting the cart before the horse.

Even so, on 13 February 1916 de Broqueville issued a second circular, in which he prescribed the introduction of Dutch lessons in military training camps. A verbal language test would now count towards the candidate's overall training results. A day later, de Broqueville also discussed the same matter with the king.[57] Van Cauwelaert's own newspaper - *Vrij België* (Free Belgium) – subsequently learnt that junior officers would receive 8 hours of Dutch tuition during their four-week training period, with reserve officers receiving 24 hours during a four-month period. In June 1916, the paper commented that this was too little, too late: it was almost impossible to learn the language in such a short period, particular when the training covered so many other different subjects. Might it not be better, suggested the paper's editorial, that the officers should learn their Dutch 'in the field', through daily contact with their own Flemish troops? Yet this was essentially a step backwards in terms of what the Flemish nationalists were seeking to achieve. The reasoning of *Vrij België* is illustrative of the strategic failure of the Flemish Movement during the early decades of the century. As already suggested, the wider use of Dutch at all levels of the education system was the crucial factor: if this could be achieved, many of the Movement's other aims would almost automatically follow. Sadly, this was a lesson which the occupying German authorities quickly understood.

1916: activist fireworks and a failed government declaration

On 15 March 1916, the German Governor-General von Bissing issued a proclamation to the effect that the University of Ghent would become a Dutch-language university during the academic year 1916-1917. This news sent shockwaves through Belgian society, since it was now perfectly clear that the language question could no longer be confined to meaningless matters such as circulars in the army or crackdowns on a few harmless activists. More and more politicians were coming to the conclusion that a comprehensive approach to the language question was required. King Albert was also coming around to this same opinion. But what exactly could be done? The Belgian government seemed at a loss for answers, while her allies were beginning to look more and more suspiciously at what was going on in "brave little Belgium".

With this in mind, Albert wished to reassure his allies by attuning his policy to the international position of Belgium in European politics. In many ways, this seemed the obvious thing to do. Since the Treaty of Vienna in 1815, a neutral Belgium had been one of the cornerstones of the balance of power in Europe, particularly in its role as a buffer between those perpetual enemies, France and Germany. The German invasion of 1914 had shattered this balance, removed the buffer and precipitated a world war. A desire to restore the pre-war situation was therefore an obvious card for the Belgian government to play. A free and neutral Belgium was a guarantee of a peaceful Europe. It was for this reason that King Albert, even while he was leading his army on the IJzer, sought to revive the tried and trusted policy of his predecessors, which had kept the nation safe since the time of his grandfather, Leopold I. Albert maintained consistently that Belgium was not a member of the Allied camp, but rather an innocent – and independent – third party which had been dragged into the conflict against its will. Consequently, it was his aim to stress this independence at all times. This was a position which the British – for geo-political reasons of their own – were able to accept. An independent and truly 'Belgian' Belgium presented much less of a threat to British interests than if the country was under French or German control. France, however, viewed this situation from a very different perspective. Paris wished to integrate Belgium firmly into the Allied coalition, in order to enlist its more active help in the fight for the complete and final destruction of Germany. If France was successful in this goal, Belgium would be ripe for the picking during the course of any subsequent victory negotiations. This also explains why the French were happy to associate themselves with the few radical Walloon politicians who dreamed of incorporating Wallonia into the French Republic. France's geo-political strategy ensured that King Albert adopted a very cautious approach. Throughout the war he continued to emphasise that Britain and France were not 'our allies' who had rushed to Belgium's aid, but were only 'guarantors' of Belgian neutrality and independency

4 Albert I (until 1918)

The French Field Marshall Foch, with King Albert I and Prince Leopold, De Panne, 4 May 1915 (photograph by Queen Elisabeth).

Belgium and the Monarchy. From National Independence to National Disintegration.

De Panne, 4 May 1915 (photograph by Queen Elisabeth)

under an international treaty obligation. For similar reasons, he was determined to keep the Belgian Army on Belgian soil and refused to take part in the futile offensives in which the British and the French sacrificed the cream of their youth. He hoped for a 'drawn' war, which would lead to a compromise peace and (as far as possible) to a restoration of the pre-1914 situation. This old balance still represented his nation's best hope for a free and peaceful future.

It is hardly surprising that this policy of active neutrality caused King Albert to be viewed with suspicion in the Allied corridors of power. Some slanderous tongues even accused him of being pro-German, casting doubt on his loyalty by virtue of his German grandfather, his Austrian mother and his German wife. To make matters worse, many figures in the essentially pro-French Belgian wartime government were inclined to share this opinion – or were at least radically opposed to his policy, which was nevertheless in keeping with the international status of a neutral country. This led to serious tension between the king and his ministers during the period February-July 1916.

Within this context, the Flemish Movement occupied an important position. French politicians had long seen the Movement as a Pan-German association. The activist collaboration of Flemings in the occupied part of the country merely served to confirm this opinion. In similar fashion, the struggle for 'language rights' within the Belgian Army was also regarded as suspect – often by many Belgians as well. Moreover, this shadow of suspicion extended deep into the very heart of the ministerial cabinet. On the other hand, the king – much like his grandfather before him – saw the Flemish Movement and the Flemish national identity as a powerful counterbalance to the strong wartime tendency to seek closer links with France. For this reason alone, it was impossible for him to ignore the language drama being played out along the banks of the River IJzer. Besides, he was not insensitive to the question of language rights for his Flemish subjects, as we have already seen. He realised, however, that there were serious limitations on his room for manoeuvre. The moment was hardly right for a full scale reorganisation of the armed forces. Any measures which disrupted the smooth running of the army in wartime would be seen as almost treasonable – and an attempt to force the high command to learn Dutch was certain to arouse great resistance from the French-speaking senior officers, who formed the backbone of the army. Even a mild attempt to support the Flemish Movement at the front would be guaranteed to strengthen the pro-French sympathies of the Walloons and the pro-German suspicions of the Allies. In this respect, Albert was more realistic than Adjutant Rombouts, whose more radical 'force-them-and-be-damned' approach was quoted earlier in this chapter. Even so, the king still wanted to do something – but what?

It has often been suggested that the de Broqueville Government should have declared that Ghent would become a fully Dutch-speaking university immediately after the war. Frans Van Cauwelaert worked tirelessly throughout the summer of 1916 in the hope of securing such a declaration, which he believed would preserve the unity of the nation. Looking back in retrospect, there is much to be said for this argument. A positive

'Flemish' message could have played a useful role at this crucial time. Such a declaration could never have bound the hands of a post-war government, but it would have put the brakes on activism and, more importantly, could have created a more positive post-war climate in which to discuss a long-term solution for the language question.

Yet in reality, it was wishful thinking to expect the government to agree to a declaration which was essentially (in the terms of the time) so radical. This type of stratagem often has a snowball effect. Who could say what the following demand might be? Universal suffrage after the war? Or full administrative separation? Besides, the de Broqueville Government was an emergency government, which only had a mandate for the duration of the conflict. It was hardly in a position to settle the issues which had split the country for the past 25 years, particularly if this meant committing a future post-war administration to a particular line of action. It was for this reason that the government announced on 1 January 1916 that it had no intention of making fundamental changes in either domestic or foreign policy. This was certainly in keeping with the government's own views on the University of Ghent: not a single minister was in favour of the complete scrapping of French-language tuition. For one thing, many of them recognised that such a policy was internationally indefensible. It was certain to raise all hell in Paris and could only strengthen the hand of the separatist Walloon Movement. Worse still, the elimination of the French-speaking University of Ghent – the beating heart of elitist French culture in Flanders – could also be seen as an overture to the Germans, who, after all, were proposing precisely the same thing. But if all these things now seem obvious to us, why were they not obvious to Van Cauwelaert, who was a shrewd and skilful politician? Perhaps they were. Perhaps Van Cauwelaert was actually hoping to force an ambiguous compromise declaration. A statement which combined the promised introduction of Dutch at the university with a general commitment to full equality of language rights in law might have killed two birds with one stone: it could have satisfied immediate Flemish aspirations, while still keeping the door open for the maintenance of a French-language presence in Ghent.

In a letter to Van Cauwelaert on 22 July 1916, Minister of Finance Aloys Van de Vyvere claimed that he was the only cabinet member in favour of the full introduction of Dutch at the University of Ghent after the war. The other pro-Flemish ministers, Joris Helleputte and Prosper Poullet, were not prepared to go as far. Poullet argued in favour of maintaining a "centre of Latin culture" in Ghent, whereas Helleputte (according to Van de Vyvere) was proposing a complex and opaque plan of his own making.[58] This letter underlines the weakness of Flemish sentiment amongst both the government and the Flemish Catholic politicians. Or perhaps it allows us to analyse the various and ever-changing political aims of 'the' Flemish Movement in their proper historical context. Amongst the politicians of the day – most of whom still sent their sons to university – there was only a small minority in favour of the complete and radical introduction of the Dutch language into all levels of Flemish life. This meant that a politician might be a supporter of less ambitious measures and still have a reputation as being pro-Flemish. It is certain that there would have been no parliamentary majority in favour of the full introduction of Dutch at the University of Ghent, with a corresponding elimination of French language tuition. This was not even the case after the full democratisation of voting rights during the period 1919-21 – and this for a proposal that all the modern-day Belgians would now find self-evident.

A few days later, on 27 July 1916, Van de Vyvere wrote a long letter to King Albert, in which he discussed the language question.[59] He said that until a few months previously the Flemish people had been prepared to sit patiently and wait for the end of the war, but that more recently (as a result of the von Bissing proclamation) there had been a change in public opinion. In the army, the Flemings were becoming more and more angry at the discrimination against them, particularly with regard to promotions. In the junior ranks, a Walloon who spoke no Dutch could still expect to be promoted, whereas a Fleming was expected to show a good knowledge of French before he could achieve the same rank. But it was the intellectuals who were most upset: being labelled a 'Flemish militant' ruled them out from any hope of promotion, no matter how good their French was. They were not allowed to go to the officer training school and they were seldom recommended for bravery awards. Van de Vyvere emphasised that this had a negative effect on their families in the occupied zone, an effect which was heightened by the fact that it was the largely Flemish families in the unoccupied zone which had borne the brunt of the recent recruiting drive. This was further compounded by the incorrect but persistent belief that the Belgian government was working hand in glove with the French, whilst making too few overtures towards The Netherlands, and that the Flemish faction was seriously under-represented in Le Havre.

At the end of his letter, Van de Vyvere requested an audience and he was received by Albert on 31 July and 1 August 1916. With regard to the language question, the king noted in his diary: "As for a solution to the Flemish question, the minister envisages a wide-ranging bilingualism and the creation of a Flemish-speaking further education system".[60] This hardly sounds as though they were discussing the scrapping of French at the University of Ghent! It seems that Van de Vyvere expressed much more moderate views in conversation with his sovereign than when he was corresponding with Van Cauwelaert, a member of his own party.

Minister Poullet also saw the king on 15 September 1916 and they, too, discussed the language question in the occupied territories. Albert asked Poullet what he thought of the idea to issue a ministerial declaration about the future of the language question. Poullet replied that this was impossible, since it had been agreed that the ministers would make no declarations about domestic matters until the war was over. In his diary, the king noted that he had warned Poullet against the annexation campaign being conducted by some politicians, since this could seriously complicate relations with The Netherlands. "I talked to Minister Poullet about the trend in Wallonia which has found considerable favour in Paris and which is sliding towards the idea of becoming a French satellite state [*"l'inféodation vers la France"*]. This movement is being supported by the friends of Minister de Broqueville."[61] For his part, Poullet noted: "[King Albert] is insistent on the danger of allowing annexation by France. There is growing pressure in this direction; hence the Flemish reaction. [He] insists on censure."[62] It is clear that King Albert was not happy about the growing pro-French faction within the small Walloon Movement, whose most extreme proponents were already pressing in Paris for the annexation of Wallonia by France.

On 25 September, it was the turn of Van Cauwelaert to be received by the king. He asked to be allowed to speak freely about the Flemish Movement. Albert gave his permission – and then noted the politician's comments in his diary. Van Cauwelaert described the situation as "alarming" and referred to the possible international implications of the language question. Some of the Flemish militants hoped to obtain guarantees for the Flemish people as part of an international peace process to end the war, a strategy which could benefit from the common interests shared by Germany and The Netherlands. The Flemings would be prepared to accept the Dutch-language University of Ghent (which, thanks to the Germans, was almost on the point of opening its doors), because they feared that the government would do nothing after the war. The king also dutifully noted Van Cauwelaert's comments about a lack of respect and a shortage of promotion opportunities for Flemish soldiers in the army. "Many complaints are coming from the army. It is not just about the linguistic ignorance of the officers that these complaints are being made, but also about the lack of appreciation which the army commanders show towards the Flemings and the ostracism to which they are subjected whenever a decent position becomes available."[63] Equally interesting in this context are the comments recorded by Marie-Elisabeth Belpaire. Madame Belpaire was a leading figure in the aristocratic circle gathered around the king in De Panne, who concerned herself with the care and spiritual welfare of Flemish troops at the front. She saw Van Cauwelaert immediately after his meeting with Albert, and he told her that the king had said: "I never cease to tell my ministers that they must find some way of giving satisfaction to the Flemings." On the army question, he added: "In my opinion, it is more important for our officers to have a knowledge of Flemish than a knowledge of physics and chemistry."[64]

The king was clearly concerned about the language question. He was probably pressing for a conciliatory government declaration on the future of the University of Ghent. A declaration was indeed issued a few days later. Van Cauwelaert must have been consulted about its drafting – he had already been in Le Havre for a number of weeks, constantly lobbying government officials and ministers. In a letter to Julius Hoste on 30 September 1916, Van Cauwelaert had written: "A declaration which seeks to avoid the issue will do more harm than good."[65] After a long meeting of the ministerial council on 4 October, the government finally agreed a plan of action and a text. A royal decree would be issued instructing that all professors at the 'Dutch' University of Ghent should be scrapped from the National Orders. The publication of this decree would be preceded by a 'Report to the King', signed by the competent minister, Prosper Poullet. Albert signed the decree on 10 October and it was published, together with the report, in the Belgian State Gazette some 10 days later. The text of the declaration bears careful reading: "Before the war, the question of the transformation of the University of Ghent was still pending in parliament. It is therefore a matter for the competent legislative power in Belgium [i.e., parliament] to find a solution for this question after the war. This is a national question which can only be resolved by a sovereign nation, acting in full independence in a Belgium which is wholly and incontestably free. The government is convinced that once peace has been restored, mutual agreement and goodwill towards the Flemings, which the government will seek to promote and enhance at all levels, including that of higher education, will ensure full equality of rights in law and in fact, such as our constitution demands."

The wording of the text seemed to confirm Van Cauwelaert's worst fears. It was imprecise and ambiguous. What exactly did the word 'transformation' mean? A complete switch from French to Dutch as the language of tuition? Or something less radical, more bilingual? And what to make of the phrase "full equality of rights in law and in fact"? This was clearly intended to conciliate the Flemings, but it might equally have applied to the rights of the bilingual French-speaking community. Van Cauwelaert was determined to make things more clear-cut. Writing to his wife on 9 October, he commented: "The only reasonable interpretation of this form of words is that it refers to the full introduction of Dutch in Ghent. But before I leave, I will try and obtain incontrovertible proof that this is – and will continue to be – the government's intention".[66] It was no doubt as a result of his intervention that the Dutch translation of the declaration which appeared in the State Gazette on 20 October no longer spoke of "transformation", but used the Dutch word *vervlaamsing* – which clearly implied the full introduction of Dutch. A press release issued by Poullet in The Hague also used this same word.

The logic behind the actions of Poullet and Van Cauwelaert is understandable. Even so, they were effectively digging their own – and the declaration's – grave. As soon as the Dutch translation appeared, the liberal minister Goblet d'Alviella protested that the ministerial council had not approved the *vervlaamsing* of Ghent, but only its *transformation*. This was perfectly true and, when pressed, Poullet was forced to confirm this fact in public. On 25 October, *Le XXe Siècle* – de Broqueville's own newspaper – wrote: "There is nothing in this document which allows one to believe that the government is considering the 'Dutchification' [*vervlaamsing*] of the University of Ghent."[67] By now, it was obvious to the Flemish people that the Le Havre administration had no intention of allowing the full introduction of Dutch in Ghent. In short, the whole declaration fiasco had the opposite effect to what Van Cauwelaert had planned: instead of winning the confidence of the Flemish people, it destroyed that confidence and led to a radicalisation of Flemish public opinion against the unitary Belgian state.

On 11 October 1916, King Albert also signed a number of other decrees, which had been prepared by the Minister of Justice, Carton de Wiart. These decrees amended the laws of Belgium to reflect the wartime situation and were probably regarded in the ministerial council as a counterbalance to the 'favourable' declaration in respect of the University of Ghent. One of the decrees reorganised the security services, which henceforth came under the authority of the General Staff. The military were given the task (amongst other things) of preventing meetings which posed a possible threat to public order. They were also empowered to read and censure the correspondence of soldiers at the front and to take action against any publication which might give comfort to the enemy or have a negative effect on "the morale of the army or the civilian population". The government undoubtedly saw this as a way to restore 'proper' discipline at the front. Nevertheless, the social unrest amongst the Flemish troops continued to find its most frequent expression through language-related matters, so that these new measures, following the clumsy mismanagement of the Ghent declaration, was like a slap in the face to the supporters of the Flemish Movement. The storm clouds were gathering, and the army was rocked by one language incident after another, often resulting in the court-martial of those involved. At the end of 1916, all was not well with the Belgian ship of state.

Spring 1917 - towards an independent Flanders

On 12 December 1916, the German Kaiser put forward a first tentative peace proposal. Acting as intermediary, President Woodrow Wilson of the United States of America contacted the warring nations to ask what their conditions for peace might be. In the weeks which followed, this resulted in great tension between Belgium and the Allies, since the Belgian government made clear its wish to submit a separate answer to the German peace initiative. On 28 December, this led to a heated exchange between a determined King Albert and the exasperated French diplomat, Philippe Berthelot. The Allies clearly suspected that the Belgians were planning to make a separate peace with the Germans.

On 4 February 1917, the activists in the occupied zone set up a Council of Flanders. This pseudo-government was charged with making the wishes of the Flemish people clear to the peace negotiators. These wishes included "sovereign independence". The reaction of the authorities in 'free' Belgium was prompt. On 11 February, the new chief of staff of the Belgian Army, the Walloon general Louis Ruquoy, banned the meetings of all groups and societies at or behind the front. This included the 'study groups' set up by various pro-Flemish soldiers and civilians, which often held fierce political debates. The discontent amongst these groups was great, and most decided to continue their activities in secret. Growing tension at home was mirrored by developments on the international stage. In Russia, revolution was brewing. Rasputin

In 1915-1916, King Albert hoped that a compromise peace might be possible. He feared that the total defeat of Germany would upset the European balance of power and might signal the end of Belgium as an independent country. Through his contacts with the British government, including Lord Curzon, the king tried to ensure the position of Belgium as a neutral buffer between the great powers of France, Germany and Great Britain (photograph by Queen Elisabeth).

Belgium and the Monarchy. From National Independence to National Disintegration.

King Albert with Colonel Fairholme, the British military attaché (photograph by Queen Elisabeth).

was murdered in December 1916. Open revolt broke out in February 1917, which quickly spread to the army. In March, Tsar Nicolas II abdicated his throne. This powder-keg situation had an effect on all the warring armies – including the Belgian – and levels of unrest amongst the rank-and-file troops began to reach alarming proportions. The failure of the peace initiative, following the failure of so many bloody offensives, led to a sharp increase in the number of desertions. The entry into the war of the United States in April – with its promise of the right of self-determination for all peoples – offered a glimmer of hope, but this was quickly extinguished by the outbreak of a full-scale mutiny in the French Army in May. There were even rumours that Walloon activists in Paris were again agitating for the annexation of Wallonia by France.

Writing in March 1917, Hendrik Borginon – a leading light in the Flemish movement, who was fighting at the front – noted what he described as "a Flemish awakening" amongst his comrades in the trenches: "a first expression of a new-born nationalism in our simple, good-hearted lads".[68] Suddenly, it was no longer just the Flemish intellectuals who were protesting about lack of language rights. Thousands of ordinary soldiers also began to stand up for their own language, even if it was only by answering 'aanwezig' (Dutch) instead of 'présent' (French) at roll calls. Some even went so far as to hang slogans in the trenches at night. The military authorities reacted nervously, alternating Flemish-friendly concessions with sanctions and transfers. One of the concessions was the royal decree of 12 February 1917, which stipulated that every division, corps, etc. would be given its own translator. This at last made it possible to issue communiqués in both languages, as had been foreseen in the 1913 Army Act. In view of what was happening in France, this was perhaps the least the government could do to show its appreciation for an army which was still trying to maintain discipline within its own ranks. Eugène Génie, the French military attaché who spent several months in De Panne, reported to Paris that this royal decree had been drafted at the express insistence of King Albert.[69] (The ever-observant Miss Belpaire noted that since his arrival in Belgium, Génie had learnt quite good Dutch and was often disparaging about Belgian officers who were unable to speak the language.[70])

On 6 March, it became known that a delegation from the Council of Flanders had been received in Berlin. Van Cauwelaert insisted that the government should act "decisively" to bring to an end "all the shameful situations in both the army and the civil administration which give the Flemish people just cause for complaint."[71] He once again emphasised the need for a clear and unequivocal public declaration about the future of Flanders and its institutions.

The king, however, looked at matters from a broader perspective. He was certainly prepared to consider measures which would conciliate the Flemings, but he expected similar efforts from others. If the Germans were trying to woo the Flemish nationalists with their cheap promises, might it not help if the French were also to adopt a more pro-Flemish stance? The king was obviously worried about the way in which public opinion in Flanders was moving. With rumours of secret peace negotiations and an imminent re-drawing of the map of Europe, it was imperative for the future of Belgium to avoid a pro-German Flanders at all costs.

On 10 March, Génie had a long conversation with King Albert, a summary of which he dutifully reported to the Ministry of War in Paris. "It [the Flemish Movement] is not a widespread German movement as such. It is a strongly particularistic movement, which the German propagandists have been able to exploit, thanks to both conscious and unconscious complicity. But nothing or no one could be further removed from Prussian absolutism than the Fleming, who is characterised by his communal traditions. A Fleming will not willingly speak French, but he neither understands nor speaks German. He will never go to Germany, whereas the number of Flemings going to France is much greater than the number of Walloons going there. It should perhaps also be noted that the greatest Belgian writers in the French language are nearly all Flemings: Maeterlinck, Verhaeren..."[72] The king reiterated his wish that the French government should show greater goodwill towards Flemish sensibilities. Génie concluded his report by commenting that King Albert was "a partisan who firmly but perhaps exaggeratedly believes in the need for concessions to the Flemish, although he fears our disapproval on this matter."[73]

Génie did not mention precisely what the king had in mind, but some kind of initiative was clearly needed, since in Belgium the situation was going from bad to worse. On 21 March 1917, Governor-General von Bissing announced the administrative partition of occupied Belgium along linguistic lines! The government in Le Havre reacted by issuing two new laws on 8 April, the first of which made voluntary collaboration with the policy and plans of the enemy a criminal offence punishable by hard labour, while the second laid down the general principle that all the legislation introduced by the occupying Germans would be declared legally null and void as soon as the national territory had been liberated. In a separate report on "the question of further education in Flanders", the government noted that this matter had been on the agenda for discussion when war broke out and that "the exemplary behaviour of the Dutch-speaking patriots" would make these discussions "more urgent and more necessary than ever" once the war had been brought to a successful conclusion.[74] Later in April, a number of other reports were received in Le Havre about the state of public opinion in the occupied territories. One of the common themes in these reports was the widespread feeling that both a Dutch-language and a French-language university should be set up in Ghent after the war, so as to meet the expectations of the Flemings but without antagonising the Walloons. This highlights just how ambiguous the official discourse over the question of the introduction of the Dutch language in higher education really was. In keeping with this ambiguity, de Broqueville reminded the public in an interview given to *Le Courrier de L'Armée* (The Army Courier) and *De Legerbode* (The Army Messenger) on 19 May 1917 that the government had already promised legal and actual equality of rights as early as October 1916. But it all made little difference: by this time the militant wing of the Flemish Movement had lost all confidence in the premier and his ministers. De Broqueville was also unwise enough in his interview to quote the inaccurate figure of 80% for the level of Flemish troops at the front – something he would regret later. The de Broqueville interview was largely in response to an article in a Flemish student magazine by Paul Vandermeulen, a well-known and much respected army chaplain, in which he openly stated that Flemish interests should take priority above Belgian interests, even if this meant maintaining the administrative separation introduced by the German occupation authorities. This Flemish cleric played an important role at the front, where he channelled and gave expression to the general dissatisfaction about the language issue felt by the chaplaincy service and the many trainee priests who acted as stretcher-bearers.

The Open Letter to King Albert of 11 July 1917

On 6 July 1917, the army high command circulated an appeal in which they encouraged officers and non-commissioned officers to learn Dutch. In theory, this was an important step forwards. The Army Act of 1913 had foreseen bilingual training for the officer corps in the future, but here was a measure which sought to improve the situation immediately. The precise details are no longer known, but it seems that it was a voluntary appeal, which had little success. On the contrary, it provoked a strong reaction from the Walloon soldiers. But this reaction was soon destined to be forgotten, in light of what followed.

In the preceding months, the Flemish intellectuals fighting with the army along the IJzer had gradually been joining forces with each other to develop a more coordinated response to the language problem. This was the beginning of what later came to be known as the Front Movement. On 11 July, this movement published its *Open Letter to the King of the Belgians, Albert I*. This 11-page document, which in essence was a romanticised nationalist discourse, caused a considerable stir. Some even regarded it as an act of insubordination against the military authorities. Moreover, it was a direct appeal to the person of the king, similar to Destrée's Open Letter of 1912.

"Full of confidence in you, who at the start of this world war reminded the Flemings of the Battle of the Golden Spurs, we, your Flemish soldiers, the Flemish army, the army of the IJzer, now turn to you and say that we are ready to lay down our lives for our country, but that this sacrifice should not serve to further bind our people in slavery, but should serve to let them breathe more freely, should allow them to live in freedom." The Open Letter complained bitterly (and extensively) about the language situation in the army, which discriminated against "eighty percent of your soldiers", and also about the treatment of the subject in the press. In all these matters, the writers of the letter saw the signs of a clear and deliberate policy, which was designed to eradicate the Dutch language, or at least ensure its subordinate status. "Officialdom is against us, and is happy to tell anyone who will listen that the Flemish Movement is finished, that the Belgians – and therefore the Flemings – will one day all be Romans. They say that we, the Flemings, are no longer fighting for freedom, for equality and for the full recognition of our legitimate Flemish rights, but that instead we are now fighting for the Latinisation of our land and the triumph of French Culture. Maeterlinck [Maurice Maeterlinck was a Flemish author who wrote in French, and was awarded the Nobel Prize for Literature in 1911] and so many others speak to packed audiences abroad or write in warm and cosy rooms to attack our race, while we must watch our Flemish heroes dying on the cold fields of battle with their mother tongue on their lips, giving their all to win freedom for their country and their people. Do they have no respect for our Flemish blood?"

The Open Letter continued to support the fight against the Germans, but commenting on the visit of the activist delegation to Berlin the writers said that the government "had provoked such an attitude by its own treason". The activists were also right to accept the German proposals for the University of Ghent. It was not important that these proposals came from the enemy: what was important was the fact that the proposals embodied a "fundamental right" of the Flemish people.

Referring to the machinations of the government, the generals and the anti-Flemish intelligentsia, the Open Letter concluded: "We have lost all confidence in our superiors, who conspire to work against us more fiercely than ever (...) We distrust the government, a government which we elected but which has misused its powers and has deceived us for the past 85 years. It is only in you, our King, that we still believe." And what exactly was the Front Movement demanding? "We want to see a Flemish army alongside a Walloon army; we want a Flemish administration in Flemish hands, since herein lies our only hope of salvation." In addition to this vague post-war federal programme, the writers of the letter specifically asked the king himself to give "a clear, written and solemn promise that our full equality, our full rights, will be granted to us immediately after the war."[75]

This manifesto caused much discussion amongst the soldiers in the trenches. An excited stretcher-bearer wrote to Van Cauwelaert: "A powerful and irresistible propaganda is at work. On 11 July, a colossal manifesto appeared, written by unknown hands. The people who previously, with a few exceptions, knew little or nothing about the Flemish Movement are now in a state of uproar. In some places, the confrontations were quite vehement."[76] If the army was not immediately reformed, then the soldiers, according to some, would be perfectly entitled to lay down their arms. And indeed, in August and September 1917 the level of desertions from the Belgian Army reached an all-time high.

The Open Letter heralded a new phase for the Flemish Movement at the front. It now began to have a serious impact on the huge majority of uneducated, ordinary soldiers, whilst at the same time placing the government in an increasingly difficult position: how exactly should they deal with this growing radicalism? The king had his own ideas on this latter point – and was about to take the initiative.

Summer 1917: General De Ceuninck acts and Albert makes himself heard

How did the king and his ministers react to the Open Letter of 11 July 1917? On the one hand, it was clear that order needed to be restored in the army. On 4 August, Albert appointed General Armand De Ceuninck as Minister of War in place of de Broqueville, who took over the Foreign Affairs portfolio. De Ceuninck was the king's nominee, but de Broqueville was also in agreement with the appointment. The king wanted a more pliable minister of war, but also someone who was a soldier and who could restore discipline in the ranks. In this respect, De Ceuninck had a reputation as a strong disciplinarian. His appointment was followed by a stream of reprisals against the soldiers in the trenches. Aloys Van de Vyvere was the only minister who protested against the new wave of disciplinary measures in the army. His other colleagues repeatedly declared that the 'trouble-makers' needed to be dealt with; that discipline must be restored; and that there must be an end to open insubordination in an army which was fighting a war of national survival. De Ceuninck's actions were wholeheartedly endorsed by the ministerial council.

On the other hand, the King also wanted to meet the Flemings half way. On 27 July 1917, Van de Vyvere wrote to Van Cauwelaert: "I hope that I will soon be able to give you some very good news. There is serious discussion about the formation of all Flemish companies."[77] The king had indeed been persuaded of the need for the formation of Flemish companies, on a trial basis. During an audience, Albert told Génie that he wanted a quick solution to the language question, by offering "reasonable concessions" within the existing legislative framework. As far as the experiment with homogeneous companies was concerned, France could help by "demonstrating its understanding for the Flemish Movement and by adopting a more positive attitude towards Flemish soldiers who combined the expression of their Flemish grievances with feelings of respect and gratitude towards the French nation." The king was critical of his own ministers – including de Broqueville – who claimed that 80% of the front-line troops were Flemish, and he also had some harsh words for the clergy: "The clergy has been most imprudent in releasing, or at the very least exploiting, a current, the effects of which it no longer has the power to control."[78]

Because the king had not yet given a public answer to the Open Letter of 11 July 1917, a new Open Letter was published on 12 August. This second letter was the work of Cyriel Verschaeve, a priest who was in close contact with members of the Front Movement. Verschaeve had become a militant Flemish nationalist during the war years, and from his position as chaplain in an unoccupied village behind the front he was able to exercise considerable influence on pro-Flemish opinion in the trenches. The new letter was more critical of the king. He had given no response to the original appeal and the number of reprisals was growing daily. "Sire, this is making us bitter (...) Give us justice, protect our rights."[79] It was the start of a widening gulf between the king and the most extreme elements of the Flemish Movement.

When the king next visited the army on 13 August, he saw that many walls were daubed with Flemish protest slogans. This was obviously a dangerous situation for an army in wartime and the very next day the disturbed king sent Secretary Ingenbleek to seek the opinion of Miss Belpaire in De Panne. She later noted: "The Flemish question was soon raised: the danger caused by the dissatisfaction it created amongst the troops; the fear that the prevailing spirit of unrest might gain the upper hand. The king is well disposed towards the Flemings, according to his secretary. He has a passionate desire to give them satisfaction and is trying to find the right way to do it. He knows that I am in contact with many people, and therefore he wanted to ask my opinion as to what could most usefully be done. I answered that the main demand was the introduction of Dutch at the University of Ghent. To which our visitor replied that the king was aware of the necessity to allow the Flemish people the possibility to develop their full potential in their own language."[80]

Not content with his secretary's report, the king interviewed Miss Belpaire personally in an audience held on 15 August 1917. He was using her to conduct his own public defence in the face of Flemish criticism. In a letter written the same day, she commented: "He confirmed to me his affection and respect for the Flemings, and asked me to make this known to them. 'You have great influence, Madame. Tell them that the monarchy is fully convinced of the right of the Flemish people to achieve complete development in their own language, at all levels.'" Albert went on to say that he was certain that the Flemings would get their own way over Ghent. By this he undoubtedly meant the creation of a Flemish university alongside a French one. And further: "He [the king] will do all that he can for them. The Flemings must be patient and trust him. Everything he can do, he will do... 'But as you know, I am not the real master... and it is not always easy to have powerful friends.'" This was an obvious reference to the limitations on his power imposed by ministerial responsibility and by the 'powerful friends', particularly the French, who were still incensed at what was effectively a state of *de facto* Belgian neutrality along the IJzer. Equally importantly, "he has recommended to General De Ceuninck that he should be prudent in his dealings with the Flemings." But in what way? At the end of August De Ceuninck declared that

4 Albert I (until 1918)

In the trenches, May 1917. King Albert is on the left, with General De Ceuninck standing next to him (photograph by Queen Elisabeth).

Belgium and the Monarchy. From National Independence to National Disintegration.

In Flanders fields: General De Ceuninck at Nieuwkapelle, 1917 (photograph by Queen Elisabeth).

he had only sent Chaplain Vandermeulen and other dissidents to a punishment camp on this island of Cézembre "because it is not permitted to shoot these traitors." They would almost certainly have been treated differently in the British and French armies, where executions of soldiers were commonplace. Even the radical pro-Flemish Hendrik Borginon later admitted that the British and the French would not have hesitated to apply the death penalty in similar cases.

On 17 August, Verschaeve sent another letter to Miss Belpaire, in which he said that the Front Movement was still awaiting a declaration from Albert in person, a personal answer to the first Open Letter of 11 July, with its appeal for "a clear, written and solemn promise that our full equality, our full rights, will be granted to us immediately after the war." Verschaeve added that the men at the front understood that the king was unable to make a binding promise as such, but he could go a long way towards satisfying Flemish opinion "with an encouraging message, publicly addressed to all Flemish soldiers or politician, better still, to the entire Flemish population." In a conversation with Van de Vyvere on 20 August, Verschaeve repeated that an unambiguous statement from the king must be made at some stage, if matters were to improve.[81]

On 17 August, the king once again discussed the language question with his secretary and they came to the conclusion that the Flemish intellectuals had made an irredeemable mess of the whole situation. This analysis, which points the finger of responsibility directly at the Flemish establishment, is reflected in the Belpaire papers. During her attempts at mediation with the Front Movement, she became increasingly frustrated at the lack of pragmatism amongst the Flemish intellectual elite. The demand that Albert should reply personally and officially to the Open Letter of 11 July 1917 was simply not realistic at that moment. It was equally impossible to quash the punishments meted out to Flemish soldiers, as the Front Movement insisted, since this would be "detrimental to military discipline, which is so necessary in time of war". And a reconciliation council to discuss possible post-war solutions for the language problem, as Belpaire had suggested, could not be made up of soldiers, since it would simply "degenerate into a Russian soviet". Her opinion of the Open Letter was equally damning: it only reflected the thinking of "a few hotheads who are constantly trying to incite the people."[82] Van de Vyvere had made a similar comment during his 20 August meeting with Belpaire and Verschaeve. Verschaeve noted coolly in his diary that the minister believed that the Movement's influence was confined to "a few screamers". Belpaire also observed that the ordinary soldiers reacted differently to the intellectuals. "The people, the Flemish people, have always had a traditional trust in the royal family, its true moral and spiritual government", and genuinely appreciated "the goodwill of their brave king, even though this may not be said." She based this assessment on the letters which she also received from 'simple' Flemish soldiers, who looked at things differently from the Fronters and who believed that the language question should remain closed until after the war had been won.[83]

Nationalist discourse and holy wars

Van de Vyvere and Miss Belpaire were right when they referred to a small group of leaders. This group consisted of just a few hundred young men, mainly university students or pupils who had only recently graduated from secondary school. Nevertheless, they were able to generate a strong and compelling militancy which was out of all proportion to their numbers. Protest movements need to make use of evocative, inflammatory language, if they wish to mobilise mass support amongst a lethargic public. Typical in this respect is the following example written by Firmin Deprez, a student leader from Leuven, who here describes his reasons for enlisting: "Nurtured from a tender age in the bosom of our most beautiful and most noble student movement, I had oftentimes promised, sung and sworn that I would devote all my powers to the revival and resurgence of the Flemish people, who are so dear to my heart."[84]

Nationalism, like religion, always creates its own form of intellectual discourse, and the two often go hand in hand. They both exploit the 'militant' use of language with the aim of securing emotional commitment to an idealistic cause. In Catholic Flanders, the people were used to this kind of 'spiritual' appeal, where rationality was frequently expected to make way for blind obedience and complete faith, often with the prospect of suffering and sacrifice, in imitation of Christ. If it were possible to make an analysis of the sermons preached each Sunday morning in the churches of Flanders during the period leading up to 1914, it would almost certainly conclude that the linguistic usage bordered on the 'totalitarian'.

The Flemish Movement at the front had much in common with the militant Catholicism of the pre-war era. It combined powerful secular slogans – "Here is our blood, where are our rights?" – with the religious battle-cries of the past. For example, in December 1917 a group of militants ended a clandestine action with the rallying-call "Long live God! Long live Flanders-land".[85] But perhaps the most famous illustration of the close links between militant Catholicism and radical nationalism was the development in 1916 of a slogan which was destined to symbolise the righteousness of the Flemish cause for generations to come: *Alles voor Vlaanderen, Vlaanderen voor Kristus* (All for Flanders, Flanders for Christ), often shortened to AVV-VVK. AVV-VVK stood for a strong political and religious commitment to the national ideal, which was also a fundamental element in the thinking of the Flemish collaborators during the Second World War and which, in other contexts, can still be seen today in fundamentalist movements throughout the world. Writing in June 1915, the pro-Flemish Jeroom Leuridan claimed that he had enlisted as a volunteer, so that he could look his "battling and suffering people" straight in the eye. "If hard days lay ahead of me, if I experience degradation and humiliation, if I am misunderstood, if I remain unhonoured, even if I die, then it is all for you, my Flanders, for you, and it will bring me eternal rest and a heavenly reward."[86] Later in the same year, Leuridan received a letter from a fellow student, Abel Louf, in which he declared what can only be described as a Flemish Holy War: "The time has come when we need to make good all those things which we have so often sung and shouted about, what we have so often written at the top of our school work, what we have used to defend ourselves against the taunts of our enemies: All for Flanders, Flanders for Christ. Yes, everything we have – our blood and our life – must show that we are faithful to Flanders and her cause. 'Victory or death' must be our cry.

In closing, for I see that the time is drawing near, I shout with all the passion of my courageous breast the same words as the heroic Rodenbach [a legendary student leader who died in 1880, aged 24], our commander:

> My Flanders, sweetest of all my pleasures,
> My life, my soul, greatest of all my treasures,
> All for Flanders, and Flanders for God
> For thee I would lie gladly beneath the cold sod."[87]

It goes without saying that many of these 'romantic' volunteers quickly became disillusioned when confronted with the harsh reality of life along the River IJzer. But the religious-nationalist undertone was never completely eradicated from their ideological thinking, and these few hundred intellectuals were destined to play a pioneering role in the Front Movement. They did this consciously, repeatedly claiming that they spoke on behalf of all their fellow soldiers, or even on behalf of all their fellow countrymen. In this sense, they saw themselves as the potential future leaders of a new Flanders. In contrast to Miss Belpaire and Minister Van de Vyvere, King Albert did not believe that the Front Movement was just a small band of like-minded intellectuals. It was for this reason that he was so disparaging of the priests and the clergy in his conversation with Génie on 10 August 1917 (see above). And indeed, it is undeniable that the Flemish chaplains and seminarists played a major role in spreading militant religious-political ideas amongst the army rank-and-file. In October 1917, the stretcher-bearer Vital Haesaert ended a funeral oration for a dead seminarist with the following words. "God has given you, O future priest, a bloody altar, the killing fields of Flanders, on which, surrounded by your true Flemish comrades, you have shed your own dear blood for God, for Flanders, for Belgium."[88] This typifies the prevailing mentality of the Flemish priesthood, which was prepared to pay lip-service to the Belgian national ideal, while simultaneously attempting to capture the hearts and minds of Flemish youth with their own particular brand of pseudo-religious nationalism, in which the old Flemish virtues of Catholic idealism and purity were mingled with a clear traditionalist distaste of the 'sinful' culture of modernist France. Based on its analysis of soldiers' letters, the army censorship service concluded that the language question was spreading like wildfire throughout the army during the second half of 1917. "We suspect that this is the result of non-stop propaganda, and the chaplains and the stretcher-bearers are often cited as being the most strident propagandists."[89]

Summer 1917: King Albert's two-pronged policy

The king felt that the time had come to tackle the language question. Nevertheless, in the meetings of the inner cabinet held on 19 and 26 August and during the sessions of the ministerial council held on 24 and 25 August and 9 September 1917 the only decision of consequence was the confirmation that General De Ceuninck should attempt to ensure strict compliance with the language law of 1913. In the anti-Flemish atmosphere of the ministerial council, this was probably about as much as could reasonably be hoped for. The same council also confirmed that the "sowers of dissension" should be dealt with severely. The Front Movement had endangered the unity of the nation in time of war and therefore deserved the harsh punishments they received. To prove the point, the ministerial council held on 31 August approved the harsh penalty which De Ceuninck had recommended for Chaplain Vandermeulen, notwithstanding the objections of Minister Van de Vyvere. It is not clear what the king thought, but we do know that he attended the meetings on 19 and 26 August and 9 September, all of which were held in De Panne.[90]

Meanwhile, De Ceuninck tried to do what the ministerial council had asked of him. In a circular dated 22 August he let it be known (amongst other things) that promotion to the rank of second-lieutenant would henceforth take greater account of the candidates' language ability. The cabinet had also instructed him to ensure that each company should have at least one Dutch-speaking officer and that each platoon should have at least one Dutch-speaking non-commissioned officer and corporal. However, the idea of single language companies was quickly forgotten.

What role did the king play in these developments? The records are not clear on this point, with one important exception. In a draft of an address which he was planning to give to the ministerial council on 1 February 1918 (see below), Albert wrote: "You will remember that I was in favour of a declaration six months ago. It was then said that the moment was not right, that it was necessary to choose the moment freely, without duress." This comment probably refers to the meeting of the ministerial council on 9 September 1917. According to the minutes of this meeting, de Broqueville had suggested that the king should "speak at an appropriate time". However, the idea of a 'personal' message issued by the king himself aroused the furious opposition of Minister Paul Hymans, supported by the rest of the council.[91]

The only positive element (from the Flemish point of view) to emerge from these manoeuvrings were the efforts by General De Ceuninck to ensure full compliance with the law of 1913. Occasionally, the general even went further than was strictly necessary. For example, on 12 September he informed a meeting of the General Staff that every officer should be able to speak some Dutch and must therefore make the necessary efforts to learn the language. In a circular issued the following day and read aloud to the troops, he announced that every soldier had the right to be addressed by his officers in his mother tongue, especially in time of war. The officers should not be afraid of being made to look ridiculous and should instead take every available opportunity to learn Dutch. Moreover, the officers should support their NCOs in this respect and the rank-and-file were encouraged to form bilingual 'friendship circles'. It was all very superficial and it failed to remove the greater irritation felt by the Flemish soldiers as a result of the continuing 'persecution' of members of the Front Movement. Alphonse Van de Perre, member of the Lower House, also thought that it was unrealistic to expect 60-year-old Walloon officers to start learning Dutch. In a letter to Secretary Ingenbleek, he warned of the possibility of a bitter Walloon reaction.[92]

There were indeed irritated Walloon reactions to the new language measures introduced by General De Ceuninck. Just as the Flemings were angered by what they saw as the anti-Flemish attitude of the government and the military authorities, so the Walloons were annoyed by what they saw as unjustified pro-Flemish concessions – largely because (in their ignorance) they tarred the Front Movement and Van Cauwelaert with the same brush as the activists in the occupied zone, who were collaborating openly with the enemy.

In the meantime, the fourth winter of the war had arrived and the morale of the troops was falling as quickly as the temperature. In December 1917, a record number of desertions were registered in the Belgian Army. The physical discomfort of the trenches, which was already considerable, was made even worse by the freezing weather. The censorship service noted with some disquiet that the Russian Revolution had made a significant impact on the troops and that support for "socialist ideas" was growing. The service also reported that there was a growing desire for the opening of peace negotiations, even amongst soldiers who had previously been regarded as "patriotic". The men in the trenches wrote less frequently about the Flemish question – largely for fear of reprisals – but the language problem remained a daily catalyst of discontent in the front line, leading to mutual irritation, mutual provocation and mutual misunderstanding. The Front Movement, forced underground by the repression, now organised secret actions for the painting of slogans or the distribution of pamphlets. These actions were assisted by an increasing number of 'ordinary' soldiers, so that the Movement began to acquire something approaching mass support. On 1 and 9 December, disgruntled Flemish soldiers even held protest meetings in De Panne! Hundreds of them marched through the streets, singing Flemish songs and shouting Flemish slogans. It would not be the last time.

Spring 1918 – the government in panic

On 8 January 1918, the American president Wilson put forward a new peace proposal based on the right of self-determination for all peoples. The level of nervousness in diplomatic circles increased dramatically. Still confronted with a demoralising military

Belgium and the Monarchy. From National Independence to National Disintegration.

De Panne, 19 August 1917. A meeting of the inner cabinet has just been held. Afterwards, the king talks to Minister Jules Renkin (photograph by Queen Elisabeth). From left to right: Paul Hymans, Paul Berryer, King Albert, Emile Vandervelde, Jules Renkin, Charles de Broqueville.

De Panne, 19 August 1917 (photograph by Queen Elisabeth).

deadlock at the front, on 22 January 1918 the ministers at Le Havre learned that in occupied Belgium the activist Council of Flanders had declared Flemish national independence. The news caused a tidal wave of panic and an emergency session of the inner cabinet was quickly convened. The ministers feared above all that Germany would demand a place for the new and illegal Flemish government at the peace negotiations which everyone expected to take place in the near future – and with President Wilson's commitment to self-determination, they might very well succeed.

Parallel with these events, it was becoming obvious that the Germans were preparing a major offensive on the Western Front for the spring of 1918. Against this background a crucial meeting of the ministerial council was called for 1 February 1918. King Albert planned to address the meeting and in 1991 Marie-Rose Thielemans showed the manner in which the different drafts of his speech gradually changed. The first draft was in Albert's own hand and was subsequently amended by Secretary Ingenbleek. This second version is more explicit than the first, but is still a representative summary of Albert's opinions on the language issue in the spring of 1918.

What did the first draft say? The king began by conceding the existence of a genuine Flemish Movement at the front (in a manner which contradicted the frequently offered opinion that this movement was the work of a limited number of hotheads). The Flemish soldiers felt that they were being sacrificed for no gain. The majority remained loyal to their officers and the Crown, but revolutions are not made by the passive majority: they are made by the committed minority of agitators. It might well be that in the near future the government would be forced to go much further than it really wanted. Might it not be better to act pre-emptively, and release the pressure by timely concessions of a less drastic nature, before it was too late? "Whatever we do now," wrote the king, "I have the feeling that after our return [i.e., after the war] we will have to go very far indeed. Be that as it may, the time has come for plain speaking." In other words, the king once again argued in favour of an open declaration on the language question.

He then proceeded to look at this question in more detail. His opinions with regard to education were much the same as they had been in 1910. Dutch was not an inferior language and deserved the opportunity to be developed to its fullest extent, from primary school level right through to the universities. According to Albert, it was certain that the Flemings would continue to learn and use French within the framework of this new system. The concept of monolingualism should not deter the government from propagating the French language in Flanders. And it must always be possible to study in French in Flemish schools and Flemish institutions of higher learning. As far as the army was concerned, he conceded that the intellectuals in both linguistic communities were now in favour of separate Flemish and Walloon regiments. Albert did not exclude the possibility of such a reform, but said that it was not possible in the present circumstances.

The second draft, which was developed further by Secretary Ingenbleek, looked more deeply at the 'mass' nature of the Front Movement. The secretary described the movement as being systematic, organised and led by numerous intellectuals. The ordinary Flemish soldier felt that he was being sacrificed (*sacrifié*). Even if they had no grievances to unite them – "and they do have grievances" – then they would still feel bound to each other "by a feeling of dignity and solidarity." Would the Walloon soldiers have tolerated being spoken to for so long in Dutch by officers ignorant of their own French language? No, they would have revolted long before now. It was important for everyone to accept that the Flemings had precisely these same feelings of pride and self-worth. And they did have these feelings – "this I can assure you" – because their spiritual mentors (the clergy) had made them aware of their situation and of the message which was being spread by President Wilson and the other Allied nations: namely, that every people, no matter how small, had the right to exist freely. This was a simple idea and therefore capable of appealing to simple minds, not least because so many had already died in the cause of freedom. The government was no longer faced by a hardcore of idealists, as was the case before the war, but by "a collective opinion, which at this stage is still rudimentary but which is being nourished each day by the disillusionment resulting from a seemingly endless war."

The Ingenbleek draft also added a number of more practical elements to the text. As far as the future government of the country was concerned: "There is a desire for greater administrative autonomy. It is possible to do much in this direction, but there is one boundary which we cannot cross: there must be no administrative separation." With regard to the army, the secretary summarised Albert's views as follows: "What can we do after the war? First of all, we can experiment with a bilingual system [by which the king probably meant legislation on the basis of language facilities in Flanders], but only on condition that the application of the system is strict and correct. Until now, we have sought refuge in clumsy half measures which have satisfied nobody and even the letter and the spirit of the existing laws have been trampled underfoot. This must cease and we must pass a new series of laws which will be implemented flawlessly. If these laws do not give satisfaction, (...) if the desired results are not achieved, then the time will come when only extreme remedies can provide an answer."

This last section is important, as was the first draft, which also shows that Albert was not prepared to dismiss the idea of separate linguistic regiments out of hand. However, he was only prepared to contemplate such a measure – as the immediate post-war years would show – if it was unavoidable and absolutely necessary. This pragmatic approach characterises the language policy which Albert followed all his life. It was a form of *Realpolitik*, which he adjusted as circumstances demanded, but without ever losing sight of his overriding priority: the preservation of a unitary Belgian state, by promoting and maintaining the elements which served to bind the Flemings and the Walloons together, including the use of the French language in Flanders.

Moreover, it was a policy based on reason and common sense: the socio-cultural role of the French language was so strong, that it seemed unrealistic to believe that its use would ever disappear in Flanders.

In the event, the king's address to the ministerial council on 1 February 1918 was much more moderate in tone. Even so, it was the prelude to a stormy meeting of the council, which lasted a full five hours and still failed to come to any meaningful conclusions. The group around the liberal minister Paul Hymans wished to go no further than a settlement of the language grievances in the army within the framework of the law of 1913. Hymans was also prepared to see a Dutch university alongside a French university in Ghent – which was something of a breakthrough – but the announcement of a language programme must be postponed until after the war. Premier de Broqueville was prepared to propose the immediate introduction of a small number of monolingual companies on an experimental basis, to which General De Ceuninck replied with a long-winded statement to the effect that there was no language problem in the army! De Broqueville's proposal also provoked a strong reaction from the more anti-Flemish ministers. When de Broqueville held his ground and the meeting moved on to the possible practical implementation of monolingual regiments, the king intervened: "In 1913 I was already in favour of regional recruiting, but to begin something of this kind during a war will lead to an outburst of discontent amongst the 5,000 officers, for which I am not prepared to take responsibility. I would not be able to confront or control such a wave of discontent. Apart from this, regionalism promotes competition. Look at the example of England. There, the officer corps is an army in its own right. If they choose to oppose the monarchy, they can overthrow it. This is what we have seen in Spain."[93] The meeting was unable to make further progress, at which point a number of ministers suggested drawing up a draft declaration. It was finally made by the king's secretary (Ingenbleek) and de Broqueville's cabinet secretary:

"We wish to find solutions for all the problems which may arise within the bosom of our Belgian family. Some impatient spirits have asked whether the time is not right for a thorough reform of the army. No, the time is not right. This would be playing into the hands of the enemy. Have confidence in the word of your sovereign. I tell you, I promise you: satisfaction will be given to the Flemish people in education, in administration and in the army. When I say this, I am certain that I am speaking for the entire nation, the Flemings and the Walloons, who have both shown the same spirit of sacrifice in the service of their fatherland."[94]

This text illustrates the limits of what Albert regarded as 'possible' in the circumstances of early 1918. It bears a strong similarity to the limits he had set in his address to the ministerial council on 1 February. It was more an emotional appeal than a political declaration; a solemn pledge such as the writers of the Open Letter of 11 July 1917 had always wanted. King Albert was now prepared to guarantee in person the fair and equal treatment of the Flemings: they could now rest easy and await with confidence the end of the war. As a declaration it sounded much better than the government's declaration of October 1916. It was certainly more in keeping with the spirit of the moment. But it diplomatically failed to mention – as Albert knew full well – precisely how "satisfaction" would be given to the Flemish people "in education, in administration and in the army". This was something that the king would have to leave to his ministers.

A new meeting of the ministerial council was held on 20 March 1918, attended by the king and the army chief-of-staff, General Ruquoy. Everything pointed to the fact that the Germans were planning to launch a major offensive. Yet even in this crisis situation, the language question still seemed to be the army's main source of concern. Once again, the meeting discussed the possibility of a declaration of future intent.

From the notes which the king made about the debate[95], it is evident that Hymans and Vandervelde only wished to make "a number of minor cultural concessions" towards the Flemings and pushed for even severer penalties (executions) in the army. Renkin shared their opinion. King Albert interjected that it was an illusion to think that the same harsh disciplinary measures could be introduced into the Belgian Army as in the British and French armies (where executions were regularly carried out). The chief-of-staff also replied that he would never ask Belgian soldiers to fire on their own comrades, except as a last resort when all other disciplinary means had failed. The king reiterated that in his opinion 'something more' must be offered to the Flemish people: "In any event, it is not possible to continue with the punishments without first giving tokens of goodwill towards the Flemings." Once again, King Albert failed to get his way. Hymans, Vandervelde and Renkin – a liberal, a socialist and a Catholic – were radically opposed to the king's idea.

The day after the inconclusive ministerial council, the German General Ludendorf hurled 200 divisions against the Allied lines. The situation was perilous in the extreme. The Allies lost ground around Ieper and in France. The level of desertions continued to grow. The agitation of the Flemish Movement reached new heights. It was in this atmosphere of crisis that Premier de Broqueville resigned on 11 May 1918. The main reason was a dispute with the king about the way the army should be run at this critical moment, but subsidiary factors – such as his irreconcilable conflict with Minister Hymans on the language question – also played a role. In July, the German advance ground to a halt. In August, the Allies resumed the offensive. In October, the German Army collapsed – the war was nearing its end.

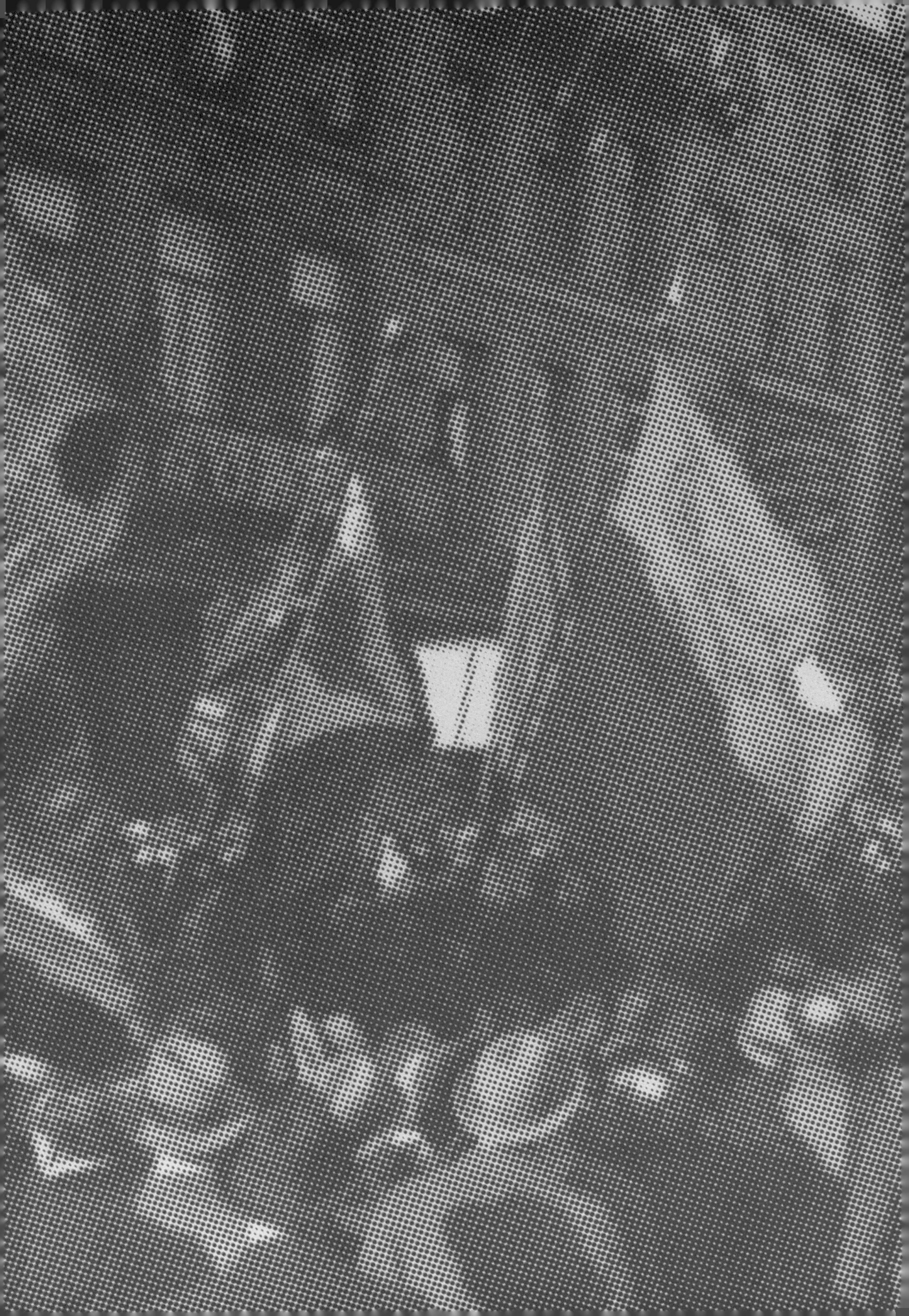

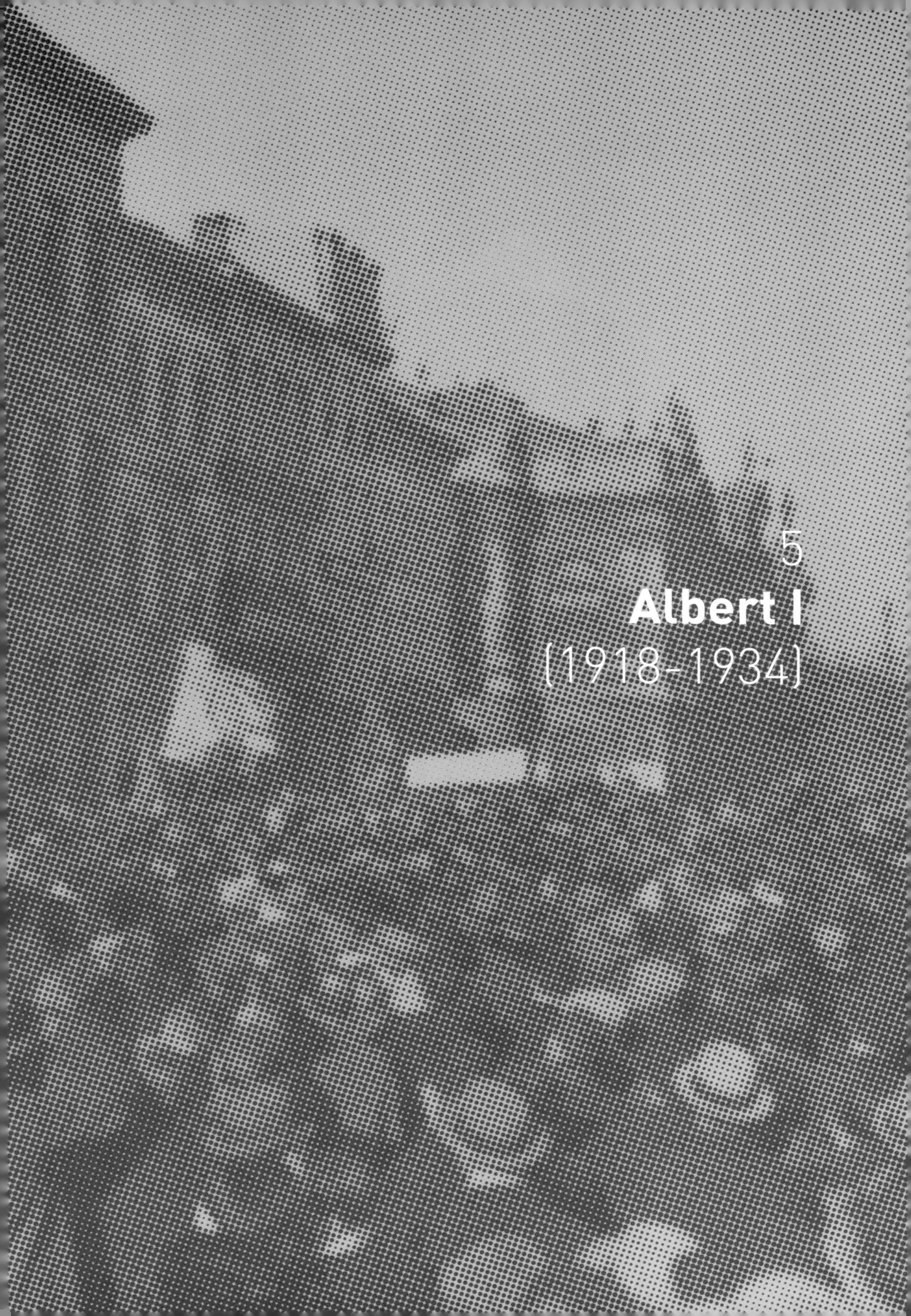

5 Albert I (1918-1934)

The Delacroix administration and the speech from the throne

After 1914-1918 the king had to work with a new type of government: coalition government, under the leadership of a prime minister. This gave the king a considerable degree of power during the formation of the different governments, principally because of his right to appoint the 'formateur' – the future prime minister, responsible for negotiating the political alliances which made each new administration possible. However, once the government was up and running, his role was less important than it had been before the war. Before 1914 Albert had been used to dealing with homogeneous governments, with just one partner – the majority party. He was now faced by administrations comprised of more than one party, which required both politicians and monarch to learn the hitherto little practiced art of political compromise. It was a slow and difficult learning curve. Nevertheless, the prestige which Albert had acquired during the war allowed him to exercise significant influence on the political process. He was often consulted and his opinions were often taken into account, together with those of the senior government ministers. In some matters, such as the army and foreign policy, it was difficult for the ministers to take effective action without him. But it would be untrue to say that Albert held the day-to-day policy strings in his hand. He was no longer the team captain, but more a kind of referee, a neutral arbiter who tried to ensure that the political players stuck to the rules, but with the option of issuing a yellow or red card, if the circumstances warranted it.

The unexpected end of the war temporarily wiped the language question off the political agenda. In contrast to what Albert and many of his political advisers had believed during the war years, the onset of peace showed that the language issue was not the most pressing problem in most people's minds. A rapidly growing and widely shared Belgian nationalism created an atmosphere in which the activists, with their limited following, were viewed with general disdain. The Front Movement disappeared almost overnight and even the Flemish Movement came to be viewed with suspicion. A large section of the population seemed to sense that there were larger and more immediate problems to solve, particularly in the economic, social and military fields.

As soon as the Armistice was signed, the wartime government submitted its resignation. On 13 November 1918, King Albert appointed Léon Delacroix, a Catholic lawyer, as formateur. He was a moderate, French-speaking intermediary figure, who had never previously played a prominent role in politics. In this respect, the pragmatic king was trying to adjust to the change in public opinion. Neither he nor Delacroix found it necessary to include pro-Flemish politicians in the new government of national unity which was sworn in on 21 November. The new administration tackled problems for which there was a broad consensus of opinion, such as the post-war

Belgium and the Monarchy. From National Independence to National Disintegration.

At the end of the war, King Albert relinquished supreme command of the Belgium army, but continued to be associated in the public mind as a soldier-king in uniform. This 1921 photograph shows the king in another – and more unusual – light.

rebuilding programme and the introduction of universal suffrage. It was agreed that this latter measure should be introduced without delay, and without the need to amend the constitution in advance. (The first elections in Belgium on the basis of 'one man – one vote' therefore took place in the spring of 1919. The constitution was only amended post factum in 1921.)

In his speech to parliament from the throne on 22 November 1918 – which like all such previous speeches was given exclusively in French – the king declared: "It would be difficult to understand if the fruitful union which the Belgian people so admirably displayed during the war years should now, at the very moment when our national territory has been liberated from the enemy, make way for the renewal of the sterile quarrels of the past. This union must remain a reality in the new circumstances of peace [applause]. This is the sole *raison d'être* behind the formation of the new government (...)"[96]

This was an unmistakable reference to the divisions which the language question had caused. Had this not led to the sterility and indecisiveness of the ministerial council meetings held on 1 February and 20 March 1918? During the war the king had had numerous opportunities to witness how even the pro-Flemish faction – Van Cauwelaert, Poullet, Helleputte and Van de Vyvere – had managed to disagree on this matter. Sterility and indecisiveness were 'luxuries' which the Belgian nation could no longer afford. Having said this, most of the Flemish Catholic members of parliament were now prepared to formally approve Van Cauwelaert's Minimum Programme. This meant that in theory they were prepared to support the full introduction of the Dutch language in education, administration and the judicial system; the removal of French language facilities in Flanders; and the splitting of the army into separate French and Flemish units. However, behind the façade of the Minimum Programme, there was a deep disunity amongst the Flemish politicians, both with regard to short-term strategy and long-term goals. For example, even leading figures such as Van de Vyvere and Poullet were not wholly convinced of the wisdom of abolishing all language facilities. As far as the ordinary Flemish parliamentarians were concerned, the historian Emmanuel Gerard has written that their seemingly closed ranks also contained "opportunists and doubters, men who would lose their parliamentary seats if they did not pay heed to which way the wind was blowing."

In these circumstances, it is hardly surprising that King Albert did not regard the language question as an important priority in the years immediately following the liberation. This was evident in his speech from the throne on 22 November 1918. Although this speech was written in large part by the ministers of the government, whose policy for the coming year it described, there can be no doubt that Albert was consulted about its content. His ministers' words corresponded closely to his own opinion, at least as far as the language question was concerned. In a passage dealing with the need for unity amongst the Belgian people, irrespective of geographical origins and language, the government, via the mouth of the king, let it be known that it intended to introduce measures based on "the strictest form of equality and the most absolute form of justice". These principles must ensure "the unity and indivisibility of the nation". This meant, amongst other things, that "officials, magistrates and officers must learn the language of the people they administer – this is an elementary rule of fairness." Consequently, Walloon officers in the army would be required to learn Flemish. Every Belgian, the king continued, must have the right to achieve full cultural development in his own language, "including the field of higher education. [Shouts of 'hear, hear!'] The government will bring proposals before parliament to lay the foundations for a Flemish university in the near future, the precise modalities of which will be determined by parliament itself." In other words, there was to be a first, limited introduction of Dutch, but with no mention of the possible abolition of the French-speaking university in Ghent. This was little more than an extension of the position which the king had taken with regard to the 'open' declaration made during the war years. When Albert added that the activists could not count on being given amnesty and that the guilty would be pursued with "the full and just severity of the law", the whole assembly stood to its feet and cheered the king loudly. It was a telling reflection of the feelings of the time.

The liberation of Belgium: 11 November 1918 in Antwerp.

The government's own declaration on 28 November was more vague on the subject of the language question. This was the result of pressure exerted on Delacroix by Paul Hymans and Émile Janson. The prime minister now referred to "certain difficult issues" and cited higher education as being one such issue.[97] There must first be a "cooling-off period" – which suggests that for the time being the politicians were prepared to let sleeping dogs lie. Delacroix therefore decided to concentrate on matters which would be far less contentious, and where support from all sides could be more or less guaranteed.

Questions in parliament – May 1919

In the spring of 1919, King Albert summoned the minister responsible for education, Alphonse Harmignie. The 'three V's' – Van de Vyvere, Van Cauwelaert and Van de Perre – had tabled a number of parliamentary questions about the language policy of the government. The king wanted to discuss with his minister the prospects for the setting up of a Dutch-language university. When the questions were put in parliament, Harmignie answered that the time was not yet ripe for laying the "foundations" of a Flemish university in Ghent. Probably this was also probably the opinion of the king.[98] However, a commission was appointed to look into the wider organisation of higher education. The three questioners responded with a fierce defence of the Minimum Programme, pressing in particular the question of bilingualism in the army. Prime Minister Delacroix was firmly against the splitting of the army into Flemish and Walloon regiments, since in the long term this could only lead to two separate armies and two separate countries. He was prepared to tolerate a Dutch university in Ghent, but only alongside a French-speaking one. It was a view shared by most of his parliamentary colleagues. The motions of the three questioners were defeated by a large majority. Just six months after the end of the war, public and political opinion in Belgium had become anti-Flemish. In this sense, the actions of the 'three V's' were not politically astute. It was unwise to try to force reform on the army in the atmosphere of 'hooray-patriotism' which prevailed immediately after the war.

Nevertheless, the court continued to maintain its contacts with the Flemish Movement. At the beginning of September 1919, the king's secretary Max-Léo Gérard had a long conversation with the Dominican friar Georges Rutten, who in turn had recently met with a number of prominent figures from Flemish-Catholic circles. In a report to the king[99] Gérard commented that the Catholics with whom Rutten had spoken were all against outright administrative separation, but that they all wanted to be "educated, administrated and prosecuted in their own language". Some were still prepared to consider French language facilities, and in this context Father Rutten mentioned the need for freedom of language choice in secondary education, providing there were enough heads of household in a school to demand a class in

French for their children. However, the Dominican made clear that everyone was "firmly against" the full introduction of Dutch at the French university of Ghent. With regard to administrative matters, a majority of the Catholics favoured "complete undoubling" of the central administrative services. His note makes clear that Gérard was not happy with this concept, since it was little more than administrative separation via the backdoor. It meant that Flemish issues would be handled at the central level in Brussels by Flemish officials, while Walloon matters would be left to Walloon officials. However, Rutten's general attitude gave Gérard greater peace of mind: "Father Rutten recognises that the recruitment of civil servants must take place almost exclusively in the bilingual part of the country, but he believes, in time, that the Walloons will assimilate the Flemish language. This being said, his entire exposition was very moderate in tone." The king would no doubt have been pleased to hear this, just as he would no doubt have supported the idea of bilingualism for the officials of the central administration in his kingdom.

King Albert and Frans Van Cauwelaert

The most important driving force behind the Flemish Movement during the 1920s was indisputably Frans Van Cauwelaert. Working from within the Catholic Party, he proposed his famous Minimum Programme, which would have entailed the complete abolition of French language facilities in Flanders. The linguistic minority in Flanders was an elite which had helped to maintain its status and standing precisely by exploiting the system of language facilities. This system created a form of apartheid, not only in cultural terms, but also in social and economic fields. This apartheid was a phenomenon which could operate in the era of the census voting system, but it could not be justified (or made to work) in a modern democracy. Why should a bilingual Fleming have the 'right' in Flanders to hear judgements against him in French or to insist upon receiving a French version of an administrative document? If this person lives in Flanders and understands the Flemish language, an insistence on French is both unnecessary and illogical. Moreover, such an insistence can also be discriminatory. Take, for example, the question of employment opportunities. In the circumstances of the late 19th and early 20th century, language facilities implied that all magistrates and officials needed to be bilingual, which automatically excluded the majority of the Flemish population from public service. From circa 1900 onwards, it became increasingly evident that there was only one solution to this problem: the abolition of the language facilities. This in turn – and in time – would lead to the introduction of one of the principles on which the future organisation of the Belgian state would be based: the principle of territoriality in the use of language by the government for administrative purposes. This meant Flemish in Flanders, French in Wallonia and both languages in bilingual Brussels. For the more crucial domain of education, it also meant that lessons would be given exclusively in Dutch, with the exception of language subjects (French, English, German), which could be taught in the language in question – a fact which ensured that the French language would continue to play an important role in the curriculum for secondary education.

As will shortly be seen, the language facilities were indeed abolished during the 1930s. A key element in this national agreement was reciprocity: Wallonia agreed to the scrapping of French language facilities in Flanders, on condition that Flemish language facilities would not be introduced in Wallonia.

Nowadays, this is a widely accepted (and acceptable) political position, both in Flanders and Wallonia, but in the 1920s Van Cauwelaert had great difficulty in persuading his contemporaries of the validity of his arguments. He was only backed by a minority of public opinion, even in Flanders, and support from within his own Catholic Party was never wholehearted. Demonstrations against the abolition of the French-speaking university in Ghent attracted large crowds, not only in Brussels and Wallonia, but also in Ghent itself. Meetings and petition actions organised by Van Cauwelaert were much less successful. How can this be explained? The small but influential Flemish elite was bilingual, and they were not inclined to change. At best, they only gave lukewarm support to Van Cauwelaert. At worst, they used their influence to oppose him. They feared above all that the introduction of Dutch-language teaching at university level would lower the overall standard of university education. They also feared that the abolition of legal protection for the bilingual Flemings in Flanders would lead in the long term to the end of the Belgian nation. The situation was different amongst the uneducated Flemish masses, who had no knowledge of French. Here Van Cauwelaert's radical brand of monolingualism was much more popular, but to achieve political impact he needed to persuade socialist and liberal workers to vote for his Catholic party. In a nation which was so ideologically divided, this was by no means certain. In other words, the only support on which Van Cauwelaert could always rely was the support of the Catholic-voting masses in Flanders – but this was not even enough to give him a majority in his own part of the country.

In some respects, Van Cauwelaert's own strategy contributed to his political weakness. His concept of a Minimum Programme aroused much suspicion. This might be his minimum, but what was his maximum? It is doubtful if Van Cauwelaert knew the answer to this question himself. He was a skilled politician and he knew that he needed to trim his sails according to the wind. At times, in the immediate aftermath of the war, he did indeed flirt with more radical Flemish-nationalist ideas. For example, he refused to condemn the activists who had been branded as 'traitors' and he even undertook the defence of several of them in court (he was a qualified barrister). He also maintained his contacts with the Front Movement, which had devised its own post-war federalist programme, and in 1919 he allowed Filip De Pillecyn to become editor of the *De Standaard* newspaper (which had been founded by Van Cauwelaert). As a member of the Front Movement in the trenches, De Pillecyn had supported deserters who crossed over to the German lines and who then (with German encouragement) 'informed' the population of the occupied zone about the language problems along the IJzer. Another provocative incident occurred in 1920, when Van Cauwelaert went to Switzerland as part of a parliamentary commission set up to investigate the workings of other federal countries. After his return, he gave an interview to *Het Laatste Nieuws*, in which he said that the Flemings were only asking for things which already worked perfectly in the Swiss cantons![100] This 'radical' element in Van Cauwelaert's thinking was also reflected in the slogan which the Flemish-Catholic Union (*Katholieke Vlaamse Landsbond*) – one of his propaganda organisations – devised to express its feelings about the Belgian nation in 1924: "Is our Union indifferent to the fate of Belgium? Completely! – if a choice needs to be made between a Belgian interest and a Flemish interest!" [101]

These intellectual and political manoeuvrings – one minute a firebrand radical, the next a conciliatory pragmatist – led Van Cauwelaert and his followers to be labelled as 'neo-activists' after 1918. It also explains why many politicians and – more importantly – the king viewed him with growing suspicion.

Yet having said all this, it must nevertheless be remembered that after 1920 Van Cauwelaert rejected the transformation of Belgium into a federal state. In this respect, he was not a Flemish nationalist – a term which must be understood within a specifically Belgian political context (as explained in the introduction). After some initial hesitation in 1919 and 1920, Van Cauwelaert opted for the 'Dutchification' of Flanders, in the sense that he pressed for the full and exclusive use of the Dutch language in education, administration and legal affairs, but without wishing to alter the structure of the unitary Belgian state. He hoped that the legally enshrined use of Dutch in Flanders, without any language facilities for French-speakers, as foreseen in his Minimum Programme, would provide a permanent solution to the language problem in Belgium. In this, he was sadly mistaken.

Van Cauwelaert's position was a party-political one, influenced by the foundation of the Front Party. This new party – which grew out of the wartime Front Movement – was a strong advocate of the federalisation of the Belgian state and can therefore be described as 'Flemish-nationalist' in the narrow, 'Belgian' sense of the term (in the 1930s it would evolve into a separatist party). Moreover, the Front Party quickly began to win votes from the Catholic Party, a development which was clearly unacceptable to the Catholic Church. It is open to question whether or not this growing split in the Catholic movement now persuaded the devout and highly pro-church Van Cauwelaert to turn against federalism – a move which was strongly encouraged by the Catholic religious establishment and had the potential to heal the rift in the Catholic fold. If this was his intention, then he clearly failed. The Flemish nationalists continued to grow stronger, notwithstanding their separation from the Catholic Party, and they continued to argue with conviction and success for the structural division of the Belgian state. This success was linked to the development of an emancipation movement which not only sought to 'elevate' the status of the common man and to make society more democratic – aims shared by Van Cauwelaert – but which also found it harder and harder to reconcile itself with the authoritarian thinking of the Church, in which there was too little place for individual freedom.

The first post-war elections, held in 1919, did not see the breakthrough of the pro-Flemish parties which had been hoped for. The Front Party and its federalist programme won just 60,814 votes and five seats in parliament. More significantly, the Catholic Party lost considerable ground – a sign that even in Flanders the Minimum Programme did not enjoy majority support. With a few exceptions, the Flemish liberals and socialists were still strongly opposed to Van Cauwelaert's radical programme.

However, Van Cauwelaert did receive welcome backing for his strategy from elements within the Catholic Church. Bishop Rutten of Liege (not to be confused with the Dominican friar of the same name) and Bishop Seghers of Ghent both openly encouraged their priests to preach support for the Minimum Programme from their pulpits. Their example was followed by Bishop Waffelaert of Bruges and Bishop Heylen of Namur. It was almost a repetition of the war years: like the chaplains in the trenches, ordinary priests were once again being used to promote the Flemish Movement. King Albert was concerned by these developments and supported the efforts of Cardinal Mercier – head of the Catholic Church in Belgium – to nip them in the bud. In December 1920, Albert even invited the papal nuncio to the palace for a long discussion about the Flemish Movement. In his subsequent report to Rome, Monseigneur Nicotra wrote that the king had started the audience with the announcement that he wished to discuss the "provocation" of the Flemish nationalists, who wanted to promote a federal state along the lines of the Swiss model – a clear reference to the perceived influence of Van Cauwelaert and his recent visit to that country with the parliamentary commission. Albert also complained about the behaviour of Bishop Rutten, who had allowed his feelings as a Fleming to get the better of him. Moreover, dixit the king, his attitude threatened to "infect" the other bishops. Nor was the trouble confined to the top of the Church hierarchy: the parish clergy, supported by various religious orders (most notably the Jesuits, who were fiercely divided by the language question, notwithstanding their 'elitist' reputation), were also believed to be fervent supporters of this revolutionary movement which sought to destroy the kingdom! It is clear that Albert was worried and he intervened in the activities of his bishops on several occasions during this period.[102]

In 1922, Cardinal Mercier obtained a papal letter in which Catholic agitation for the further introduction of the Dutch language in secondary education was condemned. The Church hoped that by acting in this authoritarian manner it would restore unity within the Catholic ranks. Disunity (it was said) not only weakened the Church, but also the Catholic Party, which was still the Church's best hope of achieving its secular aims, even though it had lost the absolute majority which it had enjoyed during the period 1884-1914 (as a result of the introduction of the single vote system after the war). Cardinal Mercier's heavy-handed approach, supported by the king, certainly helped to slow down the progress of the Dutch language in secondary schools, but the king's old 1910 plan – a complete Dutch-language system alongside a complete French-language system in Flanders – was now dead and buried. The battle was now being fought for monolingual education in Dutch, and this was something that the king and the cardinal (for the time being) were prepared to resist to the best of their ability.

Language legislation: 1921-1923

However, neither the monarch nor the Church were able to control matters of state as they had done in the past, and new institutional mechanisms soon led to a breakthrough in the language question. The government needed a two-thirds majority to push through its planned constitutional reform – necessary in order to 'regularise' the single voting system which had been introduced immediately after the war – and the only way it could obtain this majority was to 'buy' the support of Van Cauwelaert and his Flemish Catholics. The price was the government's acquiescence in a new language law for administrative matters, which was passed in 1921. Little is known about the king's role in the approval of this legislation, although there are indications that in January 1921 (at the request of Van de Vyvere) he tried to persuade the Catholic senators to be more reasonable in their persistently negative approach.

In the meantime, a new and separate issue was brewing. In Belgium local burgomasters were appointed by a decree issued by the king and the minister of the interior, following a proposal put forward by the ruling coalition which had been formed following the municipal elections in the town in question. In Antwerp a new coalition had been formed between the socialists and the Christian-democrats – an almost revolutionary innovation in Belgian politics. This 'travaillist' (i.e. leftist) majority proposed Frans Van Cauwelaert as burgomaster, but there was a delay in confirming his appointment. The government in Brussels always found a reason for postponing the signing of the royal decree. Liberal and Catholic-conservative opposition to the 'neo-activist' Van Cauwelaert and his leftist coalition led to considerable dissent within the ministerial council. This dissent was supported by the king. He was gravely concerned by the possibility that this institutional precedent might result in the formation of a similar coalition at national level, since the socialists and Christian-democrats were both known to be in favour of shortening the length of military service and were seen as being 'anti-militarist' in general. There was also concern about the possible repercussions for the Flemish question. Writing to Prime Minister Carton de Wiart on 30 September 1921, the king commented that Van Cauwelaert "is not representative

In 1928, Crown Prince Leopold married the Swedish princess, Astrid. On 19 May, the princess arrived in Antwerp by boat. Burgomaster Frans Van Cauwelaert (left) welcomes the princess at the town hall. Prince Leopold is on the right.

of all Catholics, but is the personification of a majority from which we have everything to fear. We would become estranged from that portion of the population on which we should be building our own support."[103] The constitutional reforms were completed on 15 October, and just days later the socialists resigned from the national government, following an incident concerning a pacifist demonstration. This meant that the cabinet now needed the support of Van Cauwelaert and his followers to stay in power. Minister Van de Vyvere forced the cabinet's hand by threatening to resign, and the signing of the royal decree appointing Van Cauwelaert soon followed. This, however, was too much for the liberals, who actually did resign, thereby forcing a new general election. But by then Van Cauwelaert was already safely installed in the burgomaster's office in Antwerp.

After the 1921 election, in which the Catholics won an additional seven seats in parliament, the creation of a Dutch-language university in Ghent soon found itself back on the national political agenda. The king had appointed the Catholic Georges Theunis as 'formateur'. The choice of this financial expert from outside the world of politics was acceptable to almost everybody, including the opposition. The country was in the middle of a serious financial crisis and Theunis seemed like the right man at the right time. Marie-Rose Thielemans has sketched the genesis of the new government's programme, which was drawn up by the king's secretary, Max-Léo Gérard. The king's most important priorities were:1 – finance, 2 – reparation payments, 3 – the Army Act, and 4 – Ghent. Had the question of a Flemish university suddenly become an important issue again? Yes and no. Financial recovery was dependent on forcing the Germans to make the reparation payments agreed under the Treaty of Versailles. But it seemed that this would only be possible if the former Allied powers occupied the Ruhr valley. This in turn would require the strengthening of the Belgian Army via a new Army Act. But this could only be passed with the support of the Flemish Catholics, who were supporting Van Cauwelaert. And the price for their support was to be... Ghent.

Even so, the government was still bitterly divided on the issue, and so it was decided to allow the governmental majority a free vote on the proposal in parliament. This meant that the individual members of parliament did not have to vote en bloc in accordance with the policy of their party, but were free to vote in accordance with their own consciences.

The king's 'old' 1910 position – the foundation of a Flemish university alongside the existing French institution – was on this occasion defended by the liberals. This was also the opinion of the king[104], but finally he changed his mind. In June 1923, the Lower House approved a national compromise, the Nolf proposal (named after the minister responsible for education, Pierre Nolf). The idea of separate Dutch and French universities in Ghent was buried once and for all. Henceforth, all students at the unitary University of Ghent would be required to follow at least one third of their tuition in Dutch. This represented a first breech in the French monolingualism which dominated higher education in Belgium and was an important victory of principle for the Flemish Movement. The precedent had now been set – all that remained was to build upon it. Writing to Van de Vyvere, King Albert commented (my italics): "I cannot tell you how happy I am that a ministerial crisis has been avoided on the question of a Flemish university. This would have been disastrous. The government has acted wisely in agreeing to *this intermediary measure*."[105] That the king should refer to the Nolf proposal as an "intermediary measure", while many others regarded it as the limit of what was acceptable, shows that the monarch already recognised in 1923 that the full introduction of Dutch in Ghent was unavoidable in the long run. We have already seen how Albert, in his drafts of 1 February 1918, first wished to experiment with a two language system in the army, before eventually agreeing to more "extreme" solutions. He now seemed to be applying the same principle to the University of Ghent.

Albert's ability to be both flexible and pragmatic with regard to the language question was demonstrated elsewhere in 1923. Following their successes with regard to the use of Dutch in public administration and at Ghent, the Flemish Catholics now turned their attention to the army. Minister Devèze, a liberal from Brussels, was not prepared to contemplate the linguistic splitting of units in any way, shape or form, not even through an expanded programme of regional recruitment. However – and to the great anger of the Walloons – he was willing to strengthen the commitment to full bilingualism within the officer corps. This was an attitude typical of many politicians and people in Brussels, where bilingualism was strongly entrenched. In contrast to his minister, Albert was willing to consider the linguistic separation of units at platoon level. A majority of the government, as well as a growing number of pro-Flemish Catholics, also seemed prepared to consider this option. However, the Flemish Movement was dismissive of the proposal: the platoon (10 men) was almost operationally irrelevant as a unit: the crucial levels were the company (75 men) and the regiment (300-350 men). Moreover, Devèze was also unwilling to accept the proposal for Flemish platoons, arguing that they endangered the unity of the nation. As a result, the language question in the army was postponed until further notice.

In December 1923, Prime Minister Theunis briefed his new minister of war, Pierre Forthomme, with regard to "the clear and definitive opinion of the king concerning the matter of Flemish companies." In his report to the king of this briefing, Theunis wrote: "I told him that in the opinion of Your Majesty this concession would be the first step towards the division of the army and then the nation".[106] Prime Minister Delacroix had used exactly the same words when talking about the regiments in answer to the parliamentary questions tabled by the 'three V's' in May 1919 (see page 137). This is an opinion which Albert seems to have repeated to successive postwar administrations. During the war, with all the pressures which it entailed, he had nevertheless given serious consideration (in July 1917) to the more "extreme solution" of Flemish companies, albeit on a limited trial basis. Prime Minister de Broqueville had suggested something similar in the meeting of the ministerial council on 1 February 1918. In his preparatory notes for this meeting, we have also seen how Albert and Ingenbleek first intended to make a statement about Flemish regiments, although they conceded that this was not a viable option in time of war. This illustrates clearly the way in which the Belgian monarchy in general and King Albert I in particular was prepared to adjust its position to reflect the prevailing circumstances. In this sense, the monarchy is like a weathercock: it moves with the wind.

Yet is it possible that the political establishment, including King Albert, made a capital mistake during the first years after the Armistice, by attempting to put the brakes on the development of meaningful language legislation? This brings us back to the question of whether the negative national spiral which was precipitated by the electoral reform of 1893 was irreversible – or not.

1921-1923: the first cracks in the Belgian national fabric

Nationalism and the writing of history: it is a difficult combination. In Flemish historical literature, the administrative language law of 1921 and the Nolf compromise of 1923 are regarded as 'bastard' legislation of the worst kind. This opinion is an almost natural concomitant of the Flemish nationalist discourse which developed in the years between 1918 and 1923. But is this a fair assessment of the laws in question?

The administrative law of 1921 actually introduced a fundamental change in many of the public services in Flanders and it represented the first real step towards the abolition of French language facilities in the region. In contrast to legislation passed before the war, the law of 1921 was applicable throughout Belgian national territory and it introduced for the first time the concept of 'local language = administrative language'. Apart from a bilingual zone around Brussels and the bilingual province of Brabant, the nation was now officially divided for administrative purposes into regions which were either exclusively French-speaking or exclusively Dutch-speaking (although there were still many loopholes and anomalies – far too many for the liking of the Flemings). In this sense, the law gave legal definition to the reorientation which the Flemish Movement had been demanding since 1893: monolingualism throughout its own territory. It was the same principle that the Walloons had always demanded for their own territory – and the law now recognised this fact.

More concretely, the 1921 Act established monolingualism for all municipal and provincial administrations in Flanders and Wallonia, and for the central administrative services of the state (in the capital Brussels), in respect of their contact with civilians and for internal communications between the various services and departments. It did not, however, apply to the Brussels region – which then comprised 16 municipal districts – or to the provincial administration of Brabant. This seemed clear enough, but there was still much discussion about the language rights which should be accorded to the bilingual Flemings. The central administrative services were always required to use the language of the citizen with whom they were dealing, which seemed to imply the bilingualism of these services. In contrast, at municipal and provincial level the citizen had no absolute right to language facilities. Nevertheless, in towns with a high level of bilingual inhabitants such facilities often continued to exist, albeit in a more limited form. The law foresaw 'external' bilingualism in municipalities where 20% of the registered voters requested it or where 15,000 voters requested it in towns with a population greater than 70,000. This was the case in a significant number of Flemish towns. In addition, the municipal and provincial administrations could decide by a simple majority vote to add the other national language as a second 'internal' language. In practice, this meant that a particular matter might be dealt with in either French or Dutch.

The Flemish nationalists tended to focus their attention exclusively on the exemptions to monolingualism in Flanders and on the specific provisions for the Brussels region. They were not happy with these provisions, since the principle of a free choice of language had already strengthened the predominance of French in the capital since the end of the 19th century. Even so, archive research under the supervision of historian Lode Wils has shown that, with the exception of Brussels, the law of 1921 meant a radical change for the administrative services of many municipalities. The 1921 Act led to the rapid advancement of Dutch in Flemish towns and cities which in the past had almost exclusively used French for their administration, such as Kortrijk, Halle, Leuven, Tongeren, Ostend and Ghent. If anything, the effects were even more dramatic at provincial level. The impact of the facilities system on the total volume of administrative activity after 1921 was very limited throughout the country.

The law of 1923 dealing with the partial introduction of Dutch into the University of Ghent was equally radical. Henceforth, students only had the 'right' to follow a maximum of two thirds of their tuition (lectures, tutorials, etc.) in French. The remaining third had to be followed in Dutch. Moreover, this provision only applied to the four largest faculties: Law, Medicine, Letters and Sciences. In the remaining, smaller faculties, such as Art History, Archaeology and Geography, the teaching was given exclusively in Dutch. Equally important, the new law applied not only to newly appointed professors, lecturers, etc., but also to the existing teaching staff – a measure which went further than Van Cauwelaert's original proposal.

So why was Flemish public opinion not satisfied with these two important steps forward? Simply because they were subjected to the influence of a new, more aggressive, more radical form of Flemish nationalism. In politics, a victory is only a victory if it is perceived as such. Van Cauwelaert thought that he had 'won', but he failed to convince Flemish public opinion that this was the case. Instead, public opinion was hijacked by the Front Party, who opposed the Catholic Party at every turn and painted the laws of 1921 and 1923 as a kind of Flemish sell-out. They had at their disposal a widely-read popular press and their federalist views even found favour in some of the more respectable papers, such as *De Standaard*. At the beginning of the 1920s the Flemish Movement, as redefined by the Fronters, was becoming more and more radical, first in favour of federalism, but soon thereafter in the direction of separatism. This was the result of the recruitment of an increasing number of activists to their ranks. Important in this respect was the influence of the radicalised Flemish nationalists on Flemish students. A large section of the Flemish student movement was convinced by the message of the nationalists and became fanatically pro-Flemish in their turn. This was to have a major impact on the future, since the young students of the 1920s were destined to become the future civil servants and politicians of the 1930s and the 1940s.

Belgium and the Monarchy. From National Independence to National Disintegration.

COMPAGNIE MARITIME BELGE   STEAMER SUR LE FLEUVE

PAQUEBOT "ANVERSVILLE"

Menu -:- Spijskaart

Déjeuner

HORS D'ŒUVRE	VOORGERECHTEN
Médaillon d'Arles	
Filets de hareng fumé à l'huile Parmentier	Radis noirs
POTAGES	**SOEP**
Potage Miss Betsy	Consommé Garibaldi
ENTRÉE	**INLEIDING**
Tomates farcies Ménagère	
PLAT DU JOUR	**DAGELIJKSCH GERECHT**
Tête de veau en tortue, pommes nature	
BUFFET FROID	**KOUD BUFFET**
Roastbeef pickles	Gigot d'agneau
Saucisson de Jambon	de Mortadelle
SALADES	**SALAAD**
Céleris-raves	Laitue
FROMAGES	**KAAS**
Port-Salut	Hollande
DESSERT	**NAGERECHT**
Tarte aux fruits	
Café	Thé

Lundi 7 Mars 1938

Seconde Classe

During the inter-war period, the 'Dutchification' of the Flemish elite continued to make progress. The passengers on the steamboat to Congo were now given a menu in both national languages! Even so, Dutch still continued to lag behind French in many spheres of daily life – including the culinary. For example, Dutch had words for 'everyday' foods such as 'onions' and 'potatoes', but had no vocabulary to describe finer dishes (e.g. the difference between 'potage' and 'consommé').

This new and radicalised Flemish Movement made its first serious breakthrough onto the political scene in the years 1923-1924. It was characterised by revanchism and a fierce hatred of everything that was 'Belgian', which in political terms was expressed in policies which were pro-separatist and anti-royalist. In a worrying sign of things to come, there was also a tendency to glorify the activist leaders, who in a 'Belgian' political context could only be regarded as national traitors. The continuing influence of the *Flamenpolitik* and the distorted representation of the laws of 1921 and 1923 played a crucial role. In the hands of the ultra-nationalists, the politicised Flemish masses which had come into existence after 1893 were first mobilised and then moved steadily towards the right. From the end of the 1920s, this would lead to a disturbing growth in anti-parliamentary behaviour amongst many of the movement's followers. Perhaps this was inevitable. The radical, anti-Belgian wing knew that it could never achieve its objectives within the framework of 'Belgian' parliamentary democracy. The fact that Flanders was so predominantly Catholic also gave an added impulse to this swing to the right. Catholic traditionalism was the ideal breeding ground for the development of a critical view of the democratic system, the system of the 'liberal' French Revolution. The Liberty of 1789 was increasingly depicted as licentiousness, whereas Equality was despised because it meant that the ultras would never achieve power. All that remained was Fraternity: the fraternity of the Flemish brotherhood.

In absolute terms, the radical Flemish nationalists did not constitute a particularly large political group during the 1920s. During the 1921 elections the Fronters fielded candidates in every electoral district for the first time. They polled just 59,000 votes, a lower total than they had achieved in 1919. In some districts they did much better, in other districts less well. While the bilingual '*Franskiljons*' (a term of abuse for the bilingual Flemings, roughly equivalent to 'Frenchies') still held sway in the cities, the Flemish nationalists made good headway in the countryside and in the smaller towns and villages, the places where in many respects the Ancien Régime had effectively continued to exist up to 1914.

At the same time, the new Flemish nationalism was also a powerful emancipation movement, based in a socio-economic environment that was already intellectually well-developed but had little real influence. After the electoral reform of 1893, the power of the ordinary, educated Flemings had been kept in check by the use of the multiple vote system, but this restriction was removed with the introduction of 'one man – one vote' in 1919. This not only enhanced the electoral strength of the Flemish masses, but also led to a hitherto unseen flourishing of Flemish 'life' and culture. Flemish student and youth movements blossomed as never before. A distinct social grouping began to emerge, a network of societies and organisations which united people around the common denominator of their 'Flemishness'. The visual arts, music, theatre and literature all found new and more overtly Flemish expression in societies which promoted their nationalist virtues, often in the traditional Catholic manner of street parades and processions. The most successful of the new Flemish societies were the Union of Front Veterans (*Verbond der Vlaamse Oud-Strijders*, VOS) and the Flemish Tourist Union, whose nationalist-cultural activities allowed them to reach hundreds of thousands of ordinary Flemings. In 1923, the militants also began the famous IJzer Pilgrimage, under the slogan "All for Flanders, Flanders for Christ" (AVV-VVK). The atmosphere at this annual event became increasingly aggressive. Veterans who marched under the banner of "No More War" in 1923 were marching through the streets in paramilitary formations just ten years later.

The electoral progress of the radical Flemish nationalist movement was not only reflected in the growing electoral success of the Front Party. Tens of thousands of nationalist votes were also cast for the Catholic Party. Religious motives no doubt played a part in this more 'traditional' voting behaviour, but Van Cauwelaert also had the advantage of working from within the parliamentary majority, which obviously gave him more chance of achieving practical nationalist goals. Van Cauwelaert's strategy was to win language concessions which at first seemed limited, but actually offered a real prospect of much more at a later stage. Moreover, he could also be classed as a radical, since his chosen strategy was potentially damaging to the national unity of Belgium: if necessary, he was prepared to use the numerical superiority of the Flemings to impose new language laws on the less numerous Walloons. This would inevitably have provoked a fierce Wallonian reaction, as had been the case in similar circumstances in 1912. Nevertheless, in the years after 1921 it appeared as if history was about to repeat itself. The Flemings once again seemed ready to use their parliamentary majority to push the Walloons into a corner.

As a result, the debate about federalism and separatism also continued to play an important role in the thinking of the small but influential Walloon Movement. The separatism expounded by the Flemish Movement seemed more threatening, because it was backed by a mass movement, but the greater threat to the unitary Belgian state actually came from Walloon separatism. The idea that Flanders might one day secede from Belgium and unite with The Netherlands was never a realistic possibility: the two peoples spoke the same language, but they were light years apart in terms of culture and mentality. This was not the case with the Walloons and the French. The possible incorporation of Wallonia into France was much more 'emotionally acceptable' to both parties and was no doubt discussed at length in the corridors of the Elysée Palace and the Quai d'Orsay – as it probably still is.

Albert I and the Flemish question, 1925-1928

In February 1925, King Albert asked Prime Minister Theunis to discuss with his ministerial council the problem of the civil servants who had been removed from their posts because of their political collaboration with the Germans during the occupation of 1914-1918. He also requested that the public prosecutor's office should not pursue activists who had been convicted in their absence but who were now gradually returning to Belgium, following their exile in The Netherlands. Theunis complied with the king's wishes, and in his letter of thanks to the premier Albert once again demonstrated his ability to be politically flexible: "Posed in this way, the problem seems to me to be capable of a solution which can give full satisfaction to the Flemish element, but without requiring the government to compromise on matters of principle."[107] In short, the king was suggesting a pragmatic, individual approach, in order to avoid discussions about a general amnesty, which could only lead to further division of the country.

In December 1926, Van Cauwelaert nevertheless tabled a motion in the Lower House, formally requesting that an amnesty be granted. This meant that a parliamentary debate could no longer be avoided. The head of the king's cabinet, Louis Wodon, put pressure on the French-speaking liberals to avoid provoking a political crisis on this issue. If they did, new elections would inevitably follow: "And what elections! The whole campaign would turn on the question of the amnesty and the language problem. This is a frightening prospect, which could be dangerous for the very existence of the country and which therefore must be avoided *at all costs*."[108]

The liberals did as they were asked and remained calm. The same, however, could not be said of August Borms. As a leading activist collaborator, he had been convicted and heavily sentenced after the war. He was still in prison, where he intended to stay until a general amnesty had been granted. He had been offered early release, but had refused to accept it, because of a condition which stipulated that he should not engage in political activity. The king discussed this delicate case with Minister Rubbens in 1928. Rubbens said: "We consider this man to be more dangerous in prison than outside it," to which the king replied: "I agree entirely, but I could never persuade a Brussels minister to release this prisoner."[109]

At roughly the same time, the question of the army reappeared on the political agenda. In 1927, the general staff devised a new military strategy, which was based on a smaller army but one which could be mobilised more rapidly. Regional recruiting would have undoubtedly speeded up the mobilisation process. It would also, of course, have solved the seemingly never-ending language problem in the army. In January 1928, General Galet, the chief of the General Staff, put forward a proposal for strict regional recruiting. The Flemish nationalists were delighted – it was what they had been demanding for the past 15 years. Surviving archives tell us little of Albert's involvement in this matter, but it is unthinkable that Galet would have acted without first consulting with the king. The general told the ministerial council that (this time) the need for bilingualism in the more senior ranks of the armed forces would be taken seriously, because the creation of regional units implied that "a casual acquaintance with Flemish" would no longer be sufficient. The training of the rank-and-file would take place exclusively in their mother tongue and they would be recruited in their own provinces. The Flemish Movement was even able to secure a promise that the language division of units would take place at company level. These companies would in turn be amalgamated to create single-language battalions, which opened up the prospect of single-language regiments at some stage in the future. The new army language law of 7 November 1928 represented a major step forward for the supporters of monolingualism in Flanders. There was, however, a downside. The need for unity of command necessitated the use of a single language for the issuing of orders – and this language would still be French. Van Cauwelaert and his followers understood this and accepted it as unavoidable. However, the more radical nationalists were irritated that the language for use between officers had to be French. Yet perhaps this was splitting hairs. In the final analysis, the far-reaching division of units on a linguistic basis meant that the senior ranks had no option but to become bilingual.

The Walloon radicals were strongly opposed to the new law. The Walloon Movement saw the enforced bilingualism of the officer corps as being essentially to the benefit of the Flemings, since the vast majority of the Flemish officers already spoke acceptable French, whereas the French-speaking officers hardly knew a word of Dutch. Less understandable was the reaction of the extreme wing of the Flemish Movement: notwithstanding the fact that the use of their own Dutch language in the army now increased dramatically, the radicals were incensed by what they saw as the institutionalised bilingualism of the army.

As might have been expected, the practical implementation of the new law led to a number of organisational problems. For this reason, in December 1929 General Galet put forward a new proposal for even larger single-language units. Minister of War de Broqueville was not easily convinced. The current situation was already delicate enough, notwithstanding the fact that the new army language examinations were made almost laughably easy, for fear of having too brusque an effect on the largely French-speaking officer corps. In this context, it is noticeable that two successive ministers of war – de Broqueville and Devèze – were opposed to monolingual units at higher than company level. The majority of the army high command was also against any such move, since they feared the anti-Belgian feeling which might result from the creation of larger Flemish units. This was an opinion shared by the British and French military attachés in Brussels. Moreover, it was an opinion which the often virulent outbursts of the radical Flemish nationalists in the press did little to alter. Every day the Flemish popular papers were full of new articles which expressed extreme radical views in language that was openly inflammatory, with an obvious hate for everything Belgian, coupled to an aggressive separatism and strong anti-royalist feelings. How could the Flemish troops be regarded as loyal, if this was the attitude of their ideological representatives? Were they not hostile towards King Albert, their own commander-in-chief?

As Laurence van Ypersele has shown, the king's status was one of the main issues at stake in the Flemish-national debate. The more the king became identified with the unitary Belgian state and its 'inadequate' language laws, the less inclined the Flemish press became to write about their monarch in respectful terms, let alone to raise him to the pseudo-mystical status of a national hero, as was the tendency in some elements of the French-language media. The growth of anti-monarchist feeling amongst the Flemish people after 1918 has not yet been properly studied, but it is undeniable that there was a growth – and that it was widespread. In 1924, the provincial governor of Limburg reported to the Ministry of Home Affairs that a group of scouts had recently marched through the streets of Hasselt shouting "Down with the king. Off with his head!" In 1929, a teacher in the village of Zwijndrecht was accused by a town councillor of praising August Borms, of refusing to stand during the national anthem and of referring to the sovereign as "Albert" instead of "King Albert". As the centennial anniversary of the founding of the Belgian nation approached, this kind of Flemish radicalism began to crystallise into a new and harder form. The Flemish Union of Front Veterans (*Verbond der Vlaamse Oud-Strijders*, VOS), supported by the newspaper *De Standaard*, called upon its members to boycott a march-past in front of the king. Nor was this type of behaviour confined to the hard-line ultras. Even more moderate Flemish organisations, such as the influential Davids Fund (*Davidsfonds*), were reluctant to take part in the 1930 celebrations. This was symptomatic of the penetration of Flemish-nationalist sentiment in traditional Catholic thinking.

The *coup de grâce* for bilingualism in Flanders, 1928-32

From 1928 onwards, there was a growing consensus that the time had come to put a definitive end to the language question and the unsatisfactory stop-gap laws which it had produced. The celebration of the 100th anniversary of the founding of the Belgian state seemed an ideal moment to bring this about. Might it not be possible to settle the nation's linguistic tangles once and for all by 1930? If not, the demands of the radical Flemish nationalists could only become even more extreme. Prime Minister Jaspar was already alluding to a "total solution" for the language problem at the beginning of 1928, and as the year progressed there were growing signs that a rapprochement between the various parties was in the making. In the Catholic Party, this willingness to compromise was strengthened by the fear of a split in its own ranks and a possible collaboration between the Christian-democrat faction of the party and the Belgian Workers Party. Things seemed to be moving gradually in the right direction when – as so often in the past – the language issue suddenly exploded without warning.

The reason for this explosion was the death of an elderly liberal member of parliament in Antwerp. As a result, a by-election needed to be held and a suitable date was agreed: 9 December 1928. It was the custom at this time that only the party of the deceased member should put forward a candidate. This candidate would be automatically elected and the status quo in the Lower House would be restored. In keeping with this custom, the socialists and the Christian-democrats did not participate in the Antwerp by-election, and so the only candidate was the liberal, Paul Baelde, a bilingual lawyer and a well-known member of the Antwerp establishment, with a strong dislike of Flemish nationalism. This was like a red rag to a bull for the ultras, and so the Front Party decided to break with convention and put forward a candidate of their own: no less a person than August Borms, who was still in prison for his collaborative activities during the war! With this simple manoeuvre, the radicals ensured that the by-election would now become a plebiscite on the question of the nation's language politics. The margin of Borms' victory stunned the political world. He polled 83,053 votes against just 44,410 for Baelde, with 58,052 spoilt ballot papers. There were different ways of looking at these figures, but the most common interpretation was that 45% of the Antwerp electorate had voted in favour of radical Flemish nationalism. True, 24% of the electorate had not been prepared to vote for someone who had been condemned to death for collaboration and treason, but they had not been prepared to vote for Baelde either: by spoiling their ballot papers they made clear their disapproval of the nation's language laws. This meant that Baelde had been elected with just 31% of the popular vote, since Borms' conviction meant that he was unable to take his seat in parliament.

Perhaps this result was not such a surprise, after all. The great port city of Antwerp had long 'enjoyed' a reputation for political radicalism. In the 1860s a group of leading local citizens had formed the Meeting Party, which operated across the usual party political lines to protest against the building of a new ring of forts around the city. The party won several seats in the Lower House and also held a majority on the city council. It attracted widespread support from amongst the popular wing of the nascent Flemish Movement, and was seen as being both anti-establishment, anti-Brussels and anti-monarchist (it was King Leopold I who was insisting that the forts must be built). This political culture had also manifested itself during the Great War, when the city had boasted a higher than average number of activists, not only amongst the Catholics but also (more unusually) amongst the socialists. Yet even by Antwerp standards, the result of the December 1928 by-election was something out of the ordinary. It was immediately interpreted as a serious warning to the political establishment about the urgency of dealing with the language question. If the Jaspar administration did not implement Van Cauwelaert's Minimum Programme with a minimum of delay, the field would be left to the radical Flemish nationalists – and the fate of the unitary Belgian state would be sealed.

Faced with this situation and having no real alternative, the Jaspar government, supported by King Albert, threw its weight behind the immediate realisation of the Minimum Programme. This meant that (this part of) the establishment now opted to scrap the much-disputed language facilities in Flanders, in the hope that this would

August Borms was released from prison on 17 January 1929. A huge demonstration was held by his supporters in Antwerp on 3 February.

restore national calm. With this aim in mind, the premier set up a parliamentary commission, consisting of members from the three traditional parties, whose task was to draw up a permanent solution for the language problems which had plagued the country for so long. It was a noble aim – and one which has been revived on several occasions in subsequent Belgian history. However, on this occasion the situation looked promising – at first. The Catholic Party was favourable to the proposal. The Flemish and Walloon wings of the party had agreed a kind of armed truce, and both were prepared to support Van Cauwelaert, if only to avoid a new split in their ranks and to keep the socialists out of government. Moreover, it was becoming clear that the Christian-democrat faction of the Catholic Party was proving to be an effective bulwark against the Front Party. At the beginning of 1929, the Christian ACV trade union and the Catholic Party (both of which contained Walloon members) declared themselves to be in favour of administrative monolingualism for Flanders, outside Brussels – which represented a radical change of position.

Initially, the liberals continued to oppose the Minimum Programme. They were supported by the socialists, who actually fought the 1929 general election on a programme which promised a "Belgian Compromise". The text of the compromise was somewhat obscure, but it was clear that its intention was to maintain a degree of language facilities for French-speakers in non-bilingual municipalities. In this manner, it was possible for the socialist BWP – as historian Maarten Van Ginderachter has pointed out – to preserve its unity with no loss of face for either of its regional wings. As an electoral policy, however, it was not a success. The socialists' share of the national vote fell from 39.4% to 36%, whereas the Front Party leapt from 80,407 votes in 1925 to 132,567 votes in 1929. Sobered by this electoral defeat, the socialists held a congress on 10 and 11 November 1929, which now agreed to support the principle of administrative monolingualism in both Flanders and Wallonia. Nevertheless, the BWP, under the leadership of the pro-Flemish Camille Huysmans, continued to defend the rights of the bilingual French-speaking minorities in Flanders. In particular, the party continued to emphasise the cultural differences between Flanders and Wallonia. For this reason, the BWP argued for the continuation of a limited degree of bilingualism in the Flemish education system. With this aim in mind, the Troclet Report proposed the approval of second-language education in cases where more than 25 parents had requested it, whereas Huysmans favoured a scheme whereby a third of all lessons during the last four years of secondary education would be given in French. This was something very different from what the Minimum Programme had foreseen: full Dutch language education in Flanders (but with an important place for other languages, including French, in the school curriculum).

Given the complexities of this situation, it was perhaps inevitable that the Catholic-liberal administration of Prime Minister Jaspar – like so many before it – would eventually get bogged down in the quicksand of the language question. Encouraged by the socialist position, the liberals continued to resist full Dutch monolingualism in education. They were prepared to accept a fully Dutch University of Ghent, but in return they demanded guarantees in primary and secondary education for the (bilingual) French-speaking minorities in Flanders. The Catholics refused to agree to these concessions – and so the government fell. Given the heated political atmosphere, it was unthinkable that new elections should be held so soon after the previous ones, particularly as the socialists were adamant that they would remain in opposition. Consequently, King Albert refused to accept the resignation of the Jaspar administration. This pressured the liberals into withdrawing their objections to a fully Dutch-speaking university in Ghent. From the opposition benches, the BWP held its ground for a brief while longer, but eventually agreed that its MPs could vote freely on the matter, following which all the Flemish and a number of Walloon socialists switched their support behind the government's proposal.

In April 1930, the University of Ghent became a fully Dutch-speaking institution, with effect from the following academic year (1930-1931). King Albert defended this decision in a speech which he gave in Ghent itself on 13 July. Throughout the rest of the 100th anniversary celebrations he confined himself to pleading for greater national unity, which he felt could best be achieved through greater cultural exchange between the regions and by a more widespread bilingualism. To underline his point, he made his speech in Brussels in both national languages.

On 28 September 1930, the king wrote a letter (in Dutch) to Minister Van de Vyvere: "I hope, as I know you do, that the future will see a period of greater calm with regard to the language question. This is still our most serious problem. It is regrettable that so many remained blind for so long to a situation which was so obviously alarming. Do you remember a certain council meeting in De Panne [the ministerial council meetings of 1 February and 20 March 1918], when we were with three or four against ten? It is important that the wealthier classes show more goodwill towards Flemish language and culture."[110]

By May 1931 the Jaspar government was back in trouble, partly because of the worsening economic crisis, but more particularly because of internal divisions relating to the language question. This time it was public administration and primary and secondary education in Flanders which stood at the top of the agenda. "The King's preoccupations with regard to the language question are also mine," the harassed prime minister wrote to Albert.[111] The government's 1929 programme, which foresaw a general settling of all outstanding language matters, still needed to be finalised. To achieve this, Jaspar needed agreement on a new language law for public administration, to replace the legislation passed in 1921, which still granted a limited degree of language facilities. He managed to persuade his ministerial colleagues to agree a draft text for both public administration and for primary and secondary education, but thereafter he was unable to hold his liberal-Catholic coalition together: the differences between the partners were just too great. Jaspar resigned. Albert wanted to replace him with a more overtly pro-Flemish premier. The king first approached Van Cauwelaert, but he was unwilling to accept the task. After further searching, the royal choice finally fell on Jules Renkin. This immediately aroused the suspicions of the liberals: Renkin was a French-speaking Catholic from Brussels, but in recent years he had adopted a strong pro-Flemish stance in the interests of party unity. The liberals' suspicions proved to be well founded. During the hard negotiations which led to the formation of the new administration, it became apparent that Renkin expected the pro-French Flemish liberals to give the government a free hand in language matters. This was confirmed by the government's (admittedly vague) policy statement issued in June 1931. Moreover, the Catholic representation in Renkin's cabinet consisted almost exclusively of strongly pro-Flemish ministers, while the Walloon nationalist faction – which was also strongly in favour of monolingualism in Flanders – also obtained a representative, the liberal François Bovesse.

From their position on the opposition benches, the socialists had already decided not to take a party political position on the language question, since it was an issue which was capable of dividing them unlike any other. Now that the liberals took the same decision, by agreeing to join the Renkin government, the future for the bilingual minorities in Flanders looked very bleak. There were more than sufficient Flemish and Walloon MPs who would be happy to vote the remaining language facilities out of existence. With good cause, the headline of the pro-French *Flandre Libérale* newspaper for 17 June 1931 screamed: "*M. Devèze a trahi*" (Mr. Devèze has betrayed us!). It was the Brussels minister who had finally persuaded his party to take the plunge with Renkin.

Even the Walloon members of parliament turned their backs on the bilingual Flemings, since in return for their abandonment of administrative bilingualism the government was willing to offer them legal recognition for the language homogeneity of Wallonia. Writing on this subject as far back as October 1929, the future Minister Bovesse had complained: "It is hard to let go of the French-speaking community in Flanders, but it would be more difficult and more dangerous to sacrifice our linguistic unity!"[112] It was a sign of the times when in January 1930 the *Association Wallonne du Personelle de l'État* and the *Verbond van het Vlaamse Personeel der Openbare Besturen* – the civil service unions of Wallonia and Flanders – signed an agreement on the basis of the monolingualism and language homogeneity of their respective regions. Chantal Kesteloot has rightly described this agreement as a symptom of the change in mind-set which was taking place in Wallonia.

A further contribution was made to this process by Flor Grammens. From 1931 onwards, he campaigned on behalf of a number of Flemish communities situated on the language border. As already mentioned in the introduction, the provincial boundaries did not always perfectly coincide with the linguistic boundaries, so that a number of (more or less) Flemish villages along the language frontier found themselves in Walloon provinces. In January 1930, using a mixture of cunning and deception, Grammens was able to gather together enough signatures from 25 municipalities in the Walloon provinces of Hainaut and Liege to force the government to apply the bilingual provisions of the administrative language law of 1921. Not content with these successes, Grammens took his anti-Walloon campaign a step further in the summer of 1931. Following a heated meeting at 's Gravens Voeren – a Dutch-speaking village in the Walloon province of Liege, but close to the border with the Dutch-speaking province of Limburg, to which it more properly belonged – he instituted legal proceedings against a group of excited locals for defamation of character. He had the case brought before the competent civil court and that was in the city of … Liege, the very heart of Wallonia and the Walloon Movement! Not surprisingly, Grammens' barrister, Maurice Ponette, insisted on his client's right to plead his case in Dutch, since the incident had occurred in a Flemish village, even though it fell under the jurisdiction of the French-speaking province of Liege. Angered by this obvious act of provocation, the court in Liege rejected Ponette's request. The Flemish press had a field day and even the French-language newspapers in Flanders felt compelled to criticise the Walloon judiciary for its narrow-mindedness. *Le Matin*, a liberal newssheet in Antwerp, complained that the incident had weakened the position of the French-speakers in Flanders, precisely at the moment when "their rights" needed to be defended. The Brussels journal *La Libre Belgique* commented that the court in Liege had handed the Flemings a powerful weapon in the linguistic war, by refusing to use Dutch, in a case which clearly involved a Dutch-speaking village.[113]

By now, it was clear that the bilingual French-speaking minority in Flanders were already losing the language war – and everybody knew it. Consequently, the Walloon politicians in parliament dropped them like the proverbial hot potato. There was nothing to stand in the way of the full implementation of the Minimum Programme, since it now commanded a large majority in both House and Senate. Some of the more far-reaching provisions were still a matter for dispute, but in these instances the Flemings simply used their numerical superiority to force these provisions through. This was particularly the case with regard to the bilingual Brussels region, since the logic of Flemish-Walloon administrative monolingualism could not be applied in that context. Yet each of these votes, regardless of their inevitability, was experienced by the French-speaking community in Belgium as a slap in the face. Much the same was true of the continuing bilingualism in the central administrative services, since this was (rightly) perceived as being for the benefit of the Flemings.

Notwithstanding these momentous developments, the bilingual elite in Flanders continued to enjoy a degree of protection from the Flemish liberals. Until 1929-1930 this had also been the case with the Flemish socialists, under the guidance of Camille Huysmans. At first glance, this seems difficult to explain. Why should the party of the Flemish workers break a lance for the French-speaking upper classes? This is connected with the importance of the Belgian national state to the development of socialism in Belgium. After 1918, when the period of 'equality' (based on universal suffrage) began, the socialists identified themselves closely with the unitary state, since it was within this framework that a network of social provisions could best be elaborated. For this reason, they were less prepared to question the basis of the state's organisation than the Flemish Catholics. And at this point in time bilingualism was an element of that organisation. Added to this was Huysmans' belief that Flanders was not as uniformly monolingual as Wallonia.

But what exactly could be done to protect the small but powerful group of bilingual Flemings? It was obvious that they could no longer claim the right to hear legal judgements or to complete their administrative formalities in French. Nor was this really necessary. Because they were bilingual, the obligatory use of Dutch did not place them at a disadvantage. The core of the problem lay in the need to perpetuate the bilingual French-Flemish culture. Moreover, if you concede this need, it almost automatically implies a further need for some form of French-language or bilingual teaching within the Flemish educational system. This explains why Huysmans, as late as the socialist congress of November 1929, was still prepared to support the concept of French-speaking secondary education in Flanders, although he was quite happy to ditch other, less crucial language facilities in matters of administration and the law.

From a cultural point of view, the French language did indeed deserve a degree of support in Flanders. From the social and socio-economic point of view it did not. The bilingual – and essentially French-speaking – Flemish elite deliberately cut itself off from the mass of the ordinary people and from the use of the popular Flemish language. The language barrier was a social barrier, which promoted ignorance and economic inequality. This phenomenon was strengthened by the increased 'Frenchification' of public institutions in Flanders, since the need to speak French made it impossible for the majority of Flemings to join their own civil service. To bridge this social divide, it was first necessary to break down the language barrier. The introduction of Dutch as the exclusive administrative language in Flanders helped to reduce the level of language discrimination against non-French-speaking public officials. Even more important was the widespread introduction of Dutch into the education system in Flanders. This hit the bilingual elite where it hurt the most – although most people failed to recognise this at the time. Many politicians, including King Albert, only agreed to the full legal introduction of the Dutch language at all levels of Flemish life because they believed that the French language would continue to survive in Flanders. Even overtly pro-Flemish ministers repeated this same claim time and time again during the political debates of the interwar years. In 1932, nobody could have imagined that within the space of two generations the small group of bilingual Flemings would be reduced to the status of a social curiosity, who (with a few rare exceptions) would be unable to speak decent French. This is indeed the situation nowadays.

King Albert and the bilingualism of the central administration

The legal establishment and official endorsement of monolingualism in Flanders and Wallonia was of fundamental importance. It was the logical conclusion of the trends which had been developing since 1893 and created two official and homogenous language regions, alongside the bilingual region of Brussels and a limited number of mixed language districts along the language border. This clear demarcation provided the politicians with a geographical context of homogeneous linguistic regions, which made possible the reform of the state structure by the transfer of powers from the centre to the regions. Some people thought that this possibility opened the way for the break-up of Belgium as a nation. It was for this reason that King Albert now attached even greater significance to a common core of bilingualism based around the central administration in Brussels. However, the Walloons had other thoughts on this matter.

The new Renkin government of 1931 took over the draft language proposal for administrative matters which had been formulated by the previous administration. This draft was based on the premise that the commonly-used local language would also be the administrative language. This meant that for administrative purposes

Wallonia and Flanders were regarded as being monolingual; Brussels and its surrounding municipalities were seen as being bilingual. The central administration would deal with individual cases in the appropriate local language. A bilingual counterweight was contained in the provision which stipulated that some officials in the central administration must speak both national languages, but only from the level of director upwards. In concrete terms, this involved less than 300 officials, for whom a "sufficient knowledge" of their second language would be adequate! In this way, the draft significantly weakened the stronger provisions contained in the 1921 Act. In this context Van Cauwelaert, speaking in the Lower House on 20 January 1932, declared that the Flemings had no objection in principle to the concept of bilingualism at the central level, but that the law of 1921 had proven difficult to implement precisely because of the unwillingness of the Walloons to learn Dutch.

Under pressure from the Walloons, the parliamentary committee charged with preparing a final draft of the legislation scrapped the bilingual provision. The central administration would function as far as possible with parallel monolingual departments. This administrative 'splitting' of services caused much raising of eyebrows. Would this not be damaging to the unity of the administration? Was there not a chance that different administrative practices would develop along with the different use of language? Was it not simply a precursor to a federalised state, something of which the Flemish nationalists (and a smaller number of Walloons) had long been dreaming?

King Albert thought that on this occasion the Walloon Movement had gone beyond the limit of what was acceptable. The final draft of the new law reduced the use of bilingualism – which the king still saw as a binding agent between the two different parts of his nation – to an absolute minimum. This explains why he now did something which was most unusual: he threatened to use his royal veto. In a letter of 24 January 1932 to the prime minister, he informed Renkin that he would not sign the legislation in its existing form. "Any solution which leads to the more or less avowed administrative separation of the country, or which helps to pave the way for such a situation, preparatory to a political separation and, finally, to the collapse of the nation, must be condemned without mercy." He wanted to preserve the political unity of the country at all costs. "The preservation of this unity is, in effect, closely linked to the maintenance of our national independence." [114]

This was a threat which the parliament could not ignore. The government put its thinking cap on and on 27 January 1932, after much negotiation behind the scenes, Renkin announced a new proposal to the Lower House. After a long and impassioned plea for the preservation of Belgian national unity, he rejected the parliamentary committee's amendments which foresaw the linguistic splitting of the central administration. To prevent specific issues being dealt with in different languages, Renkin proposed a new amendment. When dealing with a matter in a language which

Belgium and the Monarchy. From National Independence to National Disintegration.

The IJzer Pilgrimage, July 1930. In the background stands the IJzer Tower, a monument to the Flemish soldiers who died during the Great War. At the front, one of the men is carrying a Flemish flag and a broom. During the inter-war period, the broom was a symbol of anti-parliamentarianism (implying a need to 'clean up politics'). In the 1930s, a section of the Flemish Movement surrendered their democratic ideals and moved closer to fascism. One of the girls near the front is wearing an obviously German style of dress, which was unusual in Flanders at this time.

was not his own, a monolingual official in the central administration could now be assisted by a bilingual colleague. Van Cauwelaert immediately gave his approval: it had never been the intention, he said, to have a full linguistic splitting of the administration. The House was in agreement and voted in favour of the Renkin amendment. The idea of bilingual assistants also made the legislation acceptable to the king and so the law was approved. Time would show, however, that the new system did not work.

The next challenge for the government was to get new language legislation relating to primary and secondary education through parliament. In this instance, the continuing liberal refusal to accept the principle of local language education was likely to be the biggest stumbling block. In an attempt to sidestep this opposition, and also to rid himself of the concessions he had been forced to make to the French-speakers in Flanders in his government statement of June 1931, Renkin decided to offer his resignation. This was a purely tactical manoeuvre and the king agreed to play along: he accepted the resignation but then immediately reappointed Renkin as 'formateur'. The new administration included the Catholic Flemish politician Gustaaf Sap, a known radical in language matters. Renkin's ploy worked and the new education legislation, with its far-reaching language provisions, was also passed through both chambers of parliament.

1933 was a crucial year for Europe, culminating in the rise to power of Adolf Hitler. This awakening of a new and vital political nationalism in Germany was closely linked to the triumphant electoral breakthrough of the well-organised Nazi party. Partly under the influence of this German example, there was also a realignment of the various nationalist groups in Flanders. In this respect, 1933 also saw the founding of the Flemish National Union (*Vlaams Nationaal Verbond*, VNV). This new political party absorbed the old Front Party and re-organised Flemish nationalism along more vigorous lines, based on strict discipline and right-wing policies. Also in keeping with the German example, the VNV had a strong leader, in the shape of Staf Declercq, and from its earliest beginnings was susceptible to a further move in the direction of fascism. True, the VNV did have a less militant wing, with more 'democratic' tendencies. But historian Els Witte has rightly questioned the sincerity of the conciliatory, pro-democracy statements made by several VNV leaders during this period, since an analysis of their party programme suggests a clear desire to undermine the democratic system.

At the end of 1933, the Belgian political situation once again became tense, this time because of a proposed reassessment of the disciplinary measures against public officials who had been accused of activism. The government of the day, under the leadership of Prime Minister de Broqueville, entrusted the task to a civil service commission, which at the end of 1933 put forward seventy cases for possible 'reintegration'. These recommendations split the de Broqueville government down the middle. Public opinion was also restless and divided. It was rumoured that the cabinet had already approved the recommendations. On 31 December 1933, a large demonstration of war veterans protested against the proposed reintegration. They were received by the king, who assured them in his speech that the government enjoyed his full confidence and that officials "whose unworthiness has been clearly proved" would not be rehabilitated. This was a clever remark, since the problem relating to most of the activist officials in question was precisely a lack of reliable evidence. Albert attached great importance to the survival of the de Broqueville administration, which needed to take crucial financial measures to combat what had become a full-scale economic depression. At the suggestion of Devèze, he proposed to the premier that he should allow the disputed cases to be re-examined by magistrates, since the civil service disciplinary procedures offered insufficient guarantees. De Broqueville read the king's letter and accompanying note to the ministerial council and was finally able to persuade his ministerial colleagues to approve the plan. Minister Sap was not happy with the idea, but it was finally agreed to forward the case notes within the framework of an appeal procedure to a group of magistrates, the Goddijn Commission. A strategy was devised whereby it was intended to make the king's letter public, albeit in a slightly amended form. This letter, believed de Broqueville, was composed in such a direct and authoritative manner that there could be no question of winners or losers. However, he was mistaken. The personal position taken by the king on this matter lost him further credit in the eyes of Flemish public opinion. Yet this was destined to have no long term repercussions – two weeks later King Albert was killed in a climbing accident.

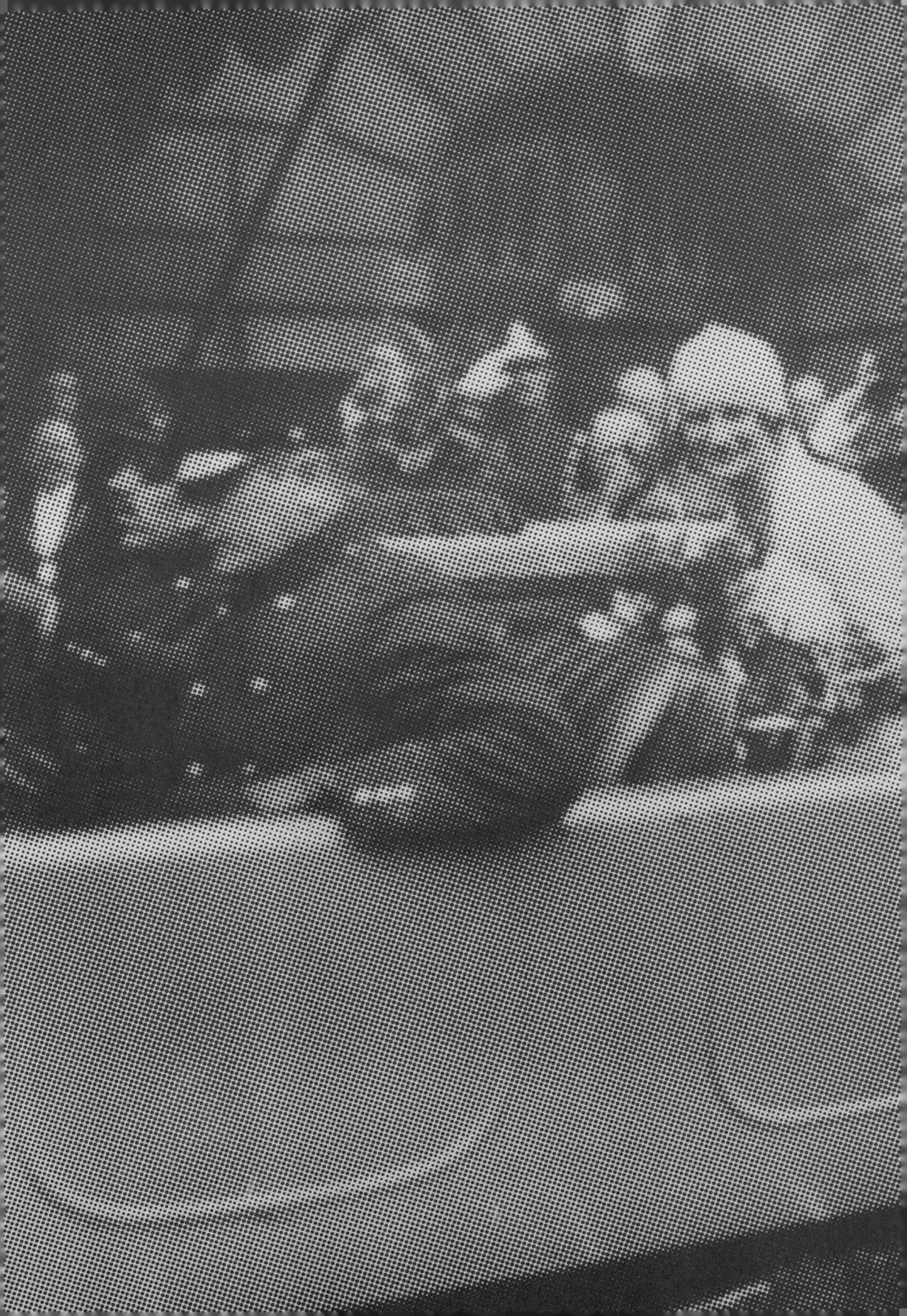

6

Leopold III
(1934-1944/1950)

The Radical King

In continuation of King Albert, 1934-1940

The marriage of Prince Leopold in 1926 to the charming and informal Swedish Princess Astrid helped to bring about a certain rapprochement between Flanders and the monarchy. After her tragically early death in 1935, the radical right-wing magazine *Nieuw Vlaanderen* (New Flanders) wrote an obituary for the Princess which was little more than an ethnic-nationalist declaration: "We will honour her memory with respect and gratitude, and also as Flemings. She came from a country whose race is related to our race. She came from a people so few in number as our own, but a people who are amongst the most civilised in Europe. She came from a nation which still knows the difference between justice and injustice. This created a bond of affection which all of us felt and which was gradually reflected in tangible realities, particularly in the upbringing of her children."[115]

In 1934, Prince Leopold succeeded his father as king. He took the constitutional oath in both Dutch and French, and for the very first time the inaugural speech from the throne was also given in both languages. Like his father before him, Leopold III was not inclined to meekly tow the French line. In the meeting of the ministerial council held on 14 October 1936 he gave a long speech with the purpose of convincing his ministers that a change in Belgian foreign policy was necessary. Prime Minister Van Zeeland and Foreign Minister Spaak had already announced such a policy and had defended it in parliament. Belgium now intended to follow a 'hands-free' strategy, which would allow the nation to steer an independent course, free from French influence. In 1920, Belgium had signed a military agreement with France, but since the rise to power of Hitler in neighbouring Germany, this agreement had become more and more compromising. Leopold's speech was intended for the council's ears only, but at the request of the socialist minister Emile Vandervelde it was made public. In this manner he hoped to persuade his fellow party members of the virtues of the new policy, which would not be easy, given the strong sympathy of the Walloon socialists for French interests. By allowing his speech to be published, Leopold was endorsing the difficult decision taken by his ministers, thereby offering them a degree of protection. Yet it was inevitable that people would see Leopold as being personally responsible for the change in course. The German press praised him to the heavens, while the French media tore him to pieces. In Belgium, the Walloon papers were mainly against the new policy, while the new ultra-right-wing Flemish Nationalist Union (VNV) had thousands of posters printed, proclaiming *'De koning geeft ons gelijk!'* (The king is on our side). The Flemish Union of Front Veterans (VOS) were also delighted, since they had launched a controversial campaign in 1935 with the provocative title *'Los van Frankrijk'* (Free from France). For the outside world, the publication of the speech placed the king squarely in the Flemish camp. Yet in reality Leopold was ill-disposed to all nationalist efforts to seek greater political autonomy, efforts which were growing in intensity with the increasing radicalisation of the Flemish Movement.

Princess Astrid and Crown Prince Leopold in Antwerp, 19 May 1928

Nevertheless, under Leopold III successive governments worked further on the language laws which would finally see Dutch introduced as the exclusive language for administration in Flanders. The king's personal opinion about the law of 1935 relating to the use of language in legal trials is not known. However, this law confirmed the basic principle of the administrative law of 1932 that the common local language should also be the administrative language, and now extended this principle to the judicial process.

The general election of 1936 totally changed the political landscape in Belgium. The Catholic Party was punished heavily by the voters, losing 16 seats in the Lower House. For the first time since 1884, it was no longer the largest party in the land. The French-speaking fascist party Rex went to the polls for the first time and immediately won 21 seats, mainly in Brussels and Wallonia. The VNV doubled its parliamentary representation from 8 to 16 seats. On the other side of the political spectrum, the communists won 6 seats, all of them in Flanders, bringing their total to 9. In keeping with developments elsewhere in Europe, Belgian politics was becoming more and more extreme. This was even more the case in Flanders. Rex would eventually be wiped out in the general election of 1939; but the VNV held its ground, increasing its number of seats from 16 to 17. In the Flemish electoral districts it was supported by 12% of the electorate, equivalent to 185,000 votes.

The breakthrough of the extremist parties in general and the VNV in particular forced the traditional parties to offer further concessions to the Flemish Movement. On 4 November 1936, the government put forward a proposal which would effectively mean a general amnesty for activist collaboration between 1914 and 1918. This was a running sore which had continued to fester since the Armistice of November 1918. The new policy of reconciliation was supported by the royal court. In a note to the king dated 2 October 1936, Secretary Robert Capelle had suggested that "substantial concessions" should be made to the Flemings.[116] Even so, the Flemish nationalists found the text of the draft legislation too vague, while the patriotic, pro-Belgian organisations feared that 'the traitors' would now be pardoned on a grand scale. The atmosphere was tense when the debate began in the Lower House on 19 May 1937. For a number of days previously, demonstrations and counter-demonstrations had been held in Brussels and several other major cities. After much heated debate, both the Lower House and the Senate passed the new law by a narrow majority, on 2 June and 10 June respectively. The king ratified the law on 11 June and it was published in the Belgian State Gazette just two days later. Nevertheless, the pro-Belgian groups refused to give up the fight and during the weeks which followed political tension remained at fever pitch. Minister Hendrik De Man, who was standing in as a temporary replacement for Prime Minister Van Zeeland, was summoned to the palace almost every day. There were even fears that the forces of law and order might be forced to fire on the demonstrators, who were incensed at King Leopold for his willingness to sign the Amnesty Act. Matters reached crisis point when a large and angry anti-amnesty crowd took to the streets of Brussels on 23 June. Two days earlier, the head of the National Security Service had reported that: "The general spirit of the people is currently hostile towards the King." The demonstrators shouted "Long Live King Albert I" and openly jeered Leopold.[117] They demanded the resignation of the cabinet, the dissolving of parliament and a referendum over the amnesty. Several hundred of the protestors actually broke through the neutral zone and occupied the square in front of the royal palace in Brussels, demanding that the king should meet a delegation. The police and army knew that any attempt to clear the square would lead to bloodshed. To prevent this possibility, Leopold took matters into his own hands and agreed to see the delegation, without referring the matter to his ministers. He promised them that he would do everything within his constitutional power to meet their grievances.

When De Man heard of this development, he rushed to see the king. He made clear that he was against concessions of any kind to the 'mob' and that any such action would almost certainly precipitate the fall of the government. Faced with this ultimatum, Leopold had little option but to agree – and so he changed his mind again. The ministers were anxious to hide behind the person of the king and so it was Leopold who met the representatives of the veterans' associations on 2 July 1937. He read to them a declaration in French and Dutch, which had been approved in advance by the government. First of all, he underlined the general supremacy of parliament and the rule of law, but then he went on to defend the Amnesty Act itself. "In my opinion it is not correct that some people – no doubt for honourable but mistaken reasons, inspired by misplaced fear – have sought to represent the new amnesty law as an attack upon the dignity of our nation and the honour of our war heroes. Whatever one thinks about the amnesty, that dignity and that honour will never be tarnished. This I can assure you."[118] Leopold added that it was impossible to reopen matters which had been correctly dealt with by an official commission at the instigation of his father before his death. Current cases would be dealt with in accordance with the law and with due deference to national dignity and national honour. The king ended by encouraging the veterans to abandon their plans to hold a protest ceremony at the memorial to King Albert in Marche-les-Dames. They agreed, and in the weeks that followed calm was gradually restored.

In 1938, the new round of language legislation was completed with the passing of a new Army Act. The experiences of recent years had convinced everyone – including the opponents of the Flemish nationalists – that the provisions of the law of 1928 were no longer workable. There was a growing consensus that a division of the army along

Brussels, 1937. A demonstration in favour of an amnesty for the Flemings who had collaborated with the occupying German forces between 1914 and 1918.

linguistic lines must be based on larger units, such as regiments. As had been the case with the preparations for the administrative language law of 1932, the introduction of bilingualism in the senior ranks met with strong Walloon resistance, while the Flemish also had a number of practical (as opposed to principled) objections. The end result was a kind of watered down bilingualism: not really enough to please the Flemings, but more than enough to irritate the Walloons.

Belgium – on the road towards federalisation, 1936-1940

The bickering which accompanied the completion of the Minimum Programme and the granting of the amnesty can, in retrospect, be seen as the last throes of a politics which increasingly belonged to the past. During the 1930s, it was replaced by a new political debate which was increasingly focussed on the 'federalisation' of the Belgian state (which, as we noted in the introduction, has an inverted meaning in the Belgian context: Belgian federalisation does not involve – as is usually the case – the unification of the component federal units, but rather the splitting up of the unitary Belgian state). The path which led in the direction of this new development was smoothed during the period 1932-1935 by the legal redefinition of Flanders and Wallonia as quasi-homogenous monolingual regions.

The militant Catholic student movements of the 1920s now provided the storm-troops for a new and more radical Flemish Movement. These young men and women in their thirties did not seek to promote their ideology through the traditional parties, but through their membership of various cultural organisations with a strong Flemish accent, since they felt that this was the best way to reach and mobilise the masses. 1930 saw the founding of a Flemish Football Union, which quickly won much support, followed in 1933 by a more elitist Flemish Tennis Association. Most of the Flemish associations still had very clear Catholic links and the three most important of these associations – the Davids Fund, the VOS and the Flemish Tourist Board – signed a collaboration pact in 1935. Notwithstanding their Catholic background, these organisations began to take a line which was increasingly independent from that of the Catholic Church. In short, they began to act as an extra-parliamentary pressure group for an outspoken Flemish agenda.

Olivier Boehme demonstrated in 2008 that these radical demands for greater federalisation were not simply confined to the use of language in the central administration and in the cultural life of the nation. There was a clear and growing desire for the right to determine social and economic policies at regional levels. Not surprisingly, this led during the 1930s to a further widening of the gulf which already separated Flanders from Wallonia. On the Flemish side of this divide, the socialists were one of the few parties who remained fully committed to the Belgian state, since they still believed that this was the best framework for the further development of a national social insurance system. Yet it was open to debate whether or not social insurance was really a unifying national issue. It certainly had a strong regional component, which came prominently to the fore in the 'transfer debate' which compared the income and expenditure statistics for the two halves of the country.

This explains why, for example, the Liege MP Van Belle argued in favour of federalisation as early as February 1930, claiming that Wallonia had been disadvantaged for years. He pointed out that between 1919 and 1927 the government had invested more than a billion francs in work on the largely Flemish River Schelde and just 113 million francs on the largely Walloon River Meuse, while Wallonia as a region had contributed more than 60% of the budget. Destrée used similar arguments, bemoaning the fact that Flanders drew more than Wallonia from the national treasury, while putting less in. Moreover, the Flemish seemed to have no sense of gratitude for the financial contribution being made by the French-speaking community. Antwerp, a city in which the national government invested heavily during the inter-war period, had often chosen more expensive German materials instead of placing their orders with Walloon manufacturers and producers.

The transfer debate reached a fever pitch of intensity during the discussions surrounding the national child benefit system. Child benefit was intended as compensation for the loss of purchasing power suffered by workers as a result of post-war inflation. It was a way of ensuring that employers made a contribution towards the increased cost of keeping a family, but without increasing wages, whilst at the same time encouraging a higher birth rate. This demographic element was a source of great ideological and inter-regional dispute. The birth rate had been falling in Wallonia since the pre-war period, which was the result of a deliberate birth control policy in what was essentially a socialist-liberal environment. Things were viewed in a very different light in largely Catholic Flanders, where a large family was not only seen as a Christian duty but also as a political weapon to strengthen the region's grip on the central Belgian state. The child benefit system in the 1930s was a national system, which was based on the concept of inter-regional solidarity. This meant that employers from all over the country made contributions to the national treasury, which then redistributed these contributions to the regions in the form of benefit. It is obvious that this system favoured the more populous regions at the expense of the less populous. Valère Fallon, a Jesuit monk, tried to disarm this explosive issue by pointing out that the demographic distribution of large families did not neatly correspond with the linguistic frontier between Flanders and Wallonia: there were large families everywhere. Large Flemish cities such as Ghent, Leuven, Antwerp and even Brussels all had a relatively low birth rate, whereas the birth rate in the French-speaking province of Luxembourg was as high as in many of the most fertile regions in Flanders. But Fallon might as well have saved his breath. In their efforts to strengthen their own regional identity, both the Flemings and the Walloons were determined to interpret the child benefit debate within a Flanders-Wallonia geographical context.

In December 1933, there was a major debate in the Lower House on this divisive issue. The dispute over the question of financial transfers was central, but the supporters of the existing system won the day, arguing that throughout Europe it was standard practice for taxes collected in wealthier regions to be spent in poorer regions. Even so, the government felt obliged to make further adjustments to the child benefit system as the 1930s progressed, which on each occasion served to anger the Walloons even further. In 1938, it was decided to reduce the level of benefit for the first and second child, a measure which was described in a congress of the Walloon socialists in Charleroi as further encouragement for "the Flemish rabbits". The Liege MP Leon-Eli Troclet complained in 1939 that during the previous nine years the child benefit system had cost Wallonia 200 million francs, all of which had been poured into the pockets of Flemish families. This, he said, was equivalent to 3.75% of all salaries paid in Wallonia during that period. He was angry that there were plans to broaden the system, so that the transfers from 'South' to 'North' would increase still further, in both relative and absolute terms. He emphasised that there were also fiscal transfers, since the government settled the deficits run up by the (largely Flemish) child benefit funds with money drawn from national treasury, to which the Walloons were the major contributors. Troclet even saw a third form of transfer, since the reduced rates for first and second children also penalised Wallonia, where families were generally smaller. He even added that, in view of the higher rate of infant mortality in Flanders, the South was paying for "dead children" (implying that this was another 'wasted' Walloon investment). Boehme has rightly noted that Troclet was exaggerating his case to make a point: public opinion in Wallonia was not as extreme and not everyone looked at the question in the same black/white, Flanders/Wallonia terms. "Nevertheless, this does nothing to detract from the fact that an analysis of the child benefit debate shows conclusively that inter-regional issues in the 1930s went much further than the language question. We cannot escape the conclusion that as soon as the government created new financial mechanisms for social and economic purposes, the resulting 'profit-and-loss' calculations became a new bone of contention between two separate and rapidly 'consolidating' regional communities, which became ever more tightly-knit by the very process of calculation."[119]

The whole debate over transfers was intensified even more by the government's need to find new measures to combat the growing economic crisis, which had a serious impact in Belgium from 1930 onwards. Almost every government in Europe was struggling to find a way to inject new life into its failing economy. Many countries – including Belgium – opted for a Keynesian policy, which allowed for coordinated action

Belgium and the Monarchy. From National Independence to National Disintegration.

A Flemish-Nationalist choral concert in Antwerp, July 1938. The slogan on the right reads 'Gelooft in de teksten die gij zingt en gij zult overwinnen.' (Believe the words you sing, and you will triumph).

to regulate the rhythm of economic evolution and to control consumption priorities. In theory, according to Boehme, this type of planned economy has the potential to strengthen 'national' feeling, but in practice (and like the social insurance issue) it can also weaken this feeling if the economic area to which the policy is applied is not homogenous. This was clearly the case in Belgium, where there was no longer any question of national homogeneity. "To the extent that the state either becomes an investment mechanism, or a redistribution mechanism, or a combination of both, questions relating to the resulting financial circuits will usually arise – and almost always in divided countries. The central questions will be who pays most and who gains most. In this 'we – they' situation, one side will very quickly get the impression that they are paying for the other side, certainly if only two partners are involved."[120] The 1930s saw numerous and heated debates over an economic policy that was increasingly analysed in terms of Flanders versus Wallonia. This was essentially a debate about the future of the Belgian nation. It was a debate carried out within the context of income and welfare distribution, but shaped by different Catholic, liberal and socialist views of man and society. More importantly, it was a debate which contributed strongly to the development of federalist thinking in the 1930s.

The creation of two official, homogeneous language regions, as well as the development of dynamic socio-economic and cultural relations which were analysed from a Flanders-Wallonia perspective, were also the logical conclusion of the electoral reform of 1893, which first allowed the Flemish masses to exert their influence on the political process. Moreover, it also created a framework which made possible yet another development, which would have been unthinkable before 1914: the splitting of the national political parties along linguistic lines.

It was the Catholic Party which first set the ball rolling in 1936. Now that the Minimum Programme had more or less been achieved, during the 1930s more and more Flemish Catholics began moving in the direction of a *Maximum* Programme. But would it be possible to achieve this from within the political framework of the Catholic Party? This party lost heavily during the general election of May 1936, a defeat made all the more bitter by the success of what seemed to be a new and more extreme Catholic alliance between Rex and the VNV. This setback prompted the reform of the party in October 1936. The new party had a federal structure, with separate Flemish and Wallonian wings: the Flemish Catholic People's Union (*Katholiek Vlaams Volksverbond*, KVV) and the Walloon Catholic Social Party (*Parti Catholique Social*, PCS). Together, they formed the Belgian Catholic Bloc, but this scarcely functioned as a viable political entity. The new structure was a prelude to full regional separation, which would allow each wing of the party to go its own way.

This is well-illustrated by the 'declaration of principles' which the Flemish Catholic KVV agreed in December 1936 with the separatist VNV, which since its foundation in 1933 had been drifting further and further towards right-wing authoritarianism. In this agreement, the general principle of federalism was accepted. There was even consensus on the question of corporatism, with the preservation of a freely elected parliament. The declaration was not, however, a great success. It was never popular with the workers' groupings within the KVV and in 1937 the VNV decided to terminate the agreement. Even so, this episode shows that the Flemish Catholics were prepared to seriously consider an alliance with the anti-parliamentary and separatist VNV – a development which would never have been possible before the 1936 reorganisation of the old Catholic Party.

The Socialist Party also underwent a process of regionalisation. The inter-regional problems did not have the same impact on the socialists as the Catholics, but during the 1930s differing Flemish and Wallonian ideologies nevertheless began to develop. The Keynesian Labour Plan put forward by the Fleming Hendrik De Man won much more support in Flanders than in Wallonia, where the party was more traditionally Marxist and doctrinaire. De Man became a focal point for a circle of prominent like-minded Flemish socialists. This group was united by its desire to improve the backward economic position of Flanders, particularly vis-à-vis Wallonia, and to prevent the decline of the socialists in Flanders into a minority party. In 1937, a successful Flemish Socialist Congress was held in Antwerp. Its programme contained a clear emphasis on inter-regional issues and it was able to attract the support of almost all the leading Flemish socialists. Amongst the matters discussed were cultural autonomy, the language border communities, the problem of Brussels, and the disadvantaged position of agriculture in Flanders. These were all topics which would not have appealed to the Walloon socialists, or on which they would have taken a different standpoint from their Flemish comrades. It reflected a nationalist way of thinking, similar to the approach being adopted during the same period by the Flemish Catholics. And as might be expected, the Antwerp congress of 1937 prompted the Walloons to organise similar congresses of their own in 1938 and 1939. This shows the extent to which the Flemish and Walloon socialists were slowly moving apart. Perhaps the clearest confirmation of this development was the growing willingness of the Flemish socialists under De Man – and under the influence of his magazine *Leiding* (Leadership) – to consider more authoritarian and less parliamentary measures as a solution to the economic crisis. The leftist Walloons were appalled at this 'treason' – but it was nonetheless a sign of the times.

During the 1930s, the Walloon Movement also experienced a period of unrest. This was a consequence of many different factors, not least of which was the fact that compulsory bilingualism continued to be an issue in both the central administration and the higher echelons of the army. This sense of unease was further accentuated by a number of subsidiary factors: the growing economic self-confidence of Flanders, combined with the gradual decline of the economy in Wallonia (which was too heavily reliant on coal and steel); the growth of anti-parliamentarianism in Flanders, especially following the declaration of principle between the KVV and the VNV; and, above all, the fear that the rising birth rate in Flanders would doom the Walloons to a permanent minority status in the national parliament. Anyone who was impartial enough to make a rational assessment of the structure of the Belgian state must inevitably come to the conclusion that this last point was destined to be a continuous stumbling block. It is significant, for example, that during the 1937 debate on the Amnesty Act the Walloon socialist Emile Vandervelde explicitly called upon the Flemings not to exercise their numerical superiority on this delicate issue.

In May 1938, Paul-Henri Spaak formed a new administration. As a gesture of reconciliation, he wished to include the pro-Walloon Emile Jennissen in his cabinet. However, Leopold III considered that Jennissen did not represent public opinion in Wallonia and consequently the ministerial portfolio was given to the Brussels politician Octave Dierckx. Shortly thereafter, three Walloon senators put forward a proposal for the federalisation of Belgium. A similar proposal by the Flemish nationalists in 1931 had been based on a division of the nation into two regions: Wallonia and Flanders, with Brussels as a part of Flanders. The 1938 proposal foresaw three autonomous regions: Wallonia, Flanders *and* Brussels.

These various political influences ensured that the national politics of Belgium began to evolve in the direction of a federalisation of the country through a reform of the state structure. This process was initiated in the least contentious of all sectors: culture. In the first instance, it was the Catholic Party which was most insistent on the principle of cultural autonomy, but after 1937 the Flemish socialists also lent their support to the campaign. This demand for the federalisation of culture, in the broadest sense of the word, reflected the exponential growth of pro-Flemish associations during the 1930s. As a result, in 1938 the Spaak government promulgated the first measures for the formal regional separation of cultural life in Belgium. Two new cultural councils – a French-speaking one and a Dutch-speaking one – were added to the Ministry of Arts and Sciences, albeit in a purely advisory role. Even more important was the division along linguistic lines of the Royal Academy of Arts and Sciences. This resulted in the appointment of new members to what was now known as the Royal Flemish Academy – but this was not without serious incident. The Royal Decree of 7 November 1938, listing the new appointees to the Royal Flemish Academy for Medicine, included the name of Dr. Adriaan Martens, a scientist who had been sentenced to death for collaboration during the First World War but had been pardoned under the terms of the 1937 amnesty. When Spaak presented the king with the appointment documents for signature, Leopold objected. Even so, the king found himself faced with a *fait accompli*. The names of the appointees had already been made public and so he had little option but to sign. The decree incorrectly stated that the appointments had been made following consultation with the ministerial council. In fact, this was not the case, as the king was quick to point out. In a speech made on 2 February 1939, the king lectured his ministers on their dubious political manoeuvrings in general and for their duplicity in the Martens' case in particular. By this time, it had become publicly known that the Dr. Martens on the list of appointees was the same Dr. Martens who had been condemned to death for collaboration. This led to the fall of the Spaak government a few days later. He was succeeded as prime minister by the Walloon socialist Hubert Pierlot, but his administration survived for just six days. In a public letter to Pierlot, dated 6 March 1939, the king explained his decision to dissolve parliament, making clear that he felt no blame for the current crisis and that his ministers had forced him into a corner by presenting him with a *fait accompli* in respect of the Martens appointment. He emphasised that the rumours which claimed that he had known and approved of Martens' nomination in advance were completely untrue, thereby implying that he would have blocked the nomination if he had been in full possession of the facts. In an act of similar defiance, the king refused at the beginning of March 1939 to award an honour to Professor Frans Daels, a notorious Flemish nationalist and the person most responsible for proposing Martens for a position in the Academy.

Pierlot eventually formed a new government and in February 1940 his administration attempted to organise the separation of the Ministry of Education, within the framework of the programme for cultural autonomy. The proposals met

Belgium and the Monarchy. From National Independence to National Disintegration.

The young royal princes in 1937: Boudewijn (1930-1993, king from 1950 onwards) and Albert (°1934, king since 1993).

with resistance, whereupon Pierlot again submitted his resignation to the king. Liberal MPs, led by Paul Hymans, reacted with disgust to what they saw as a weak-kneed gesture. Leopold was equally unimpressed and called his prime minister to order. In a new public letter, the king told Pierlot that it was impossible to accept his resignation and that it was unacceptable that a domestic-linguistic matter should precipitate a ministerial crisis at a moment when the international situation was so perilous.

May 1940 – September 1944

The German invasion on 10 May 1940 marked the start of a period in which regional differences – much more than during the period 1914-1918 – served as an intractably divisive issue in Belgian politics. This was the result of collaboration with the German occupying forces, which was more extensive in Flanders than in Wallonia.

On 25 May 1940, at the castle in Wijnendale, there was a decisive break between the king and his ministers. The ministers thought that there was still a chance to win the war from France. The king, however, no longer believed in this possibility and expected that the Germans would conquer the entire continent. For this reason he decided to stay in Belgium. The ministers were not in agreement and departed to France (and from there, after much hesitation, later moved on to London, where they set up a Belgian government-in-exile in October 1940). The king remained behind in occupied Belgium because he had become convinced that the future lay in the hands of the New Order and he wished to secure the best possible conditions for his kingdom in a new Europe under Germany hegemony. However, he was wise enough not to immediately choose sides, and on 28 May 1940 he effectively became a prisoner of war. Throughout the remainder of the conflict he maintained a neutral position. In this sense, he was not a collaborator. He was an *attentist* – his policy was the policy of wait-and-see.

Until the end of 1942 at least, many Belgians believed that Germany would be able to hold its own against the Allies, if not win the war. This meant that some kind of compromise peace seemed likely. The likelihood of a redrawing of the European map in these circumstances would inevitably mean that Belgium – if it managed to preserve its existence – would be more dependent on Germany than ever before. It was with this prospect in mind that the Walloon Movement made overtures between 1941 and 1943 to the Vichy regime of Marshal Pétain in France: the absorption of Wallonia into France might be a form of possible compensation for the final surrender of Alsace-Lorraine to Germany, which now seemed inevitable. The thinking of the Flemish Movement was influenced by similar considerations, but with a significant difference. Whereas the Walloon Movement was still dominated by a handful of intellectuals, the Flemish Movement was a mass movement backed by tens of thousands of supporters, who during the 1930s had become increasingly anti-parliamentarian and authoritarian. This broad group was ready, willing and able to work with the German invaders from May 1940 onwards. In this sense, they were the political and intellectual inheritors of the activist collaborators of 1914-1918.

This collaboration was led by the VNV, which hoped in this manner to secure the future existence of an independent Flemish nation. But what would be the geographical limits of this new Flanders? And how would it be governed? During the period 1940-1941, the VNV did not close the door on King Leopold, seeing for him a possible role as the monarch in an enlarged Dutch state, which would include both The Netherlands and (possibly) an ethnically cleansed Wallonia. Nothing ever came of these megalomaniac plans, but their very prospect committed the VNV to far-reaching collaboration with the Nazis. With the help of Secretary-General Romsée, from the spring of 1941 onwards the VNV seized control of the 'Belgian' administration in both Flanders and Brussels. As a result, members of the VNV occupied leading positions at all levels in the war-time administration of the occupied country, a fact for which they would pay dearly when the Allied victory finally came. By the end of 1942, this unpalatable truth was beginning to become clear, but the VNV had hitched its wagon to the German star, and this within the context of a total war in which almost everything was tolerated, including co-operation with deportations and the betrayal of anti-German elements.

And what of King Leopold? As the Allied noose closed around the Third Reich, the king prepared for his own expected deportation to Germany. In the spring of 1944, he drafted a royal address for his people, which he intended to be read when the country was finally liberated. The text was largely compiled by Leopold's military adviser, General Van Overstraeten, although he obviously worked in close consultation with the king and the draft was certainly read by the head of the king's cabinet, Louis Fredericq. Van Overstraeten was not known for his finesse in political matters: his preferred weapon was the sabre, not the rapier. As a result, this 'Political Testament', which was antedated to January 1944, contained a number of forthright views on a wide range of issues. King Leopold defended his policy of neutrality during the occupation and even now refused to align himself with the victorious Allies, whom he regarded as just another occupying power. He also took up positions on a number of domestic political matters, including the relations between the Flemings and the Walloons. No Belgian monarch had ever made such radical statements. Leopold reminded his people that the period between 1914 and 1944 had been marked by what he called a crisis of nationality. It was a subject on which he had strong opinions:

"After a long period of undeniable inequality and injustice, our Flemish subjects, proud of their magnificent past and aware of all the possibilities which the future might offer them, resolved to put an end to their victimisation by a narrow-minded and egotistical minority which refused to speak their language or participate in the life of the people. The incomprehension of parliament and the slowness of successive governments to satisfy their legitimate aspirations gradually exasperated their patience. Some of them even wished to break away from Wallonia, thus damning the future of Belgium. This resulted in a Walloon reaction, the strength of which it would be dangerous to underestimate."[121]

The most important task for the post-war government, according to the king, was to ensure "reconciliation between the Flemings and the Walloons". The future of an independent Belgium depended on this reconciliation. Flanders and Wallonia should seek to fulfil their historic destiny in a new Belgium in which the citizens of both regions would be treated as equals and in which Brussels would serve as a unifying centre of bilingualism and bilingual culture.

As a programme for the settlement of the linguistic problem, Leopold's Political Testament was somewhat vague. It was to be expected that the monarchy should continue to attach importance to bilingualism as a kind of national cement.

6 Leopold III (1934-1944/1950)

During the Nazi occupation of 1940-1944, a section of the Flemish Movement – in particular, those associated with the VNV – collaborated openly with the Third Reich. Most of the collaborators were between 20 and 40 years of age and dreamt of a free and independent Flemish state under German 'protection'. After the war, many of these men and women were sent to prison. This photograph shows a Flemish 'Festival of Song' held in Brussels on 1 September 1941. The pro-German paramilitary groups march by, while the singing crowd greets them with the Hitler salute.

Albert I had hoped to achieve this through the use of both languages in the central administration, whereas Leopold, recognising that this was no longer feasible, pinned his hopes on the unifying power of a bilingual Brussels. However, his statement was destined to be overshadowed by its radical condemnation of parliament and successive administrations for their incomprehension and slowness in reacting to Flemish demands. The criticism of the bilingual elite in Flanders – this was the "narrow-minded and egotistical minority" – was even fiercer. In effect, the king was accusing the French-speaking Flemings of social apartheid, of using the language barrier as a social barrier. In this respect, Leopold was simply echoing many of the sentiments felt by his father, particularly during the period 1917-1918. However, whereas Albert I had been wise enough to make such statements behind closed doors or in private correspondence, Leopold III made them in a royal address which was intended to be heard by the entire nation. It was little short of an open attack on the political establishment and must, at the very least, cast serious doubt on his political wisdom.

As it turned out, the Political Testament only became widely known a number of years later. By this time, Leopold had already been politically sidelined. A majority of liberals, socialists and communists had decided in the summer of 1945 that the king was "no longer in a position to rule", largely as a consequence of his ambivalent position during the war years. In 1950, he abdicated his throne, following a referendum in which the people were asked to decide whether or not he should continue as their sovereign. The politicians who insisted on the referendum took a major risk by deciding that the votes should be counted by electoral district, since this seemed likely to further intensify regional tensions. Nationally, there was an overall vote of 57% in favour of the king, but the regional variations were marked. Flanders voted 72% in favour of Leopold, with Wallonia voting 58% against and Brussels 52% against. Nevertheless, it would be an oversimplification to interpret this result as a straight-forward clash of opinions between Flanders and Wallonia. The provincial results show that the real difference of opinion was between Flanders and the province of Luxembourg on the one hand, and the provinces of Liege and Hainault on the other hand. In fact, the king won a majority in 7 of the 9 provinces and in 21 of the 30 electoral districts. But where he lost – in the populous industrial regions of Wallonia – he lost heavily. Yet while these statistics illustrate that the referendum of 1950 should not be viewed exclusively from a Flanders-Wallonia perspective, it was precisely in this manner that it was interpreted at the time. In this respect, the referendum helped to further strengthen regional identities and led to a sharpening of political, ideological and social conflicts between the linguistic communities. The king who had stayed behind in 1940 to safeguard his nation's existence, left it more divided than it had ever been before.

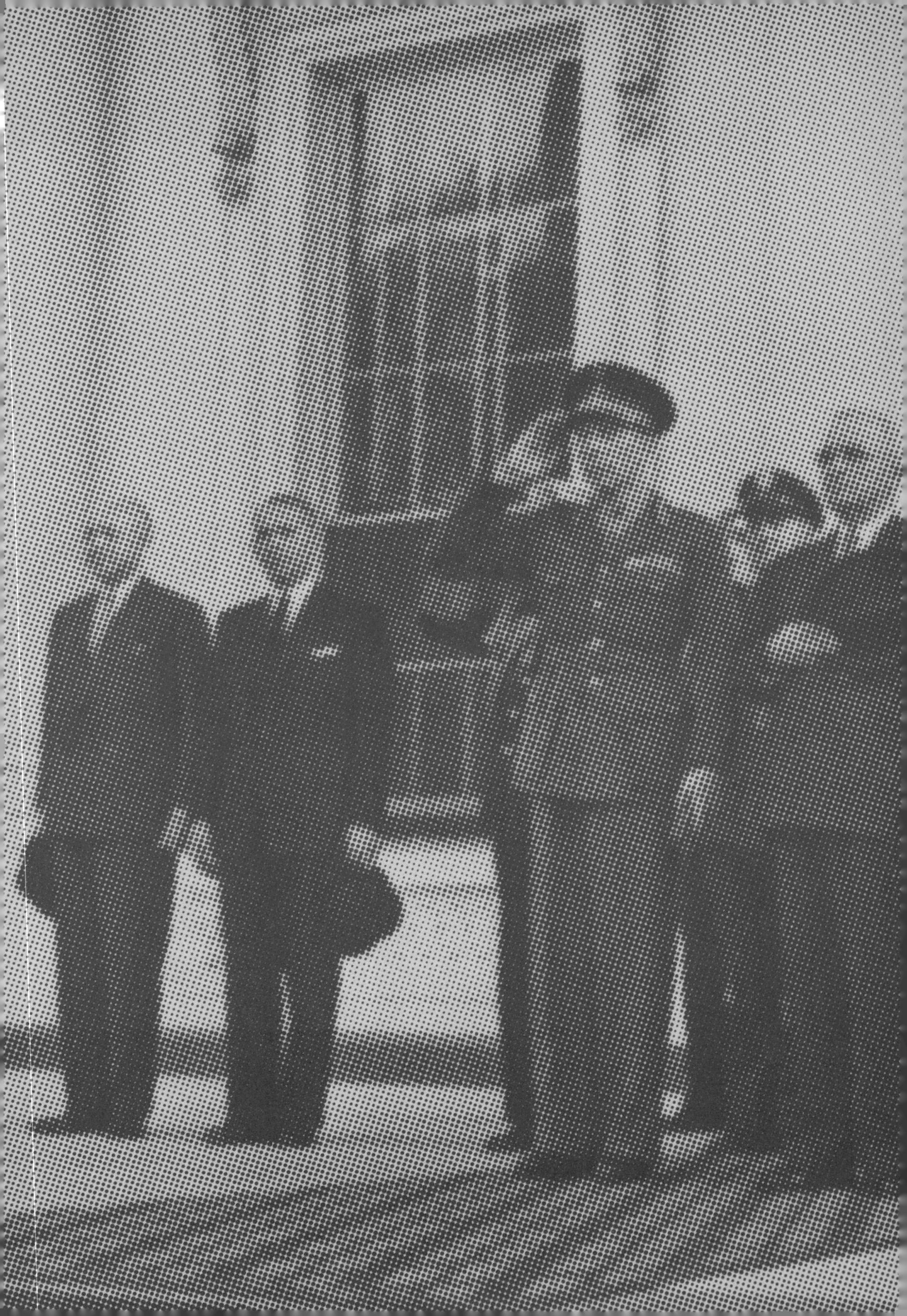

7

Prince Charles
(1944–1950)

*The Watchful
Regent of Belgium*

On 21 September 1944, Prince Charles, the brother of King Leopold, who was still being held captive in Germany, was sworn in as regent of the recently liberated Belgian nation. In a speech from the throne, given in both national languages, he said that he spoke "on behalf of the king". He praised the courage of the resistance movement and the sacrifices of the Allies, and promised that Belgium would now fight at their side until final victory had been achieved. In short, the regent – who was speaking under ministerial responsibility – did what Leopold had refused to do in his Political Testament: he accepted the line which had been followed by the war-time Pierlot government in London.

Prince Charles would eventually 'reign' for as long a period as his brother. However, the years between 1945 and 1950 were years of greater institutional stability, as inter-regional problems were largely pushed into the background in the face of the greater need for national reconstruction and recovery. As regent, Charles followed the strict constitutional letter of the law. On the one hand, he worked closely with the ministers, with whom his relationship was open. He was industrious and perceptive, and demonstrated a good knowledge of the leading political issues of the day. At the same time, he abided scrupulously by the rules governing ministerial responsibility.

In Flemish circles, Prince Charles was criticised for failing to soften the harshness with which those who had collaborated with the enemy were pursued after the war. In particular, Flemings were angered by the regent's refusal to commute the death sentences which had been passed on Flemish collaborators. This disapproval of Charles' role is a reflection of the traditional anti-royalist sentiments which permeated the more extreme wing of the Flemish Movement, combined with a one-sided analysis of the post-war executions. It is certainly true that the post-war repression was not always consistent or well thought out. In the year immediately following the liberation, a large number of relatively minor collaborators were quickly tried and severely punished, while more serious acts of complicity were overlooked. Could the regent have done more? The ruling monarch's right to show mercy to convicted offenders was a political act and was therefore subject to ministerial responsibility. The regent's cabinet only concerned itself with the most serious cases – those resulting in the death penalty – but the records suggest that it had little real influence. Attempts were made on several occasions to soften the ministerial hard line, but if the ministers would not listen, there was little the regent could do. Sometimes, however, it was possible to force a compromise, particularly as the immediate memory of the war gradually receded.

The large scale political collaboration with the Nazis in Flanders during the period 1940-1944 had a much greater impact on the Flemish Movement than the much more limited collaboration with the German occupying forces during the First World War. All traces of the steady progression towards federalism, which had been evident in

Prince Charles (Karel) is received at the White House in Washington, 6 April 1948. To his right stand the American President Truman and the Belgian Prime Minister, Paul-Henri Spaak.

the years after 1936, were eliminated completely after 1945. In this year, the Catholic party was reconstituted as the Christian People's Party (CVP-PSC). The new party was unambiguously a unitary party: there were no longer separate Flemish and Walloon wings. Much the same was true of the new Belgian Socialist Party (BSP), which sought unity around the old rallying calls of class struggle. However, pro-union and pro-Belgian sentiment was most strongly felt in the Liberal Party, which (as before the war) continued to attract many voters from the elitist bilingual sections of Flemish society. It was for this reason that the liberals failed to appeal to the old VNV voters of 1939, most of whom switched their allegiance back to the Catholic CVP-PSC.

The Flemish Movement had burnt its fingers badly during the Second World War, but this was much less the case for the Walloon Movement. The French-speaking community had become more alienated than ever from the Flemings during the war years (as a result of what they saw as 'treasonable' Flemish behaviour), but this meant that the Walloon identity emerged from the conflict with a renewed vigour. With the exception of Léon Degrelle (a much overrated figure), none of the leading Walloon politicians compromised their national integrity, while the degree of collaboration at lower levels was much more limited than in Flanders. Wallonia also had a much more active resistance movement.

In 1945, the Wallonian resistance fighters organised a National Wallonian Congress in Liege. The congress was attended by more than 1,000 delegates, including most of the Walloon MPs, under the chairmanship of a former Walloon minister. The objective of the conference was to find a permanent solution to the inter-regional problem, as this was perceived in Wallonia. The results of the congress vote sent shock waves through the Belgian political system. 486 delegates voted for annexation by France, 391 voted for a new federal structure, 154 for an independent Wallonia and just 17 for the preservation of the status quo! A second vote, a *vote de raison*, showed that the congress was almost unanimously in favour of federalism as a second option...

The war had transformed the latent discontent of the Walloon community – which had been aroused in the 1930s because of its 'minority' status in parliament – into a clear demand for federalism. Several other factors helped to increase this discontent still further: a falling birth rate, ageing industrial infrastructure, a lack of good communications and irritation at centralist planning from Brussels. In this respect, the Walloon Movement, which had always been strongly liberal-socialist, now found common ground with the Catholic Wallonian elite. The Royal Question (as the debate over Leopold's future came to be known) allowed the Walloon Movement to make greater progress as a mass movement, particularly amongst liberal and socialist voters. But the Catholic wing in Wallonia was also becoming less elitist and more populist. The Wallonian section of the Christian Union won increased representation and in 1946 the Walloons were even able to force through the federalisation of the ACW, the central Catholic trade union organisation. However, this popularisation of the Walloon Movement had reached its high water mark by 1949, the year in which the federalisation of the ACW was rescinded.

Inspired by Walloon discontent, a young Catholic intellectual from Liege, Pierre Harmel, set up a research centre to investigate the social, political and judicial needs of the Flemish and Wallonian communities. The reports of the Harmel Institute were published in 1958 and made a significant contribution towards the preparation of future language laws and the reform of the state structure – issues which were soon destined to be back on the political agenda.

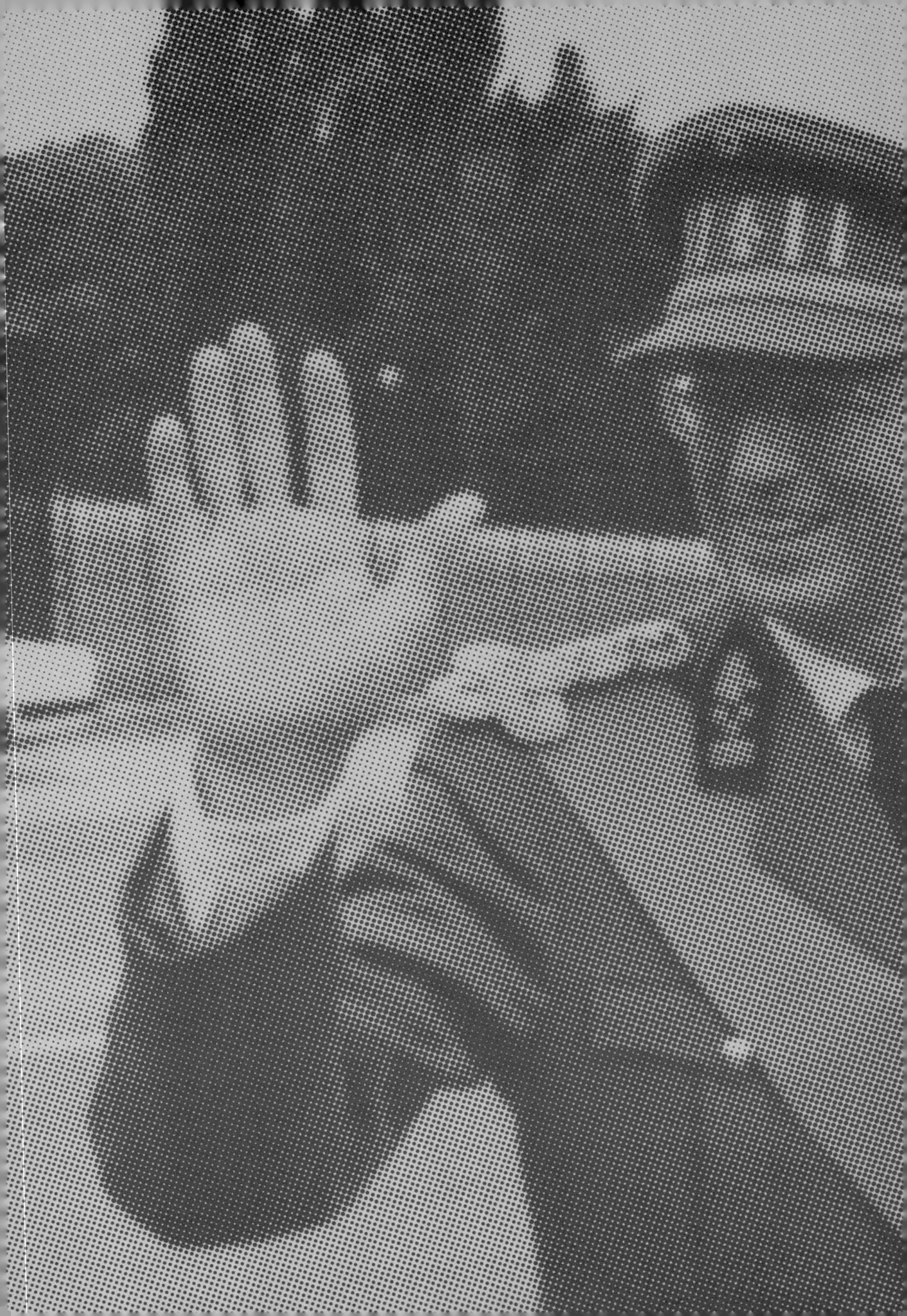

8
**King Boudewijn
(1950-1993)**

*A Chronicle of
Political Impotence*

Because national archives are only made public 50 years after the event, we know very little as yet about the role of King Boudewijn with regard to the more recent developments of the nationality question in Belgium – a question which burst into life with renewed vigour during the 1960s. Any historical investigation of this period is therefore confined to an assessment of the king's speeches, press reports, personal testimonies and the memoirs of politicians. In one respect, however, the historian has been fortunate. Notwithstanding the fact that Boudewijn's speeches were made under ministerial responsibility, there is general academic agreement that these speeches to a large degree reflect the personal feelings of the king. Even so, the role of the monarchy in the language question under King Boudewijn was much smaller than during previous reigns, since royal power and influence had been seriously limited after the Second World War. This, in part, was related to the Royal Question, which seriously weakened the position of the royal house.

Prince Boudewijn ascended to the throne in July 1950, at the age of 20. He had spent the previous 10 years in somewhat curious circumstances: first under a kind of house arrest during the period 1940-1944, then as a prisoner in Germany and Austria in 1944-1945, and finally as an exile in Switzerland between 1945-1950. When he eventually became king following the referendum of 1950, he was young for his age. "Prince Boudewijn knows nothing of Belgium and has no experience of the world," wrote the British ambassador in Belgium in 1949.[122] This background was held against him and helped to ensure – certainly in the early years – that he had very little influence. He exuded no strength, no authority – and these were the qualities which were above all needed to steer the country through the troubled waters of inter-regional dispute. It would take almost two decades before the new king was able to make an impact on national events.

The 'quiet' fifties

The 1950s in Wallonia were characterised by a smouldering discontent at the region's continuing economic decline. The Flemish Christian-democratic politician Gaston Eyskens, who was prime minister on more than one occasion after 1945, wrote in his memoirs that the solution of the Wallonian problem was one of his main concerns, but he was scathing in his criticism of the region's economic policy. After the war, the ability to attract foreign investors was crucial to the question of recovery. In this respect, Flanders possessed a number of natural advantages: its nearness to the sea, the availability of a world-class port in Antwerp and an easily accessible hinterland. Wallonia could offer none of these things, but this was not the only reason – according to Eyskens – for its further economic degeneration. The region continued to pump money into subsidies for the out-dated coal and steel industries, sectors which were clearly dying. Much less use was made than in Flanders of the new and innovative support

Belgium and the Monarchy. From National Independence to National Disintegration.

King Boudewijn and Prince Albert say farewell to King Leopold and Princess Lilian, who are about to set off by plane on a foreign visit. A photograph from the years between 1951 and 1954.

measures which various post-war governments had introduced. The large, flagship companies were too concerned with investment in their existing processes and showed too little interest in new technology and new products. Poor industrial relations only served to worsen the situation. This was compounded by the negative social-economic culture prevailing in the region. Eyskens wrote: "The spirit of enterprise is scarcely present. The Socialist Party in Wallonia has created a mentality which is unwilling to take risks and seeks solace in excessive reliance on state support. The Walloons prefer to seek employment with the government, the unions or a social organisation, rather than a private company."[123] As a result, the Walloon economy continued to go rapidly downhill, while during the 1950s Flanders was gradually climbing out of the valley of post-war depression, emerging onto the sunlit uplands of economic prosperity. In 1966, the gross domestic product in Flanders exceeded that of Wallonia (in absolute terms) for the very first time.

Throughout the 1950s, the development of the economy was the key regional priority in Flanders. The nationality question faded into the background until the end of the decade. The attempts to achieve greater federalism – so prominent in the years after 1935 – were now nowhere to be seen. Nevertheless, the question remained. For example, the Flemish Movement was upset by the results of the language census of 1947. Under the terms of the administrative language law of 1932, it was necessary every ten years to ask every Belgian which language he spoke as his mother tongue. Because the French language was still synonymous with culture, knowledge and social status, some Flemings were still inclined to claim that French was their mother tongue. The 1947 census showed that the use of French in Flanders had increased since 1932, particularly in the region around Brussels and along the language frontier. Moreover, as a result of the census, Brussels was now to be extended by the addition of three further municipalities and the linguistic border town of Ronse was required to offer external bilingual facilities. In short, the age-old language frontier seemed to be shifting – a matter of some concern, particularly to the Flemings. This situation was exacerbated by the fact that the language laws were not always correctly applied and by the extension of the transitional arrangements which the language legislation of the 1930s had foreseen. For example, the so-called 'transmutation' classes in the education system, which had been intended to speed the conversion of French-speakers into Dutch-speakers, were still operating long after the war.

However, the nationality question had now moved far beyond the issues of language and culture. It was now increasingly focussed on the key areas of political power. The Flemings were particularly irritated by the continued use of French as the language of diplomacy. Similar annoyance was felt at the closed world of the nation's banking and financial elite, almost all of whom were French-speaking. The pre-war language reforms meant that there were now many more children who had followed their secondary and university education entirely in Dutch, and who now felt offended by the continued predominance of French in the economic life of Flanders – a predominance which put them at a distinct professional disadvantage. Public administration and education might now be Dutch-speaking, but in the world of business the use of French continued to act as a social barrier. It was only a matter of time before the more radical elements of the Flemish Movement would seek to tear this barrier down.

In short, notwithstanding the fact that the Flemish nationalists had done themselves serious damage by their collaboration during the war, the language situation in Flanders – as it was experienced day to day by ordinary people – remained a source of political discontent and nationalist radicalism. As in the past, this was most often expressed through cultural and social organisations, which continued to occupy a prominent place in Flemish society. In this respect, the Catholic Davids Fund, the liberal Willems Fund and the socialist Vermeylen Fund were all trendsetting organisations in terms of shaping public opinion (a task in which they were helped by the support of the leading Flemish newspapers). In the pre-television era, these funds had tens of thousands of active members. They published books in Dutch, held lectures, organised day-trips, holidays and other cultural activities. More importantly, they helped to reconcile the radical collaborators of the war years with the principles and practices of democracy.

In addition to this moderate form of Flemish nationalism, there was still a more extreme faction which continued to work for separatism and often had close links with the Flemish Movement's Nazi past. In the immediate post-war period, these associations largely operated underground, but they continued to exist. They often met at the annual IJzer pilgrimage, where they mingled unseen with the democratic Flemish nationalists, while their young people came together in extreme right-wing youth groups.

Flemish nationalists of various persuasions took part in the general elections of 1949 and 1954. On each occasion they polled around 100,000 votes. In 1954, this resulted in a single parliamentary seat (for the Antwerp electoral district). The Flemish national movement had suffered a setback as a result of its wartime collaboration, but it had not been decimated. Immediately upon taking office in 1954, the liberal-socialist Van Acker administration officially published the results of the 1947 language census. This effectively broke the inter-regional truce which had been maintained since the end of the war. Language and nationality were back on the political agenda.

In December 1954, a new Flemish national party was formed which united – or at least coordinated – the Flemish Movement's various factions. This was the People's Union (*Volksunie*, VU). In contrast to the fascist VNV, which was de facto forbidden after the liberation in 1944, the VU was unambiguously democratic and parliamentarian. The party was Flemish-nationalist, in the sense that it declared itself to be in favour of the transformation of unitary Belgium into a federal state. In this manner the VU sought to align itself with a demand which had been very popular in Flanders back in

8 King Boudewijn (1950-1993)

The Chamberlain of the Royal Court welcomes Princess Lilian and King Leopold III at Zaventem Airport in Brussels. King Boudewijn is standing on the right. A photograph from the years between 1951 and 1954.

the 1930s, but which also implied that the new party rejected the idea of separatism. The party would eventually achieve its breakthrough in the general election of 1961. A year earlier, new steps were taken within the national Christian-Democrat Party (CVP-PSC) to re-establish a separate Flemish wing. In the Lower House, the so-called Group of Eight created a separate, pro-Flemish faction within the party's parliamentary bloc. Under the dynamic leadership of Jan Verroken from Ronse, this group exercised considerable influence through its close contacts with the extra-parliamentary Flemish Movement and the leading elements of the Flemish press. In many ways, this was reminiscent of the federalisation of the Catholic Party in 1936, and leads to the conclusion that large scale Flemish collaboration during the fateful period 1940-1944 delayed the evolution towards a more autonomous Flanders for almost a quarter of a century. Having said this, it must not be forgotten that it was not only in Flanders that people were concerned for greater regional autonomy. The Walloon politicians had some plans of their own.

The Gilson language laws, 1962-1963

In December 1960, Walloon discontent exploded in a series of strikes against the planned spending cuts of the liberal-Christian-democrat administration. These strikes were of great importance in helping to shape Walloon consciousness in the post-war era. It was mirrored on the Flemish side of the linguistic frontier by the breakthrough of the VU in the general election of 1961 and the Flemish 'Marches on Brussels' in both 1961 and 1962. The Flemish Movement still cherished the illusion that it could halt the further inroads of the French language in Brussels and these marches channelled the Flemings' general political and cultural discontent in a same manner as the strikes in Wallonia.

It was in this atmosphere that King Boudewijn appealed for greater national unity in his Christmas address to the nation, held on 24 December 1961. He warned against "rash measures which might endanger our common heritage."[124]

When Boudewijn made these comments, he was probably not thinking of Arthur Gilson, the Minister of the Interior, who put forward a series of new language laws in 1962-1963. On the contrary, speaking to historian Vincent Dujardin in 1999, Gilson claimed that the king had supported these laws and had told him that he – Gilson – deserved a statue in the royal park at Laken... The 1962-1963 legislation was a refinement of the earlier language laws of 1932-1935 in the fields of education and administration. They were inspired by a massive Flemish boycott of the language census in 1961. It was clear that the time had come to fix the administrative language frontier between Flanders and Wallonia once and for all. The boundaries of the provinces and the various judicial/administrative districts were also adjusted to reflect this frontier, with parts of 'border' municipalities being transferred from one region to the other as most linguistically appropriate. In this manner, the government was responding to the Walloon demand for a more clearly defined monolingualism and greater language homogeneity within each region, whilst at the same time meeting the Flemish demand to restrict the further spread of French into the institutional organisation of Flemish 'border' communities. This same principal of territoriality was also applied with equal thoroughness in education, where the transmutation classes were abolished. This represented the final elimination of the last legal vestiges of French language facilities in Flanders. Henceforth, all children in Flanders would receive their basic education in Dutch (although they still learnt French as a subsidiary subject). As far as the central administration was concerned, henceforth there was to be an equal 50-50 linguistic division of posts at the grade of director and above. This measure was more pro-Walloon than pro-Flemish, since there were considerably more Flemish dossiers (the national population being comprised of 56% Flemings and 44% Walloons). This meant that in relative terms the Flemish administration would have to process 25% more dossiers with the same number of staff.

But the most lasting impact of the new language legislation of 1962-1963 was destined to be made by its linguistic arrangements for the bilingual Brussels region and its surrounding districts. A good understanding of these arrangements is essential for anyone who wishes to understand the subsequent history of Belgium:

- For administrative purposes (but *not* for electoral purposes), the Brussels district was divided into the monolingual Dutch-speaking district of Halle-Vilvoorde and the bilingual district of Brussels Capital City (known as Brussels-19, because of its 19 constituent municipalities).
- In Brussels-19, both languages were henceforth accorded equal official status in administrative matters. This meant that every citizen in Brussels-19 had free choice of language. As far as the internal administration was concerned, there were guaranteed levels of Dutch-speaking staff and language parity for the more senior grades. Language examinations were introduced to ensure effective bilingualism in terms of the external administration. This last point was crucial, since it implied that all local government officials (town hall clerks, police, fire brigade, etc.) who came into contact with the public must be able to speak both languages. This reflects the fact that on this occasion the national government was serious in its attempt to place French and Dutch on an equal footing in Brussels-19, notwithstanding the fact that the Flemish-speakers formed a clear minority within the district. This obviously pro-Flemish concession was viewed, in part at least, as compensation for the 50-50 linguistic split at senior levels in the central administration, which was more in favour of the Walloons. Having said that, the basic principal of seeking to achieve parity between the Dutch and French languages in Brussels-19 was simply a matter of common sense. It was the only way to ensure that Brussels could continue to act as a *national* capital, thereby allowing the city to make a significant contribution towards the preservation of the Belgian state.
- Halle-Vilvoorde continued to be a monolingual, Dutch-speaking district (a status it had been accorded by the 1932 administrative law). However, an exception was to be made. The bilingual Brussels-19 district was hemmed in by a 'rand' of Dutch-language municipalities in Halle-Vilvoorde. (The word 'rand' literally means 'fringe' or 'ring'.) For six of these 'rand' municipalities a new language statute was devised. According to the language census of 1947, the French-speakers formed a significant minority in these municipalities. It was therefore agreed that Dutch would remain the official administrative language and the language of the internal administration in these six 'rand' communities, but that the French-speakers would be granted language facilities for the external administration. This meant that they had the right to use French in their dealings with local government officials and also the right to have their children educated in their language of preference.
- Language facilities were also granted in a number of villages along the Flanders-Wallonia language frontier. This involved a very small area of Belgian national territory (see map at the beginning of this book). The final setting of this border in 1962 had led to several bones of contention, for which a limited form of continued bilingualism seemed to offer the only solution. This was particularly true in the Voer region (henceforth a Dutch-speaking district with language facilities for French-speakers) and around the towns of Komen and Moeskroen (henceforth a French-speaking district with language facilities for Dutch-speakers).

The 1962-1963 legislation meant that Belgium was now more clearly divided than ever before into four separate and homogeneous language regions for administrative and educational purposes: French-speaking, Dutch-speaking, German-speaking and bilingual. The only exceptions to this broad, general pattern were the six 'rand' municipalities near Brussels, the villages around the Voer, the towns of Komen and Moeskroen, the town of Malmédy and the small German language zone, all of which were to be granted language facilities. In reality, this was the completion of a process which had been started 30 years earlier with the language legislation of the 1930s. It was a process which sought to establish official homogeneous, geographical regions which could formulate their own regional policy. Its successful conclusion meant that the way now lay open for the reform of the national state.

The state reforms of 1970

The state reforms of 1970 – the first since the foundation of the nation in 1830 – were the product of many years of intense political debate. In October 1962, the government had set up a work group charged with the preparation of constitutional reform. On 7 November 1963, this work group handed over its final report to the three major political parties. The liberal PVV-PLP was internally divided over the language question, but in global terms did not support the demands of the mainstream Flemish Movement, since most of the liberal voters in Flanders were members of society's higher echelons, which still sought to maintain (or perhaps even revive) the last vestiges of elitist bilingualism. This was not the case with the other two political families. In November 1962, a socialist BSP-PSB congress approved a motion in favour of equal 50-50 voting rights in all parliamentary debates involving essential Flanders-Wallonia issues. A similar Christian-democrat CVP-PSC congress held from 13-15 December 1963 had a preference for a two-thirds majority in such matters. In short, there was a general consensus that the minority position of the Walloons should not be exploited, but rather protected. This was not simply a question of the Flemings acceding to a reasonable Walloon demand, but was an essential precondition for the continued existence of the Belgian state. Even so, the problem became more acute in 1965, when the government adjusted the distribution of parliamentary seats to reflect changing demographic patterns. As a result, Wallonia lost a further three seats in the Lower House to Flanders, as well as one seat to the Brussels district, and one seat in the Senate. To compensate the Walloons for these 'losses', it was agreed that protection against their minority status would be enshrined in a future constitutional amendment. The CVP-PSC congress of December 1963 also placed a strong emphasis on the need for greater cultural autonomy and economic decentralisation. Full cultural autonomy would involve the transfer of 'national' powers to both Flanders and Wallonia, and would be the first (albeit small) step along the road towards federalisation. Economic federalisation was not yet a theme in the policy platforms of the three main parties, but the CVP-PSC motion – which spoke only of decentralisation, not of federalisation – can nonetheless be seen as a first tentative move in this direction.

In his 1963 Christmas address to the nation, King Boudewijn appealed to Flemings and Walloons to "engage in loyal co-operation" and to show respect for each other. This was a thinly veiled allusion to the Gilson language laws, where the cooperation between the two regions had been anything but "loyal" and "respectful". He called upon both sides to show "the imagination, courage and desire to succeed", in order to satisfy "the justified complaints for greater autonomy and decentralisation in different sectors of our public life". This last comment bears a striking resemblance to the motion passed at the CVP-PSC congress just weeks before!

After the preliminary report of November 1963, the discussions surrounding state reform quickly became bogged down, so that regional issues once again began to have a strong impact on national elections. Successive governments continued to bicker about what the Gilson laws actually meant and how they should be implemented. This in turn increased general political tension and provoked a number of language-related incidents in the Voer district, in Brussels and in two towns in the Halle-Vilvoorde district: in Leuven and in Vilvoorde itself. It was becoming apparent that many French-speakers not only refused to accept the language arrangements in these districts, but also questioned the precise demarcation of the language frontier. This further implied a questioning of the fundamental principle of territoriality, which had been the basis of every language law since 1932. Instead, the French-speakers substituted the principle of personality, which meant that French-speakers in Flanders were a minority who had the right to demand certain 'rights' in respect of the use of their mother tongue. In 1963, a group of 324 French-speaking inhabitants of Flanders submitted a complaint against the Belgian language laws to the European Court of Human Rights in Strasbourg. One of their main arguments was that, as French-speakers, it was no longer possible for them to obtain recognised French language diplomas in Flanders. In a judgement handed down on 23 July 1968, the court decided that the language laws in general and the principle of territoriality in particular were not in contravention of basic human rights. The court concluded that the pursuit of institutional language homogeneity in a linguistic region was reasonable grounds for 'unequal' treatment in language-related matters in the field of education.

During these years, the leading pro-Flemish pressure groups, such as the *Vlaamse Volksbeweging* (Flemish People's Movement) and the TAK (*Taalaktiekomitee* – Language Action Committee), reacted to the French-speaking challenge to the principle of territoriality with a number of radical and eye-catching campaigns in Flanders, such as protests against the excessive use of French in the commercial world or the disruption of French Catholic masses along the Belgian coast. Action was also taken again the organisation of French-speaking cultural activities in Flanders, such as the *Explorations du Monde* lecture tour. These were extreme reactions, since the pressure groups were now seeking to influence the use of language in what was essentially the private sphere. This was a new departure and was fundamentally different from the campaign to establish equitable rules for the use of language in civil administration and state-organised education.

On 5 January 1967, Gaston Eyskens sent a long and detailed memorandum to King Boudewijn, with a considered assessment of the advantages and disadvantages of a reform of the state structure.[125] Eyskens based his memorandum on two fundamental starting points. Firstly, that the majority of the population was still attached to the unitary Belgian state. Secondly, that there was a risk in political circles that this popular sentiment would be swept aside by the passion of an aggressive minority of intellectuals and radicals. It was these last groups which were undermining the position of the unitary state, with their wide-ranging proposals for decentralisation, deconcentration, federalisation, etc., etc. At the same time, it was hard to deny that the three major political parties were all split by fierce internal disputes over regional matters. By 1967, the so-called 'unity' within the CVP-PSC was little more than a façade, while the situation in the socialist BSP-PSB was little better – at least according to Eyskens. Eyskens argued for a reasoned, pragmatic approach. There were already many signs that the national state would not survive in its existing form and that it was in need of urgent structural reform. The premier therefore proposed the following package of measures as the best way to ensure the future of the Belgian nation:

- Full cultural autonomy for Flanders, Wallonia and Brussels. Each of the regions would be given new legislative powers with the right to raise taxes for matters relating to education, language, housing, spatial planning, the environment and all other competencies currently held by the Minister of Culture – in other words, a very broad definition of the term 'culture'. The central government would continue to be responsible for the basic principles of educational policy, as laid down in the School Pact of 1958, and would also provide a framework for regional taxation.
- A balanced Senate, in which the Flemings and the Walloons had equal representation, would act as a guarantee and a buffer against the minority status of Wallonia in the Lower House.
- Linguistic parity in the senior functions of the central administration must be replaced by full bilingualism for all such functions and for equivalent functions in the subsidiary administrations at national level. Eyskens knew that this proposal would provoke fierce Walloon resistance, but he saw it as the quid pro quo for Walloon parity in the Senate.

Eyskens believed that his plan involved no harm either to the unity of the country or to the integrity of government policy, since the powers which he intended to devolve to the regions did not affect the essential functions of the national state. Key areas, such as foreign policy, defence, finance, the economy and social insurance, all remained firmly under the control of the central government. In this respect, he may have been right. But the crucial question was this: would the people on both sides of the language frontier agree with him?

For the time being, they seemed unable to agree about anything. The question of the transfer of the French-language section of the University of Leuven to Walloon-Brabant was a new source of dispute in both communities between 1966 and 1968. Leuven is an ancient Flemish city, but it is located just a few kilometres from the language frontier. Its centuries-old university was the only fully developed Catholic university in Belgium. Since the pro-Flemish language legislation of the 1930s, teaching had been given in Dutch for students from Flanders, but there was still a French-language section, offering instruction to students from Brussels and Wallonia. By the middle of the 1960s, the majority of the Flemish people found the public subsidisation of a bilingual university on Flemish territory to be incompatible with their concept of cultural monolingualism for the Dutch-speaking linguistic region. This feeling was heightened by the strong influence which the French-speaking section had on the city and its surrounding districts, to such an extent that some French-speakers actually had hopes for the creation of a new bilingual region: Leuven-Brussels. By 1966 the Flemings demanded almost unanimously that this situation should be brought to an end. In this matter, the national government was the competent authority, since in the final analysis it financed the system. This allowed it to apply the language principles of primary and secondary education to the university level – at least in this instance. The French-language section was transferred across the language frontier to the newly created town of Louvain-la-Neuve. This represented a serious defeat for the Walloons, but perhaps even more harm was done by the fierceness of the protests organised by the radical Flemish student organisations, with their insulting (but nonetheless popular) slogans, such as *Walen buiten* (Walloons Out!) and *Leuven Vlaams* (Leuven for the Flemish!).

The Leuven question helped to further radicalise the opposing views of the regions with regard to the nationality debate. It also led to the split of the unitary Christian-democrat party into two separate regional parties. Freed from the limitations imposed by its French-speaking PSC partner (*Parti Socialiste Chrétien*), the Flemish *Christelijke Volkspartij* (CVP – Christian People's Party) was now able to pursue wholeheartedly those elements of state reform which had always lain closest to the heart of the Flemish Catholics: cultural autonomy. During this period, the language rift also became wider in the unitary socialist party (BSP-PSB). In Brussels the Flemish socialists appeared on separate electoral lists from 1968 onwards, while the French-

Belgium and the Monarchy. From National Independence to National Disintegration.

December 1960: the marriage of King Boudewijn and Queen Fabiola. From left to right: Prince Albert, doña Blanca de Aragón (the mother of Queen Fabiola), Queen Fabiola, King Boudewijn, Queen Elisabeth (grandmother of Boudewijn and Albert), Prince Alexander (the half-brother of Boudewijn and Albert; son of King Leopold III and Princess Lilian), Princess Lilian, King Leopold III, Princess Paola (wife of Prince Albert) speaking socialists once again began to organise their own regional congresses. Even the unitary liberal party (PVV-PLP), which was traditionally 'pro-French' in Flanders, began to show increasing signs of a more pro-Flemish approach on certain issues.

In the general election held on 31 March 1968 the most overtly regional parties made huge gains. The Flemish nationalist *Volksunie* (VU-People's Union) increased its number of seats in the Lower House from 12 to 20 and the alliance between the *Front des Francophones* (FDF – the Brussels-based Francophone Union) and the *Rassemblement Wallon* (RW – United Walloon Front) won a total of 12 seats, mainly in the capital. The traditional parties which had formed the previous government lost over 900,000 votes. This regional radicalism made the formation of a new administration that much harder. In 1965, Prime Minister Harmel had needed 65 days before he was able to form a new ruling coalition – an unusually long period, which resulted in words of warning from King Boudewijn. However, this was nothing in comparison with what was to come. In the years ahead, the formation of new administrations would require successively longer periods, largely as a result of regional complexities which made it increasingly difficult to find sufficient common ground at national level. 1968 was a case in point. The government fell in February 1968, as a result of the Leuven crisis. This meant that the election was held in an atmosphere of regional tension, which was intensified after the results were known. Writing of this period in his memoirs, CVP minister Leo Tindemans commented: "Looking back, it is difficult to convey to today's generation just how divided the nation was at that time. Opinions were so divergent, so irreconcilable, that there was no serious commitment to dialogue, which made discussions about the future almost impossible." [126] It took no fewer than 132 days to form the new Eyskens-Merlot crisis administration. Speaking in the Lower House on 25 June, Premier Eyskens promised that his Christian-democrat-socialist government would seek to win the support of the opposition, so that outstanding regional differences could be settled "quickly and completely". This was a repetition of what Prime Minister Jaspar had promised in 1928: but would Eyskens be any more successful?

Eyskens later claimed that King Boudewijn had wanted him as prime minister because of his conciliatory approach towards the Leuven issue. The January 1967 memorandum had also helped to create a bond of trust. "The king was anxious that I should become prime minister. When he spoke to me on this matter for the first time, I declined (...) But the king continued to insist strongly in subsequent conversations that I should accept the premiership. It was only because of his personal request that I agreed to do it."[127] The new administration had two Ministers for Regional Affairs – the Fleming Leo Tindemans and the Walloon Freddy Terwagne. They were given the difficult task of working out the policy on regional issues which would be included in the new administration's policy statement to parliament.

In Belgium, reform of the constitution is carried out in two separate phases. Parliament first approves a declaration of constitutional reform. This is the so-called *preconstituante* – a kind of preliminary constitutional assembly, which enumerates the articles of the constitution proposed for amendment. The *preconstituante* is then followed by new elections, so that the people can have their say on the matter. Once the new parliament – now referred to as the *constituante* or constitutional assembly – has been chosen, it can implement the proposed changes, providing that a two-thirds majority of the *constituante* is in favour.

The proposals for constitutional reform put forward by the Eyskens-Merlot administration went much further than the *preconstituante*, the previous Vanden Boeynants government. Vanden Boeynants' constitutional plans had foreseen the establishment of cultural councils in both Flanders and Wallonia, with powers to submit draft legislation to the national parliament. Eyskens-Merlot now wanted to give the regions the power to pass laws of their own on certain matters, without further reference to the national parliament. Tindemans justified this measure in the following terms: "The will of the people has been clearly expressed in the election of 31 March 1968, which (...) represents the second phase in the process of constitutional reform. The opinions put forward by the *preconstituante* – and this must be emphasised – date in reality from 1965. These opinions have been superseded by the results of the 31 March election. These results lead us to the conclusion that a large part of the electorate wishes to see a far-reaching degree of autonomy in the two main linguistic regions."[128] In other words, the regionally-charged election results of March 1968 had brought about a fundamental reorientation of the nationality issue in Belgium. It was also a clear example of the impact on national life resulting from the democratisation of the franchise in 1893. The electorate was now pushing the parliamentary parties slowly but surely in the direction of federal reform. It was in keeping with this trend that Premier Eyskens would declare to parliament on 18 February 1970: "The unitary state, with its existing processes and structures as currently defined by law, has been overtaken by events."[129] Reform was coming – and nothing could stop it.

The constitutional amendments of 1970 can be divided into three different sections:
- The first set of amendments offered *protection to the Walloon minority*. A number of (regional) issues could only be agreed on the basis of what became known as 'special majority laws'. These laws could only be passed if there was a majority in favour in both the Flemish *and* Walloon groupings, in both the Lower House *and* the Senate, on condition that a majority of the members of each language grouping was present during the vote and on condition that the resulting number of votes in favour of the law exceeded two-thirds of the total number of votes cast. In addition, an 'alarm-bell' procedure was introduced. If a proposed law threatened to seriously disrupt relations between the Dutch-speaking and French-speaking communities, it was

possible for the parliamentary passage of this law to be temporarily suspended, if this was requested by a motion of deferment signed by three-quarters of the members of a particular language grouping. In this case, the proposed law would be forwarded to the ministerial council, which would issue its findings on the matter within 30 days. As a final safeguard for the Walloon minority, linguistic parity was introduced into the ministerial council: henceforth, there would be equal numbers of Dutch-speaking and French-speaking ministers (if necessary not counting the prime minister).

- The second set of amendments dealt with *economic* matters – or rather failed to deal with them. A new constitutional article – article 107 quater – stated that Belgium consisted of three regions, namely Flanders, Wallonia and Brussels, but that the laws for the practical implementation of the economic devolution implied in this article still needed to be defined. Moreover, these laws would need to be passed as special majority laws. Article 107 quater gave no indication of the powers that might eventually be entrusted to the regions, but did specify that language and cultural matters would not fall under their jurisdiction. In other words, the question of economic autonomy – at this time essentially a Walloon and Brussels demand – was postponed to the future.
- The third set of amendments recognised three distinct *cultural* communities: the Dutch-speaking, the French-speaking and the German-speaking. These amendments essentially reflected the wishes of the Flemish people. The cultural councils were given their own legislative powers, and their regional 'decrees' would henceforth carry the same weight as national 'laws'. It was also agreed that the six 'rand' municipalities near Brussels formed part of Flanders (not Brussels). The French-speaking parties were prepared to support this pro-Flemish measure, but in return the Flemings agreed to recognise the head of family's right to opt for his language of preference in educational matters in Brussels, free from government interference.

The constitutional reforms of 1970 were first and foremost an effort to hold the Belgian unitary state together. The protection mechanisms offered to the French-speaking minority helped to disarm a potentially explosive political situation, which might otherwise have led to the disintegration of the Belgian nation. At the same time, the other measures also did as little as possible to rock the boat of regional discontent. The transfer of powers to the cultural communities was relatively limited, while the potentially more radical transfer of economic powers was neatly postponed to the future. In short, everyone got something, but nobody got everything: it was a typical compromise. Viewed in these terms, it is hardly surprising that a number of the negotiators responsible for the constitutional reforms of 1970 later claimed that it was not their intention to introduce a federal state. In the Senate, Minister Terwagne went to great lengths to explain the difference between the new state structure and a truly federal structure. In 1971, Minister Tindemans told the Senate precisely the same thing: the new system was not a federal system, since a truly federal system could never work in Belgium![130]

To a large extent, the claims of Terwagne and Tindemans were true. According to Jan Clement, a specialist in public law, the regions referred to in article 107 quater "were seen more as a kind of institutional decentralisation."[131] Even so, it is beyond doubt that the door leading to a future federal state was first pushed open in 1970. Jan Clement continues: "The new Constitution made this evolution possible, because article 107 quater (...) is a blank cheque for the future." This makes clear why Gaston Eyskens could continue to claim until the end of his life: "I was always faithful to the federal idea. The constitutional reforms of 1970 made possible the later federalisation of the Belgian state."[132]

The ageing King Leopold III, who had abdicated from the throne in 1950, viewed these developments with concern. From his castle in Argenteuil, he wrote to Premier Eyskens. "King Leopold III sent me a letter to express his anxiety. I assured him that the proposed system was a kind of 'ripening' federalism: sufficient autonomy was given to the component parts, but strong central authority was maintained, following the example of major federal countries, such as the United States of America and the Federal Republic of Germany. After the Second World War and during the constitutional process of 1970, it was above all the example of [West-] Germany which influenced me most strongly."[133] The 'memoirs' of the king, published in 2001, do indeed contain a number of petulant comments about the continuing problems between Flanders and Wallonia. Leopold's authorship of these comments (and of other parts of the memoirs) has been doubted by historians, but this is almost beside the point. The real question is this: were the comments right?

Belgium in the 1970s – lost in the mist. Region forming, Voeren and the 'rand' municipalities

Although the constitutional reforms of 1970 may originally have been intended to hold the unitary state together, the realities of the political situation soon made clear that a number of other options were also possible. The Liberal Party had supported the cause of state reform, which won it increased support in Flanders during the elections of 1971, but was also responsible for severe losses in Brussels and Wallonia. This forced the French and Dutch-speaking wings further and further apart, so that the unitary party finally split in the autumn of that year. This meant that two of the three mainstream political parties – the Christian-democrats and the liberals – were now divided along regional lines. They would be followed in 1978 by the socialists, who also agreed to go their separate ways because of regional differences and the continuing regionalisation of electoral results. This disintegration of the unitary national parties was also destined to have an effect on the further disintegration of the unitary national state. Unlike other federal states such as Canada, Germany and the USA, Belgium no longer had any centralised political parties which could unite the different parts of the country.

In a speech given on 21 December 1971, King Boudewijn defended the decision of the Flemings to voluntarily surrender their numerical superiority in parliament – this protection of the Walloon minority had been heavily criticised by the more radical elements in the Flemish Movement. The king pointed out that "respect for others, particularly when they are not the strongest, is the mark of a true democracy." Moreover, he warned all the Belgians, including "those who have helped to create this reform", to be on their guard against "an ill-considered step which may take us further than we want to go. We must act wisely and must know in advance where our decisions will lead us."

This was, indeed, the core of the problem. Where exactly did the nation want to go? And how did it intend to get there? The amended constitution of 1970 postponed the question of 'region forming' (as the further elaboration of article 107 quater was known) to an indefinite date in the future. In this manner, the reformers had introduced an element of constant uncertainty and instability into the political life of the nation. The almost intractable problem of region forming undermined one government after another. This is hardly surprising. The question of how you create coherent regional socio-economic politics touches on the most fundamental organisational processes of a modern nation state. In this sense, 1970 – like 1893 before it – represented a critical juncture in the development – or rather, the disintegration – of Belgium. It soon became apparent that article 107 quater was not only "a blank cheque for the future", but also a Pandora's Box of mischief. Once it had been opened, it could never again be closed. The result was an increasing radicalism, which quickly moved from support for economic decentralisation to support for the devolution of autonomous economic decision-making powers. As early as 1974, the policy statement of the new Tindemans' government argued that the powers of the cultural councils set up in 1970 should include, "amongst other things", urban development, spatial planning, regional economic expansion, housing, public health and tourism.

The transfer of socio-economic powers and their related financial contributions to the regions, within the context of a situation in which national party organisation was becoming increasingly fractured, was destined to be a powerful force for the break-up of the Belgian state. The constitutional reforms – perhaps unwittingly – had forged an institutional link between socio-economic nationalism and cultural nationalism. The regional question, which was continually pushed forward by successive election results, soon began to develop a strong internal dynamic of its own. Both the Flemish Movement and the Walloon Movement realised that they had within their reach an institutional lever with which they could obtain a high degree of socio-economic autonomy. As a result, the regional identities of Flanders and Wallonia became much more strongly defined after 1970. Between them lay the hybrid region of Brussels, without a clear economic profile but with very specific language problems. This meant that the largely 'technical' socio-economic issues related to article 107 quater were overloaded with more 'emotive' cultural matters, such as the use of language in the capital and in the villages along the language frontier. This was perhaps most famously the case in the municipalities of the Voer district.

The Voer district had been transferred from the French-speaking province of Liege to the Dutch-speaking province of Limburg in October 1962, as part of the arrangements foreseen in the Gilson language laws (see map at the beginning of this book). This transfer had been forced through by the Flemish majority against the wishes of the Walloons, who experienced this cultural and parliamentary defeat as a slap in the face. People who are not familiar with the cultural and social history of the Belgian state will have difficulty in understanding the level of emotion which the 'battle' for the Voer district caused on both sides of the linguistic divide. This Dutch-speaking district (but with a sizeable French-speaking minority) comprised just six villages, with a total population of some 4,000 souls. How could the language problems of such a relatively 'unimportant' community threaten the future existence of the nation? Yet this is precisely what happened. Between 1970 and 1990 the Voer district was constantly in the news, largely because of the refusal of the local burgomaster, a farmer named José Happart, to use the Dutch language. Happart, a colourful figure, was not a native of Voeren, having moved there from Wallonia with his family in his teens. He was perfectly justified in demanding language facilities for his French-speaking neighbours – this right was enshrined in law – but he was wrong when he demanded the right to remain burgomaster without the need to learn Dutch, and this in a district which was historically Dutch-speaking and where Dutch-speakers still formed a majority. Happart's principled stand not only led to street fights in the otherwise peaceful villages of the Voer, but also became a *casus belli* between the Flemings and the Walloons, splitting national political life neatly down the linguistic middle and occasionally leading to the fall of the government. The history of nationalist movements is littered with examples of similar non-issues which have been whipped up into ritual *causes célèbres*, around which the most fervent nationalist sentiments can crystallise. Consider, for example, the problems which surround the Orange Marches in Northern Ireland or the Serbian celebration of the Battle of Kosovo. The Voeren conflict falls into the same category, and for more than a decade demonstrated the extent to which regional antagonisms had become deeply rooted in public thinking on both sides of the language frontier. The Flemish press portrayed Happart as little more than a gang leader, whereas in Wallonia he was elevated to the status of national hero. In the 1984 European elections he polled 230,000 personal votes and later went on to become a minister in the Walloon regional government. He ended his political career as chairman of the Walloon regional parliament.

Events in the Voer district not only complicated the national political picture, but also allowed the use of nationalist sentiment to exert pressure in the continuing negotiations for the transfer of socio-economic competencies to the regions. The key issues in Voeren – whether or not the minority language could legally be used at council meetings, and how the local French-language primary school should be financed – concealed important matters of principle. Equally important, they served as an example for the six 'rand' municipalities near Brussels, which were also becoming increasingly restless. French-speakers in the Flemish communities of the 'rand' often belonged to the higher social strata. They were therefore willing and able to pay higher prices to live in pleasing locations within easy commuting distance of Brussels, but in so doing they gradually forced out the original – and poorer – Flemish population. As a result, these Flemish towns and villages gradually became more and more French-speaking, to such a degree that the newcomers eventually began to question the language arrangements in their new homes. In particular, there were growing demands that the language facilities which had been introduced for private citizens in 1962-63 should now be extended to the holders of public office. The most important of these demands was that the use of French should be permitted during council meetings in these six Flemish municipalities. However, the arrangements for language facilities in the 'rand' had been worked out as part of a more wide-ranging national compromise under the terms of the 1962-63 language laws. And to question this compromise was to question the entire balance of language legislation in Belgium.

Belgium in the 1970s – the monarchy under fire. Voeren and the amnesty question

In May 1979, King Boudewijn had a secret meeting with the still relatively unknown José Happart. The meeting took place at a motorway exit and was intended to be a brief affair. The king would wind down the window of his car and accept a petition from the Voeren activist. Unfortunately, Boudewijn's good manners got the better of him. He stepped out of his limousine and the two men talked for a number of minutes. When this later became known in Flanders, there was a storm of protest.

The memoirs of ex-premier Wilfried Martens shed more light on this curious episode. The meeting was arranged by the Walloon minister, Georges Gramme, and Jean-Marie Piret, from the king's cabinet. The Flemings, urged on by an indignant press, considered the king's action to be partisan. On the other side of the language barrier, the Walloons wondered what all the fuss was about. The king had the right to receive petitions from his subjects, providing he had ministerial permission. And Gramme had arranged this permission.

The king was most disturbed by the row he had caused and liaised closely with his prime minister in an attempt to put things right. A number of conciliatory gestures were made. For example, the king travelled to Hasselt in Flanders, to meet a number of pro-Flemish inhabitants of Voeren. In the short term, however, it was all to no avail. Gramme and Piret had gambled with the royal reputation and had lost. When Boudewijn soon afterwards attended an academic ceremony in Ghent, his car was pelted with missiles by an angry crowd of Flemish students. In his memoirs Wilfried Martens puts most of the blame on Piret, who (in his opinion) lacked political insight. Nevertheless, Piret remained in post until the end of 1981 and therefore was closely involved in the crucial state reforms of 1980.

Voeren was not the only regional problem with which Boudewijn became entangled during the 1970s. In 1976 the king celebrated the 25th anniversary of his ascension to the throne. For the more radical Flemish nationalists, this seemed like an ideal moment to reopen their demands for an amnesty for the collaborators of the Second World War. From March onwards, the amnesty campaign began to grow, supported by Cardinal Suenens and the Catholic newspaper *La Libre Belgique*. The ruling CVP party also indicated its approval, while the liberal Minister of Justice, Herman Vanderpoorten, had been seeking to find a consensus for a number of months.

Unfortunately, at national level the issue was completely deadlocked. This was largely the result of the attitude which the post-war Flemish Movement took towards its own wartime collaboration. In France and The Netherlands after 1945, there was general agreement that the collaborators had made fundamentally wrong choices. However, in Flanders from 1950 onwards the Flemish collaborators began to defend and legitimise these choices. They claimed that they had acted from a kind of anti-Belgian resentment: in other words, they only became collaborators because of the 'unjust treatment' of Flanders before the war. In time, this unilateral view came to be largely accepted in Flanders, where nationalist sentiment aroused by contemporary issues helped to colour people's perception of this less than glorious episode from their region's past. The focus came to be fixed on just one aspect of the collaboration – its naïve idealism. The collaborators were portrayed as being almost saint-like in their devotion to their Flemish homeland, while the liberation came to be increasingly associated not with the restoration of freedom, but with the repression which followed. This repression was common to all countries, but in Flanders its memory continued to linger. At the same time, less convenient memories of the collaboration – its anti-democratic nature, its support of the inhuman Nazi regime, its betrayals and its treasons – were quickly and quietly forgotten. For many years, a large body of public opinion in Flanders – particularly in Catholic circles – was able to reconcile itself to the actions of the collaborators. It was only at the end of the 20th century that this mentality began to change significantly, due to the passing of the war generation, a number of controversial television documentaries and the publications of historians.

In the meantime, it was impossible to reconcile Flemish public opinion on this matter with the Walloon position on collaboration. After 1944, the French-speaking community had never been able to forgive its collaborators in the same way that the

Flemings had done. Most of them had no sympathy for anyone who had worked with the Germans, even when there were extenuating circumstances. Not surprisingly, they took a similarly hard line with the more far-reaching collaboration which had taken place in Flanders. What many Flemings saw as Flemish idealism, was viewed in Wallonia as an attempt to break up the national state to the benefit of the former and the disadvantage of the latter. As a result, Walloons tended to tar all collaborators with the same brush: without exception, they were 'fascists', 'Nazis', 'war criminals', etc. In their collective memory of the war years, there was no place for any understanding. These diametrically opposed positions – Flemish forgiveness and Walloon vengefulness – meant that the two communities would never be able to agree on the question of an amnesty. But it also meant that the problem would continue to fester in the body politic, making its own contribution to the further disintegration of Belgium.

If the amnesty question was discussed at government level in 1976 – and we can assume that Minister Vanderpoorten had tested the waters – it is certain that these discussions led nowhere. In this context, a direct appeal to the king for an amnesty could only place him in a compromising position. When Boudewijn addressed parliament on 31 March 1976, he touched on the delicate issue of state reform but made no mention of the amnesty. For this reason, the members of the Flemish nationalist *Volksunie* (VU) refused to applaud at the end of the speech. In May 1976, the king was booed by supporters of the amnesty when he arrived for a ceremonial visit to Bruges, and the reactions were even more hostile when he later visited Antwerp. (On a return visit to the city four years later, the king was pelted with firecrackers, eggs and tomatoes, so that he was forced to cancel his programme: no Belgian monarch had ever been treated this way in public – and by his own people.)

In these tense circumstances, Boudewijn proceeded carefully with the amnesty dossier. During the formation of the new Tindemans government in May 1977, it became known that the premier was considering the possibility of offering the Justice portfolio to Frans Baert of the VU. The king told him that it would not be wise to give such a delicate ministerial position to a member of a strongly regional party. It was a shrewd assessment: the Ministry of Justice is above all a national ministry, which needs to be run by a national – and not a nationalist – politician. Because he knew that the Walloons would continue to block a general amnesty, Boudewijn feared that a VU Minister of Justice would seek to deal with collaboration cases on an individual basis under his own authority. The king wanted no repeat of the Dr. Martens episode which had caused his father so much embarrassment at the end of the 1930s.

"The king refuses to give an amnesty." "The king is a friend of Happart." As a result of these issues, the press and public opinion in Flanders turned against King Boudewijn. Yet the reality behind the scenes was very different. Neither of these situations was really the king's fault: by the mid-1970s the monarch no longer had any real influence in such matters. He did, however, still have his own opinions and as the 1980s dawned he was keen to press on with the federalisation of his kingdom.

King Boudewijn wants progress, part I: The Egmont Pact

In December 1972, King Boudewijn appealed to his politicians and his people "to find as soon as possible a lasting answer" and "to seek a global long-term solution to our inter-regional difficulties". The country must "develop without further delay a new but enduring institutional framework." In his 1973 Christmas speech, the king said that the economic crisis which had broken out in the course of that year made a solution of the regional problem even more urgent. A few days before this speech, Boudewijn had had a meeting with Leo Tindemans, who at the time was vice-premier with special responsibility for institutional reform. Tindemans later recorded in his memoirs: "He was concerned about the lack of unity being displayed during the preparations for the new state reforms. He was anxious to do all in his power to prevent the nation from making another blunder. Finally, he told me of a deep, personal wish, which actually sounded more like a guideline: 'May I ask you something? If at the end of long and often painful negotiations, when people are tired and more inclined to accept a compromise proposal that does not bring about any real improvement in the existing situation, if you are not personally convinced of the merits of this proposal, please do not accept it.' With these words he expressed the hope which he had placed in me." Tindemans continued: "Naturally, he did not speak of his own preferred solution or even indicate the extent to which he had considered the various options. He certainly asked many questions, but it remained unclear to me whether or not he understood the full consequences of particular scenarios."[134] It is remarkable that as late as the mid-1970s the vice-premier thought it was 'natural' that the monarch did not reveal to him his own feelings about the future of the nation. It is one of the essential conditions of a parliamentary monarchy that the king and his ministers should be able to exchange ideas freely in private; it is only in public that the king needs to maintain a neutral position. While his public speeches are covered by ministerial responsibility, internal consultation between monarch and politicians should be open and confidential. This is the 'normal' state of affairs in most countries, but not in Belgium during Boudewijn's reign. The king always found it difficult to trust his ministers. Perhaps this is not surprising. Boudewijn had arrived in Belgium in 1950 as a schoolboy with a deep-rooted distrust of all politicians. This meant that he only grew into his function as king very slowly. The conversation with Tindemans shows just how slowly. This more 'mature' Boudewijn had confidence in Tindemans, but he still kept his distance – and his thoughts to himself. This is undoubtedly symptomatic of the weakening of the monarchy which resulted from the crisis created by Leopold III.

The radicalisation of the inter-regional situation in the 1970s was not based on a global or well-considered policy, but was more a response to an irregular series of government crises, most frequently caused by unexpected – and uncontrollable – incidents in Voeren or the municipalities adjacent to Brussels-19. However, there was one structural development of considerable importance: the arrival on the political

8 King Boudewijn (1950-1993)

During the visit of King Boudewijn to Antwerp in June 1980: an anti-royalist demonstration in favour of the amnesty. A Belgian flagpole is pulled down by the manifestants.

stage in 1972 of a new generation of more militant Christian-democrat CVP-PSC politicians. This brought men like Wilfried Martens and Charles-Ferdinand Nothomb to the fore. Martens' thinking on regional matters was far more radical than the views of Tindemans and Eyskens. Both men have harsh words for Martens in their memoirs and had little sympathy for his strong federalist convictions. At its party congress in October 1972, under Martens' chairmanship, the CVP declared itself to be in favour of a far-reaching approach to article 107 quater, with "completely" autonomous regions which would be empowered to deal with "all matters of regional importance". Looking back on the congress, Martens wrote in his memoirs: "For us, it was necessary to use the further definition of article 107 quater of the Constitution to take a decisive step forward in the direction of federalisation."[135] He added that this step went much further than what Eyskens and Tindemans had intended with their 'region forming'.

According to Martens, it was he – first as party chairman and later as premier – who did most to 'convert' King Boudewijn to the federalist cause. Perhaps this was made easier by the fact that Martens was a believer in 'unionist federalism'. Alongside the legislative autonomy of the regions, which were to be provided with their own financial resources and a clear recognition of their boundaries and territorial integrity, he was convinced of the need to maintain a strong core of federal powers at the centre, which must be in balance with the powers devolved to the regions. This division of powers would be based on an assessment of which government – the regional or the national – was best placed to solve a particular problem. Choosing the wrong institutional level – either too high or too low – would result in less efficient solutions. This is the so-called principle of subsidiarity. Alongside subsidiarity there was also a need for solidarity between the component elements of the federation. In particular, a national social insurance system was seen as one such mechanism of solidarity.

A first echo of unionist federalism is perhaps to be found in a speech given by King Boudewijn at the town hall in Brussels on 31 March 1976, during the celebrations of his silver jubilee: "Uniting different bodies means accepting their diversity." It was an idea which he repeated on a number of occasions, such as on 20 July 1984: "People need to understand clearly that a regionalised state, in order to work harmoniously, has a vital need for a strong central authority, which can promote the interests which the Constitution defines as 'common'. This means that everyone must abide by the rules. In other words, federation does not mean greater division, but closer union."

The difference of opinion between Martens and Tindemans on the regional question contributed to the development of a remarkable form of particracy during the years 1977-1978. In 1977, a new administration was formed under Tindemans, based on alliance between the Christian-democrats, the socialists and the regional parties VU (Flanders) and FDF (Brussels). This alliance of opposites resulted in the drafting of the Egmont Pact (which was named after the palace where it was negotiated). This pact –

which at the time was believed to offer a final solution for the structure of the Belgian state – came into being in two distinct phases. A first version of the text was drawn up during the formation of the new administration in May 1977. Between August and October 1978, a number of inconsistencies and problems in this draft were eliminated. The main stumbling block was Brussels, and the final agreement on this delicate issue was reached by the party chairmen of the coalition partners, with almost no reference to Prime Minister Tindemans. Tindemans felt uncomfortable about this situation, but (as his memoirs show) there was little he could do when faced with the united front of the party chairmen.

What exactly did the Egmont Pact propose? Although the word 'federalism' appears nowhere in the text of the pact, it put forward a far-reaching reform of the Belgian state along federalist lines. This would be carried out in two phases. The first phase would see the creation of three distinct regional communities – Flanders, Wallonia and Brussels – with directly elected 'regional councils' (i.e. parliaments) and 'executives' (i.e. governments). The existing cultural councils would be replaced by new community councils (Dutch-speaking, French-speaking and German-speaking), each with extended powers and also with its own executive. In a later phase, the pact also foresaw the amendment of the two-chamber parliamentary system, whereby the role of the Senate would be reduced to a number of specific tasks. For the French-speakers in the six municipalities with language facilities near Brussels and in seven other municipalities and three districts around the capital city, it was agreed that there should be a 'right of inscription' in the Brussels region, which would give them the right to language facilities and also the right to vote in the capital.

In his traditional end-of-year speech in December 1977, King Boudewijn defended the Egmont Pact: "Thanks to the flexibility of our institutions and the mutual understanding which exists in Belgium, it has been possible this year to achieve a broad consensus across all spectrums of opinion. Our task is now to ensure that these institutions are based on sound constitutional and legal foundations. This presupposes that the inter-regional agreement will be clearly formulated and properly implemented." This was indeed the problem (which Boudewijn almost certainly pointed out at the prompting of Premier Tindemans). The text of May 1977 did not represent a coherent whole, so that it was far from clear whether or not it would remain within the framework set by the existing Constitution. As yet, the present government was not a *constituante*.

But there were other problems as well. André Cools, the chairman of the French-speaking socialist BSP, refused to consider any further amendments to the text, while the Flemish Movement, angered by the language concessions in Brussels and supported by the entire Flemish press, launched a fierce and persistent campaign against the pact. This campaign was supported by the Flemish liberals, who hoped in this way to rid themselves of their 'pro-French' reputation in Flanders. Even more importantly, Premier Tindemans was not convinced by the policy which his party chairman Martens had more or less forced upon him. He asked for advice from the Council of State, which confirmed that a number of provisions in the pact were unconstitutional. Between August and October 1978, the conflict between Tindemans and Martens was destined to reach new heights.

Parallel with these developments, a nationwide debate raged about the pros and cons of the Egmont agreement. This debate was particularly stormy in Flanders, where the concessions to the French-speakers in and around Brussels caused great concern. For the more radical Flemish nationalists, it was unacceptable that the *Volksunie* (VU) – which was also a Flemish nationalist party – should be prepared to 'buy' federalism by agreeing to a special status for Brussels, which effectively meant that the capital would no longer be a part of Flanders. This resulted in (yet another) split in the Flemish Movement and led to the foundation of the separatist *Vlaams Blok* (Flemish Block or VB). The Block attempted to profit from the 'treason' of the Egmont Pact by profiling itself as the champion of an independent Flanders. During the 1990s, the new party's programme became increasingly anti-Islamic, to such an extent that it was forced to change its name to *Vlaams Belang* (Flemish Interest Party) following a conviction for racial hatred in the year 2000.

In his memoirs, Tindemans published his diary notes from 1978 relating to the Egmont negotiations. These notes show that he met frequently with King Boudewijn during this period. On 10 August 1978, the king asked his premier whether he could in all conscience sign an agreement which was causing such heated debate. On 3 October, Tindemans wrote: "I was called to see the king. Our sovereign insists on a solution 'within the framework of the existing Constitution.'"[136] In his own memoirs, Wilfried Martens was more explicit about the meetings between prime minister and monarch: "I remember that serious discussions were held in the royal palace, amongst other things about the swearing of the loyal oath by the chairmen of the executives and the parity between laws and decrees. Premier Tindemans finally reached agreement with the king that he would not sign the decrees. This was an important concession by the royal entourage, but in return it was agreed that the regional governments would be referred to as 'executives' and that the regional parliaments would be known as 'councils'."[137] In other words, the classic terms 'government' and 'parliament' would be reserved for the national level. It is also interesting to note that the negotiators of the pact thought that regional decrees must have the same legal weight as national laws, whereas the palace had a very different opinion. This shows that the circles around the king were still thinking more in terms of decentralisation than federalism. In this sense, Boudewijn was a long way behind the times. The cultural councils had been issuing nationally binding decrees at the same level as national laws since the state reforms of 1970 – it was too late to turn the clock back now.

Moreover, the politicians were determined that the function of the king should be limited to national legislation: they saw no role for him at an institutional level in the autonomous regions. A comparison was drawn with West-Germany, where the national president has no authority in the regional *Länder*. No doubt this resulted in a number of difficult conversations ("fierce discussions", according to Tindemans) at the royal palace, but it all made very little difference. The only concession which the royal court was able to secure was that the presidents of the regional executives (nowadays known as minister-presidents) should take a loyal oath before the king. Was the palace content with this minimal gesture? Or did it really think that it might be able to influence the appointment of the regional executives? Did the king ever seriously believe that he would be able to reject the candidature of a regional minister-president? In reality, the oath – like the use of the titles 'executive' and 'councils', instead of 'governments' and 'parliaments' – was little more than a face-saving manoeuvre with no real meaning, since the sacred nature of an oath had long since lost its power in West European society. The names given to the new regional institutions also mattered little: what was important, were the powers they possessed. The term 'executive' would be used again during the successful constitutional reforms of 1980, but by then the public and the press were already starting to refer to regional 'governments'. By the mid 1980s the only people talking about 'executives' were to be found in ivory towers and royal palaces. In short, it no longer reflected political reality.

During the period 1977-1978 the king had the misfortune to be wrongly advised by his counsellors. Wilfried Martens was probably right in his unflattering assessment of Piret, the king's secretary, and the negotiations between Tindemans and the palace were symptomatic of the weakness of royal power. But did the king and his entourage really have any room for manoeuvre? His cabinet was not directly involved in the political negotiations between parties, and was therefore unaware of the underlying political considerations on which subsequent agreements might be based. The king would, of course, be consulted about these agreements, but usually after they had been made. Was he in a position to add anything significant to a delicately balanced proposal, which was frequently the product of months of discussion and was based on expectations, influences and compromises of which the king and his staff knew little? Add to this the expectations and exaggerations of the press, camped outside the gates of the palace day and night, and it soon becomes clear that the modern-day Belgian monarch anno 1978 was little more than a political prisoner in his own country, with no real power except during the brief period when a new administration needed to be formed. And now even this power was to be taken away from him in respect of the regions!

Relations between Tindemans and the three party chairmen had been deteriorating steadily throughout the summer of 1978. By the autumn, the premier had had enough of what he considered to be unacceptable interference in the performance of his mandate, and on 11 October he offered the resignation of his administration.

His government fell, which also implied that the Egmont Pact was a dead letter. Even so, the pact made an important contribution as a platform for future constitutional reforms. This, of course, could not be foreseen at the time, and King Boudewijn was angry with Tindemans for torpedoing the Egmont agreement. It is certainly true that he presented the king with a *fait accompli*, announcing his resignation in parliament before waiting for the traditional royal audience. But if Egmont was dead, the spirit of Egmont lived on: the process of constitutional reform could not be halted.

King Boudewijn wants progress, part II: the constitutional reforms of 1980

Undeterred by the Egmont setback, in his Christmas speech of 1978 the king appealed once more to his politicians to conclude a new regional pact which would transform the state's institutions in a manner which would ensure the future harmony and prosperity of the nation. Boudewijn once again emphasised that respect for "legitimate diversity" must be combined with "a strong and stable central authority". This central authority must be in a position "to pursue common interests and to defend them in the international arena (...) You know as well as I do that we stand to lose much as a result of the endless confrontations which prevent us from solving our difficulties and put our place at the heart of a newly emerging Europe in jeopardy."

April 1979 saw the entrance into office of the Martens I administration. One of its first tasks was the negotiation of a new inter-regional agreement, which foresaw a programme of constitutional reform in three stages. The first draft legislation was submitted to parliament in October and contained far reaching proposals: the formation of three regions with autonomous economic competencies and the extension of cultural autonomy to include all person-related matters. In his 1979 Christmas address, the king was above all concerned to reassure the unitarist Belgians that the new state reforms held no dangers for the future of the nation.

Surprisingly, opposition to the new proposals came from an unexpected source: the Flemish Christian-democrats (CVP). This was Prime Minister Martens' own party but the chairmanship had now passed into the hands of ex-premier Leo Tindemans, with whom Martens had recently been in conflict. Under Tindemans' impulse, a CVP congress held on 16 December 1979 rejected the plan for three equivalent regions. The CVP was no longer prepared to support the idea that Brussels should enjoy the same regional status as Flanders and Wallonia. This placed Martens in an almost impossible position, and his first two administrations quickly fell as a result of the Brussels issue. However, by August 1980 the Martens III administration was able to reach a compromise with its critics and the new reforms were implemented. These reforms represented a further crucial step towards a federal Belgium. For the very first time, regions and communities were given their own institutions as part of a two-pronged, asymmetrical package of constitutional measures:

- Two *regional councils* were created – one in Flanders, one in Wallonia – each with binding legislative powers for 'place-related' economic matters, such as spatial planning, the environment, housing, energy and employment.
- The third region – Brussels – was effectively put on hold.
- Political reluctance to pursue full economic regionalisation continued to be strong. For this reason, 'national' economic activities – meaning activities which affected both Flanders and Wallonia – would remain under the control of the federal government. This control was limited to five key 'national' sectors: shipbuilding, coal, steel, glass and textiles. However, all other sectors of economic activity were regionalised.
- The two existing cultural councils were replaced by three *community councils*: a 'French' one limited to the French-speaking population of Wallonia and Brussels, a 'Flemish' one limited to the Dutch-speaking population of Flanders and Brussels, and a 'German' one for the German-speaking inhabitants of the small German districts in Wallonia. These were also legislative institutions, with autonomous powers for all cultural and person-related matters, such as health care and the welfare sector. These are competencies which are not restricted to a specific geographical area – it was for this reason that it was necessary to create 'regions' alongside the 'communities' – but are linked to the needs of the community's citizens as individuals. The services which cater to these needs – hospitals, retirement homes, etc. – must be offered in the language of the 'user'.
- As a result of these changes, after 1980 the country possessed two place-related regional councils and three person-related community councils. These parliaments (for that is what they were) each had legislative powers for their own fields of competence. Moreover, these legislative powers were equivalent to those of the national parliament in Brussels. The new institutions were not directly elected, but were made up from MPs serving in the national parliament for the region in question. In other words, if someone was elected to the national parliament, they were also elected to one of the regional councils. This was the so-called 'double-mandate'. In Flanders, the regional and community councils would eventually be merged. This was not the case in Wallonia, where the regional council and the community council would continue to work alongside each other. The 'decrees' passed by the regional 'councils' were implemented by the 'executives'. As has been previously mentioned, the fact that these designations were used is the only evidence of the attempts made by the court to influence these important constitutional changes. In reality, the 'decrees' were *laws* passed by regional *parliaments* and implemented by regional *governments*.

The law of August 1980 also foresaw a procedure similar to the 'alarm-bell' procedure which had been introduced in 1970. This was necessary in the event of a 'conflict of interest' arising between the federal government and the regional institutions in the course of the execution of their respective powers. In such instances, article 143 of the Constitution encouraged both parties to bear in mind their "federal loyalty".

King Boudewijn puts the breaks on: 1983-1988

The state reforms of 1980 did not result in inter-regional peace, or even in a temporary ceasefire. In his speech to the new Martens V government on 17 December 1981, the king declared that the work of the previous *constituante* still needed to be completed, "in particular, the creation of a positive co-existence with the institutions of the regions and communities." This finalisation of the reforms implied at least a minimal consensus with regard to who did what. Unfortunately, the fact that five sectors of the economy still remained under national control helped to create a new dynamic. The Walloon socialist PS emerged as the most radical regionalist party in this respect, as was made abundantly clear during its tempestuous congress in October 1982. On the Flemish side, the CVP politician Luc Van den Brande submitted a proposal for the regionalisation of the five national sectors. Van den Brande represented yet another new generation of Flemish Christian-democrats, which – in keeping with recent CVP tradition – was even more militant than the last.

Prime Minister Martens was still in favour of maintaining the national economic sectors. This was in keeping with his philosophy of unionist federalism, which foresaw the need for national elements to promote solidarity between the regions. For the premier, the five key sectors were precisely such "a form of solidarity which must be maintained, if we wish to preserve our country." Writing later in his memoirs, however, he conceded: "Looking back, I may have been mistaken in this conclusion, at least in part."[138] Rather than promoting unity, the five national sectors quickly became a source of divisiveness.

Between them, the PS and Van den Brande had put the cat among the pigeons. The government responded by trying to transfer the matter to a parliamentary commission, while the king in a speech made to parliament on 8 February 1983 pleaded for the status quo. "The reforms of 1980 have only been in force for a short time, and many matters are still in a transitional phase. Even so, there are voices which claim that these reforms are already outdated. New plans are being prepared which would extend the autonomy of the regions and communities still further. I will make no comment on the content of these proposals. But I must however warn against this method of working, which, by creating a rapid succession of changes, entails the risk of making the governance of our land more difficult, and, ultimately, impossible." The speech was heavily criticised by the socialist opposition parties. Jean-Marie Dehousse, chairman of the Walloon 'executive', ostentatiously refrained from applauding the king at the end of his address. The next day, the newspaper *La Wallonie* referred to the king's words as a slap in the face for the French-speaking community.

Continuing discontent surrounding the national sectors, combined with new incidents in the seemingly never-ending Happart affair, ensured that the political climate during the first half of the 1980s remained unsettled. In 1982, Happart – campaigning under the slogan *Retour à Liège* (Return to Liege) - won an absolute majority in the local elections at Voeren. This meant that the exclusively French-speaking Happart would become the burgomaster of a Flemish municipality with administrative language facilities for its French-speaking inhabitants, while Happart himself refused to use Dutch. To many in Flanders this was not acceptable, but following long and difficult negotiations in government circles it was finally agreed (at the suggestion of the Walloon Christian-democrat minister Charles Nothomb) that the king should confirm Happart's appointment in February 1983. This appointment only became effective on 31 December 1983 and it was understood that in the meantime Happart would learn Dutch. However, when he came to take his oath of appointment on 30 December, it was clear that he had made no effort to keep his side of the bargain. His appointment was rescinded in January 1984, when he refused to sit an examination in Dutch. Happart appealed against his dismissal to the Council of State, but his removal from office was confirmed in a judgement handed down on 30 September 1986. This led to the start of what later became known as the 'Voeren Merry-go-round'. Happart now took up a new position as 'acting burgomaster'. This appointment was also nullified, but he was reappointed by his French-speaking majority no fewer than nine times!

The necessity to complete the reform of state became increasingly more urgent as the decade progressed. Resolutions passed at the Flemish Christian-democrat CVP congress held at Ostend in November 1986 proposed that the Belgian state structure should eventually be subsumed within a European structure. This was a very radical position for a 'traditional' party, which at the same congress also proclaimed itself to be in favour of "a far-reaching federalism" and opened the door for a discussion of the status of Brussels. The radicalisation of political debate during these years also left its mark on the socialists and the liberals. In contrast to the Christian-democrats, the other two major Flemish parties tended to remain fairly neutral on regional issues at their public political meetings, although individual party members could (and did) make more outspoken pronouncements. It was not until 1987 that the liberals first addressed the question of institutional reform at their annual congress. In this sense, the congresses of the CVP are the best barometer for assessing the level of political radicalisation during the 1980s. A study by Jan Velaers, a Belgian expert in constitutional law, has also shown the extent to which CVP congress resolutions relating to state reform were actually translated into policy practice.

In April 1987, Hugo Schiltz – at that time the leading politician in the Flemish nationalist VU – attempted to start a regional dialogue. According to Hugo De Ridder, a well-informed journalist, Schiltz launched his initiative following "a nod from court circles".[139] The "nod" in question probably came from Jacques van Ypersele de Strihou, who since 1983 had been King Boudewijn's cabinet secretary. Van Ypersele de Strihou was a politically experienced, French-speaking Christian-democrat, who had previously worked as an economic adviser in several government ministries. In 1978, he had also been deputy cabinet secretary to Premier Tindemans at the time of the Egmont Pact.

The Schiltz initiative was swept away in the storm created by the latest Happart crisis. The king referred to this issue in disparaging terms during a speech given on 20 July 1987, but it made little difference: the situation in Voeren led to the fall of the Martens VI administration on 15 October. A new interim administration – Martens VII – could do little more than call a new general election. This election resulted in no clear cut winner and the formation of the following government took no less than 6 months, notwithstanding the best efforts over a period of 106 days by *formateur* Jean-Luc Dehaene of the CVP.

Dehaene eventually succeeded in finally neutralising the political threat of José Happart. Even so, it was not Dehaene who became the new prime minister. The Martens VIII administration was able to take office on 9 May 1988, armed with a new agreement for further state reforms. Hugo De Ridder has suggested that the king played an important part in unblocking the discussions on state reform, by persuading the Walloon Christian-democrats to accept the federalisation of the education system. This represented a major change in PSC thinking, since in 'socialist' Wallonia Catholic schools were very much in a minority position. At a later stage, the king helped to stabilise the negotiations by informing the party negotiators that he was no longer prepared to put his signature to the appointment of José Happart as burgomaster of Voeren, as long as Happart could not speak Dutch. De Ridder even went so far as to suggest that the final choice of Martens as premier in preference to Dehaene was also at the explicit request of the king, who believed that Dehaene wanted to go too far in matters of state reform.

This was a belief shared by Martens himself. "From the contacts which I had with Boudewijn at that time, I became aware that he was concerned at the direction which the question of state reform seemed to be taking. The radicalism of the CVP, inspired by its congress in Ostend, was part of the reason for this concern. The policy agreement of the new administration scarcely made mention of the preservation of monetary and economic union. Moreover, the third phase of reform was described so briefly that it was possible to see in it a range of measures which moved in the direction of confederalism. This did not appeal to the king. When the time came to implement the agreement, he even wrote to me on the matter. He regarded my premiership as a guarantee that things would not get out of hand."[140]

The letter in question was handed to Martens by Boudewijn on 11 July 1988. He expressed his unease about the draft legislation being prepared by the government for the implementation of its policy agreement. "It is unnecessary to express my agreement for a system which will result in a federal structure and an extension of the powers allocated to the regions and communities. However, this greater autonomy must – as you have already stated in Parliament – be linked to a strengthening of the central state. If it is carried out in balanced manner, this double transfer can enhance the mutual trust and unity between those who will be responsible for exercising the divided powers of the state. I am afraid, however, that these aims and that global vision are no longer being clearly expressed and that – as a result of the failure to use the classic structures of a federal state – the outcome will be ambiguous, so that some people will refer to this outcome as a federal state, while others call it a federation of states or even a confederation of separate states. I have serious doubts about some aspects of the proposed changes." It is evident that King Boudewijn had little confidence in the policy agreement negotiated by Dehaene. He had a number of unanswered questions and was particularly anxious about two specific themes: foreign policy and the so-called 'residual powers'. (The constitution was based on the assumption that only limited and well-defined powers would be allocated to the regions: all other 'residual' powers would be vested in the central federal state.) During the formation period and later, he continued to warn of possible problems in a variety of different fields: "Economic and monetary union, scientific policy, foreign trade, infrastructure, the status of public servants, etc."

Other sources also confirm that during the Dehaene period and afterwards the palace made efforts to have draft legislation amended. One such instance related to the planned implementation in Belgium of economic and monetary union, which was designed to eventually lead to the introduction of a single European currency: the euro. The king considered the government's policy to be insufficiently unionist. He questioned how a national monetary policy could still be possible and how management of the state debt could be controlled if important economic levers were being systematically regionalised. It was factors such as these which explain why the moderate Martens, rather than the more radical Dehaene, now became prime minister for the eighth time (although the latter was given the Institutional Reform portfolio).

In a speech which he planned to give on 20 July 1988, Boudewijn once again wished to touch on the subject of the regional and community agreement, the first partial elements of which were scheduled to be brought before parliament a few weeks later. He wished to emphasise that the devolution of further powers to the regions and communities did not, by itself, constitute federalism. Premier Martens asked him to remove this sentence from his address, since it could create the impression that the king and the government were not on the same wavelength. After a long discussion with van Ypersele de Strihou, Martens finally got his way. Instead, Boudewijn repeated his favourite idea, which was also shared by his premier: federalism is union, not separation: "The reforms of state must ensure solidarity and cooperation between the different federal units (...). The new state organisation will transform our political structures into the structures of a true federal state. As in all other important federal states throughout the world, we need a strong central authority which can properly exercise its residual powers and which is not constantly being held to ransom by the

King Boudewijn during his speech on 20 July 1988.

arbitrariness of regional demands. I am talking about a federalism which must promote unity, which must maintain solidarity between the different federal institutions, and which rejects every form of open or concealed separatism (...). Federalism is bringing together, not forcing apart." The fact that the king was prepared to call Belgium a federal state and was willing to defend the government's state reform programme made – as was intended – a strong impression on pro-Belgian circles. This was underlined later the same month, when Boudewijn reprimanded Vice-premier Hugo Schiltz for stating that he no longer had any interest in Belgium. Schiltz publicly withdrew the remark.

In August 1988, the government brought its first legislative proposals for the new wave of state reforms before parliament. These 1988 reforms can be briefly summarised as follows:
- Responsibility for education was now transferred fully to the communities and the five remaining national economic sectors were divided amongst the regions. The regions would each receive 40% of their funding from national financial resources. This financing would be granted on the basis of a Flanders-Wallonia-Brussels distribution formula, to be introduced over an 11 year period.
- The Brussels 'Capital City' region, which was still limited to the 19 municipalities of Brussels, was to be further developed. Flemings in the Brussels parliament and the Brussels executive were given the same protection against their minority status as the French-speakers had been given at national level.

A new Pacification Law of 1988 also confirmed the existing system of language facilities (many Flemings claimed that the facilities granted in 1962 had only been intended as temporary) and strengthened their legal position, by providing that future changes could only be made by a special majority law. In return for this concession, the French-speakers agreed that Dutch must be the language used at council meetings in the Flemish facility communities. Even so, the French-speakers continued to contest this provision for 'ordinary' council members, claiming that it only applied to the burgomaster and the aldermen.

1991-1993: state reform, confederalism and separatism

In the autumn of 1991, the eighth and last Martens administration was brought down by an incident involving a delivery of Walloon-manufactured arms to Saudi Arabia, which the Flemish socialists and the VU suddenly decided to boycott. In reaction to this pre-electoral outburst of pacifism, Vice-premier Philippe Moureaux attempted to block an ICT contract favourable to Flanders. The situation rapidly got out of hand and an angry Moureaux declared to the press that if the national government did not soon issue a license for the weapons sale to the Saudis, the Walloon government would issue one of its own. This rash statement – Moureaux did not know that the government had already worked out a compromise solution – was almost revolutionary in nature, since the unilateral seizure of powers is in breach of the most fundamental constitutional principles. Several Flemish papers said that "an institutional atom bomb" had been placed under inter-regional relations. This was, indeed, the most dangerous consequence of Moureaux's blunder, since politicians now started to talk openly about a possible split between Flanders and Wallonia. Even the traditional parties and their ministers began to discuss the possibilities of separatism. In a nationalist context, the power of words and slogans can be magnified out of all proportion to their original meaning. This was an elementary rule of Belgian politics, which Moureaux momentarily forgot.

Increasingly threatening language was used on both sides of the linguistic frontier. When a new administration was finally formed following the election of 24 November 1991, King Boudewijn asked the national ministers to refrain from using the word 'separatism' in public. But it was already too late: the taboo had been broken. From early 1991 onwards, prominent French-speaking politicians would refer on more than one occasion to *séparation*, meaning the possibility that Flanders might unilaterally withdraw from the Belgian union. It was a powerful image, which had haunted Wallonian politicians and the Wallonian public for decades. When in 2006 a Walloon television station broadcast a fake programme about an unexpected Flemish declaration of independence, the vast majority of French-speaking viewers instantly believed that it was true – and reacted accordingly!

The election of 24 November 1991 reflected the extent to which the regions were drifting apart and the extent to which the public on both sides of the linguistic frontier were losing their faith in the traditional parties to solve the regional question. The separatist *Vlaams Blok* (Flemish Block) scored a spectacular success in Flanders and the nihilistic Van Rossem Party also did well. The ruling Flemish coalition partners lost almost 290,000 votes to the Block, which now had two more seats than the nationalist VU. National politics was in turmoil and it seemed once again that only further reform could put the Belgian state back on the rails. Perhaps this was indeed the logical solution, since the reform of the state system was still far from complete.

During his consultations for the formation of the new administration, King Boudewijn resolutely refused to invite the Flemish Block to take part, even though the party had clearly won the election. Viewed in the context of 1991, it was evident that the king rejected out of hand any party which so openly promoted the cause of separatism. He never received a Block delegation as long as he lived.

Even so, given the current state of affairs, there was little that Boudewijn could do to avoid accepting Jean-Luc Dehaene as the new prime minister: the man (at least according to the king) who had wanted to go "too far" in 1988. Boudewijn continued to be ambivalent towards Dehaene. Earlier in 1991, he had already criticised him in his role as Minister of Transport, when Dehaene had said that Sabena – the national airline and one of Belgium's most distinctive national symbols – would eventually have to disappear. The king was not over-enthusiastic about the prospect of Dehaene as prime minister. During the formation negotiations, another minister commented: "Martens has ruined this country. He has made it untransparent, unattractive and ungovernable." To which Boudewijn replied in a flash: "Better Martens than Dehaene!"[141] But Dehaene it had to be: there was no real alternative.

On 29 September 1992, Premier Dehaene announced the signing of the St. Michiels Agreement. This was intended as the final act in the process of state reform which had started in 1970. The agreement was implemented in 1993 by a series of far-reaching amendments to the Constitution, article 1 of which would now read: "Belgium is a federal state, composed of different regions and communities."

- The constitutional reforms of 1993 introduced the direct election of representatives to the councils (parliaments) in the regions and communities. This gave the nation's political structure the hallmarks of a federal state. Nevertheless, Belgium lacked one of the main 'national' features of other federal countries: the existence of strong national political parties which were capable of operating across regional boundaries. As a result, the combination of purely regional parties engaged in a purely regional electoral process actually helped to speed up the disintegration of Belgium, rather than slow it down.

- The constitutional reforms of 1993 reallocated a number of person-related matters which had previously been dealt with by the French Community, i.e. the French-speaking communities in Wallonia and Brussels. These powers were now divided between them. This effectively cut the symbolic political link between the two communities. In 1988, the Flemings had merged their regional and community councils, but the French-speakers now opted to move in the opposite direction. Since 1993, language politics is the only link which continues to unite the Walloons and the French-speaking inhabitants of Brussels. Even so, this remains a powerful emotional bond, and one which is easily capable of mobilising voters.
- The constitutional reforms of 1993 also introduced an important extension of the powers of the regions and communities. They were now granted (at VU insistence) the right to conclude their own treaties and in principle the so-called 'residual powers' were also transferred to their authority. However, this last provision – enshrined in article 35 of the Constitution – still awaits practical implementation (an implementation which must be agreed via a special majority law). The regions and communities were also granted a certain degree of 'constitutional' autonomy, which offered them the possibility of creating their own institutional arrangements in certain fields of activity. This was a first step towards a future Flemish constitution – a natural development in any truly federal system.

These reforms seemed to confirm King Boudewijn's fear that Dehaene would "go too far". Under the pressure of circumstances, the new premier had introduced a series of constitutional measures of which the king had been critical in the past, most notably the question of treaty rights and the transfer of the residual powers. Perhaps the final insult was the official introduction of the term 'regional government' in place of 'regional executive'.

Be that as it may, Boudewijn now considered that the process of state reform was at an end. It irritated him that Premier Dehaene refused to confirm this in public. Worse still, a number of other politicians were openly contradicting the king's standpoint. In an interview given to the *La Libre Belgique* newspaper on 11 January 1993, the new Flemish minister-president Luc Van den Brande of the CVP, said that as far as he was concerned the St. Michiels Agreement was simply another step along the road to a confederal state. In a confederation there is no longer any balance between the regions and the centre, but rather a loose collaboration between autonomous and independent regional states, which agree on a consensus basis the measures which they wish to pursue jointly. History also suggests that confederations are often stepping stones on the way to full independence.

This was all too much for the king, who 'invited' CVP chairman Herman Van Rompuy and Van den Brande to the palace, where they were given a right royal dressing down. In retrospect, this was a mistake, since most Flemings reacted negatively to the king's intervention. They were quick to point out that the Walloon Moureaux had not been treated in this same high-handed fashion in 1991, when he dropped his "institutional atom bomb". Boudewijn's actions once again compromised his position in Flanders and increased the likelihood of further regional escalation.

Such escalation was not long in coming. In the Flemish newspaper *De Morgen* the socialist Norbert De Batselier stated on 18 March 1993: "In a number of areas – and here I follow the personal position taken by Luc Van den Brande – a spontaneous tendency will show that further adjustments [to the process of constitutional reform] are still necessary. This applies, for example, in the field of social insurance. If disproportional transfers [from Flanders to Wallonia] are not stopped, it will be necessary to devolve child benefit and health care to the regional communities. At my suggestion, the Flemish Socialist Party central office has accepted nine new elements for possible federalisation, as well as the distinction between replacement and supplementary incomes."

A similar change of tone was also evident amongst the Flemish liberals, and the Christian-democrats confirmed their earlier position on 1 May 1993, when Van Rompuy threw his weight behind the section of the Flanders 2002 Manifesto which stated that the St. Michiels Agreement was part of a dynamic process. "Nothing should prevent us from pursuing the political debate on matters such as the regionalisation of social provisions; of economic and social policy; of scientific policy; of transport policy; and even of general legislative powers."

A few months later, King Boudewijn died suddenly and unexpectedly. In this manner, he was at least spared the sight of an increasingly radical CVP entering into an alliance with a new and even more militant Flemish national party: the N-VA (*Nieuw-Vlaamse Alliantie*, New Flemish Alliance).

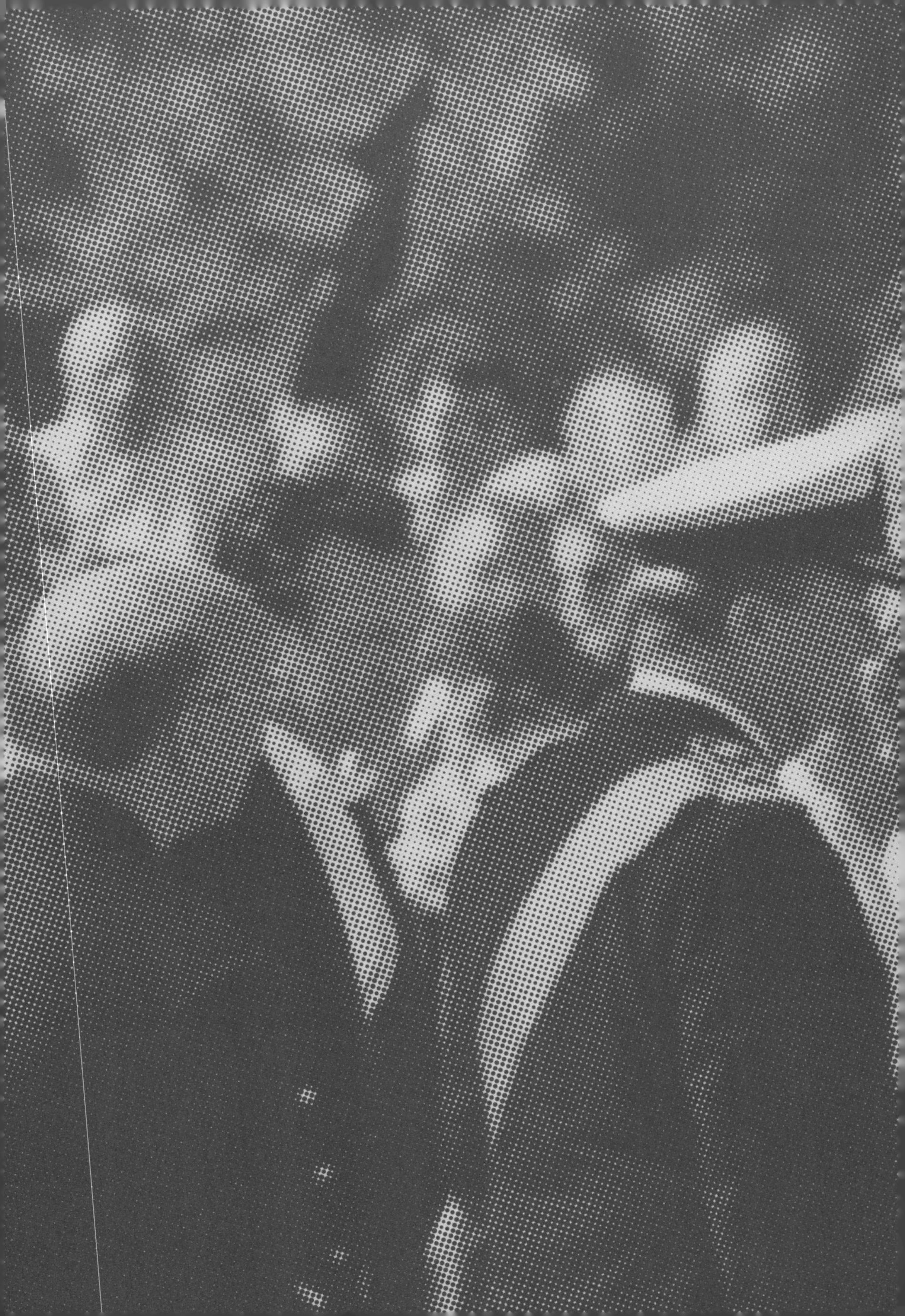

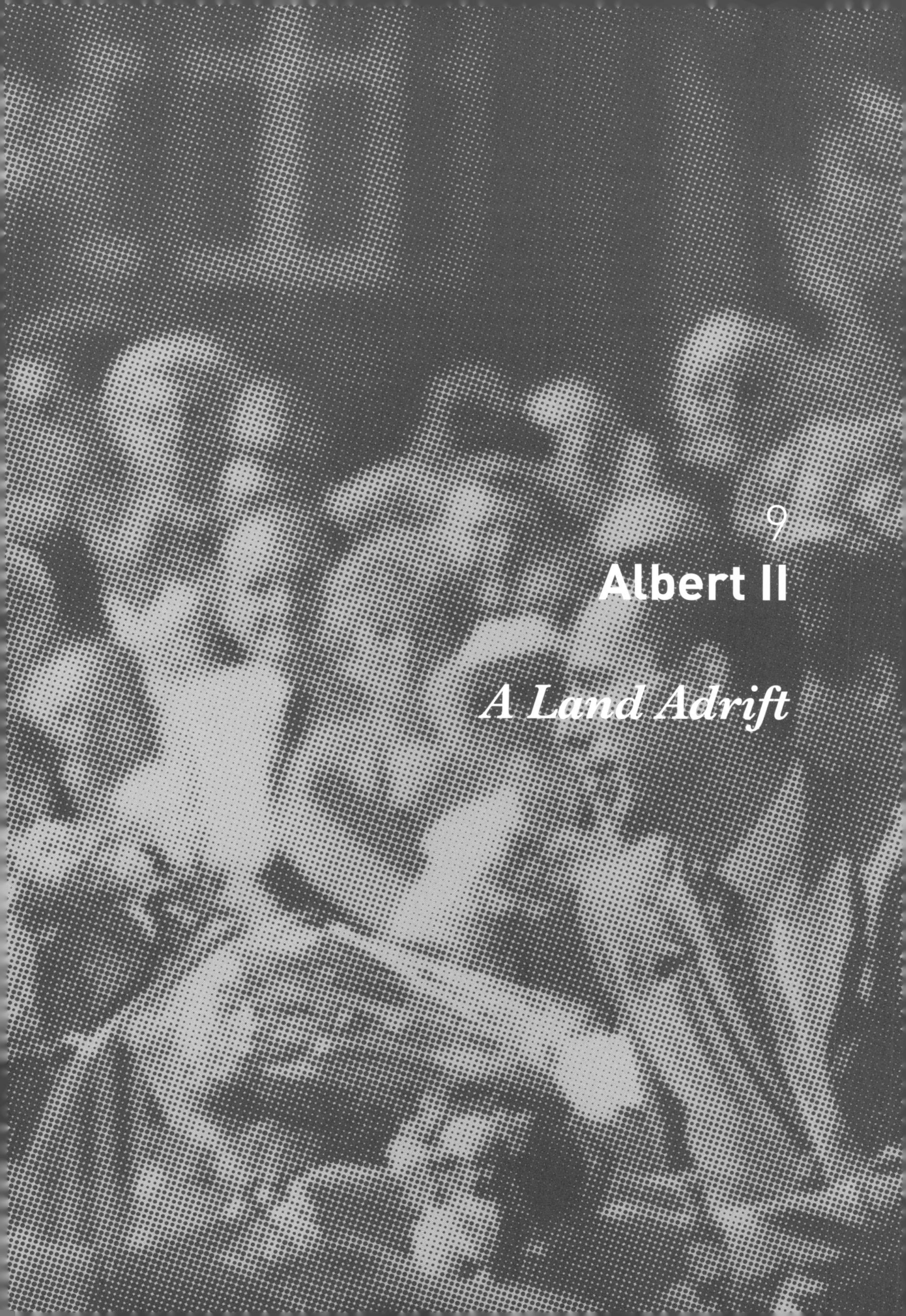

9

Albert II

A Land Adrift

9 Albert II

At the age of 59, King Albert II succeeded his deceased brother to the royal throne in August 1993. In his early speeches, he followed a similar line to Boudewijn, who in the last decade of his life had become more concerned with socially controversial themes such as poverty and human trafficking. The new king's first pronouncements on regional matters also bore a strong resemblance to the speeches of his brother, sometimes almost literally. In 1996 he said: "We must be on our guard and must reject categorically every form of open or concealed separatism". This is precisely what Boudewijn had said in his speech of 20 July 1988; he had repeated it – almost word for word – in 1992. Much the same was true of Albert's attitude towards the amnesty. In his New Year address to the nation's governments on 1 February 1994, he referred to the still lingering effects of the post-war prosecution of collaborators in the following terms. "Within the framework of inter-community pacification, we must look at measures which will help to bring about reconciliation between all the citizens of our nation." This was seen as a positive signal by the Flemish nationalists, but was moderate enough not to arouse the ire of the veterans and the Belgicists. In July 1990, the late king had made a similar appeal to mitigate the social and human consequences of the repression (an appeal which the governing coalition of the day included in its policy programme). The Dehaene government made no such commitment and in an interview with the *De Standaard* newspaper the premier suggested that this was a personal initiative on Albert's part.[142]

As time progressed, the regional elements in the king's addresses concentrated on unity in diversity, mutual understanding and harmony between different national groups, "with respect for all ethnic, religious and cultural identities."[143] On 11 July 1994, Albert attended the celebration of the Flemish national holiday in Bruges. He even hummed along to the Flemish national anthem: *De Vlaamse Leeuw* (The Flemish Lion). His presence at such an overtly 'Flemish' event was a source of irritation in Wallonia. The French-speaking press was quick to make a link with a confederational speech given by Minister-President Luc Van den Brande in Ronse a few days earlier. Albert's attendance in Bruges was seen as tacit approval of Van den Brande's message. Premier Dehaene was questioned closely in parliament on this point by Jean Gol, chairman of the Walloon liberals, and Olivier Maingain of the anti-Flemish FDF in Brussels, but he maintained that the decision to go to Bruges had been taken by the palace, and by the palace alone. As on other occasions, Prime Minister Dehaene did not seem too concerned to cover the king.

By this time, the regional question was once again gaining momentum. One reason for this was the re-emergence of the Flemish liberals as a potent political force. The liberals had been in opposition since 1988 and had used this time to change their name (from PVV to VLD – Flemish Liberals and Democrats) and to rethink their ideas. Much of this rethinking was done by the party's new leading light, Guy Verhofstadt. He concluded that the party's traditionally moderate stance on regional matters was

King Albert and Queen Paola in Brussels, 21 July 1996. Royalist supporters are wearing a message in Dutch, French and German, the three national languages: 'We want to stay Belgian'.

costing it votes, and that consequently the time had come to argue in favour of a far-reaching social and economic separation of Flanders and Wallonia. This *volte face* was accompanied by fierce attacks on the Walloon socialists, the Walloon unions and the Walloon employers' federation. In this way, Verhofstadt pushed the liberals further along the road to regional radicalism than they had ever been pushed before. But they were being pushed willingly: the 1998 VLD congress approved Verhofstadt's ideas enthusiastically, albeit in a slightly watered-down form.

In March 1999, during the run-up to a new general election, the Flemish parliament approved five new resolutions which set out the guidelines for a further major reform of the state structure. These resolutions were not only approved by the three main traditional parties – the liberals, the socialists and the Christian-democrats – but also by the more radical People's Union (*Volksunie*). VU support was important, since in the eyes of public opinion and the political mainstream it served as an indicator of the radicalism of the new proposals. But what exactly was being proposed? The new resolutions foresaw a bilateral state structure for Flanders and Wallonia, with a different status for Brussels and the German-speaking community. They also recommended a far-reaching fiscal autonomy. In the years since 1999, frequent reference has been made by Flemish politicians to these resolutions, which now occupy a mythical place in the collective past which the Flemish people have constructed for their region.

The general election of June 1999 saw the liberals return to the national government for the first time since 1988. As a result, the Christian-democrats – both Flemish and Walloon – retired to the opposition benches. During the period 2000-2003, Verhofstadt's liberal-socialist coalition worked on a new agreement for the further settlement of the regional question. This was the so-called Lambermont agreement. The regions were to be given a number of new – and, above all, symbolic – powers, such as limited rights to levy some taxes (road tax, television licenses, etc.). Agriculture and foreign trade were to be regionalised, in whole or in part. But perhaps the most important element of the agreement was the transfer of additional financial resources from the national treasury to the regions and communities. A finance law of 1988 had already introduced a new system for the redistribution of state funding, spread over a period of 11 years, whereby the regions would all receive more money from the federal state. The Lambermont agreement took this process a stage further. As a result, the regions received almost half of all state funding. However, it transpired that after these transfers had been made, the national government no longer had sufficient funds to meet its own – highly expensive – commitments in fields such as social insurance and health care. To make matters worse, during periods of high conjuncture the regions –

particularly Flanders – were able to generate huge budget surpluses, while the national treasury was slipping deeper into debt. This is still one of the biggest stumbling blocks to further state reforms. The national government has no cash to fund them and none of the regions are prepared to see their income cut through an amendment of the finance laws.

While these developments were taking place, the Flemish Christian-democrats were going through their own period in the political wilderness. Like the liberals in opposition before them, they decided to change their name: from CVP (*Christelijke Volkspartij*, Christian People's Party) to CD&V (*Christendemocratisch en Vlaams* – Christian-democrat and Flemish). Like the Flemish liberals, they also radicalised their ideas. At the CD&V foundation congress in 2001 there was open mention for the very first time of 'confederalism'. This represented a breakthrough for the more militant wing of the party inspired by the Minister-President of Flanders, Luc Van den Brande, who was also closely involved in the drafting of the famous five resolutions of March 1999. Since the CD&V congress in 2001, confederalism has become a new credo in Flanders. Confederate states are fundamentally different from federal states. Confederate states are independent states, which agree voluntarily to pursue certain common aims, such as foreign policy, defence, monetary policy, etc. If they no longer wish to pursue these aims, the agreement simply stops and the states become independent again, free to take their own individual action. However, the 'termination' of this 'agreement' is both technically and practically impossible in Belgium, since the country is moving in the opposite direction to what one would usually expect in a confederate situation: in Belgium, the desire for confederation is not the product of independent states moving closer to each other, but of a disintegrating unitary state whose regions are seeking to move further apart. As a result – and notwithstanding the regionalisation of the past 50 years – many powers are still organised by the national state across regional borders, in a manner that would be very difficult to untangle. The situation is complicated further by the existence of the bilingual Brussels community. What would happen to the nation's capital if the nation no longer exists? Moreover, most of the Flemish political parties (with the exception of the openly separatist *Vlaams Belang* - Flemish Interest Party, the successor to the old *Vlaams Blok* (Flemish Block), which was condemned in the Belgian courts for racial hatred) are at pains to stress that it is *not* their intention to end the solidarity between Flanders and Wallonia: they simply want this solidarity to be based on clear, objective and transparent criteria. This is a curious kind of confederalism.

    It means that the existing federal system must continue to work, which in turn implies a need to moderate more extreme 'nationalist' demands. Nevertheless, in February 2004 CD&V concluded an electoral alliance – a cartel – with the Flemish nationalist N-VA (*Nieuw-Vlaamse Alliantie* or New Flemish Alliance). The N-VA is the most important of the new parties which resulted from the collapse of the VU

(*Volksunie*) during the 1990s. The N-VA's position on separatism is deliberately ambiguous. The party's stated aim is an independent Flanders as a member state of a modern European Union, but in contrast to *Vlaams Belang* the N-VA does not openly preach the cause of separatism. Chairman Bart De Wever says that he simply expects the unitary Belgian state to dissolve gradually, "like a fizzy tablet in a glass of water", and that consequently his party's policy must be based on this likelihood.

The strength of this 'pragmatic nationalism' rests in the fact that many other Flemish politicians also believe that Belgium is likely to disappear in the medium or long term – but they dare not say it. In this sense, the N-VA has become a mouthpiece for a policy which many people tacitly support but which – for the time being – they prefer not to express too forcefully. This explains why the alliance between the 'moderate' CD&V and the 'radical' N-VA is regarded as a 'normal' development in the political landscape of Flanders. It also explains why the cartel won a staggering 26.1% of votes during the regional elections of 2004, a trend which was continued during the 2007 elections (with the share of the vote rising to 29.6%). In 2008, the cartel eventually fell apart, but after the regional elections in 2009 CD&V once again opted for the N-VA as a partner in the new coalition for the Flemish government.

The aftermath of the elections of 2004 witnessed another institutional change of importance, which was implicit in the state reforms of 1993. For the first time, coalitions were developed at regional level which were different in composition from the coalitions at national level. The national Verhofstadt II government, formed in 2003, was a coalition of liberals and socialists, with the Christian-democrats and the nationalist parties in opposition. But the Flemish government which came to power in 2004 was dominated by CD&V and the nationalist N-VA. It was much the same story in Wallonia. There the liberal MR was in opposition, whereas it formed an important element in Verhofstadt's federal coalition. This type of asymmetry is not unusual in federal states, but there is a crucial difference in the Belgian scenario – the lack of national political parties, which are able to transcend regional sentiment and regional divergence.

A good example of the difficulties which this can cause was seen in the DHL affair. The DHL transport company operated night-time flights out of Zaventem international airport. Given the location of Zaventem on the outskirts of Brussels, this meant that DHL flights passed over the territory of three different regions: Brussels, Flanders and Wallonia. The problems started when it was decided to reduce noise levels in the interests of the people living near the airport. Noise pollution is a regional competency, not a federal one. Consequently, there were three different noise thresholds from which to choose. The resulting dispute (it would be difficult to call them negotiations) was viewed by the three regional governments from a purely regional (and mainly electoral) perspective. This attitude resulted in total deadlock. To make matters worse, the Flemish parties were categorically opposed to any 're-federalisation' of the regional powers relating to noise levels, even though this offered a potential answer to the problem. For the first time in its history, Belgium was faced with an institutional crisis for which there was no solution. DHL drew some logical conclusions of its own and transferred its centre of European operations from Brussels to Germany, costing the Belgian economy thousands of jobs and millions of euros in revenue.

Similar problems were encountered with the electoral reforms of December 2002. The purpose of these reforms was to replace the existing electoral districts, which were based on the boundaries of the 'old' administrative *arrondissements*, with larger electoral districts based on the 'new' provincial boundaries which had been created by the regional reforms of the past 40 years. Unfortunately, there was one electoral district which (for historical reasons) straddled the borders of two different provinces – and two different regions. This was the electoral district of Brussels-Halle-Vilvoorde (known as 'BHV'), part of which was in Flemish Brabant and part of which was in Brussels-19. How was this anomalous district to be treated? How should its various municipalities be integrated into the new provincial voting system? Once again, it proved impossible for the politicians to reach an acceptable compromise. As a result the old electoral district continued to exist, in contravention of the new law. On 26 May 2003, the Constitutional Court ruled that this situation was illegal, since it resulted in the unequal treatment of voters in BHV. Consequently, the court instructed that the situation must be regularised within a period of four years – or that the law must be changed. This effectively meant that if the government wished to pursue its policy of provincial electoral districts, then BHV would need to be split. Halle-Vilvoorde could be attached to Leuven, as part of the Flemish Brabant electoral district, with the remaining towns and villages in Brussels-19 being included in the Brussels Capital City electoral district. In reality, matters were not quite so simple. French-speaking politicians in Brussels-19 were faced with the prospect of losing tens of thousands of (not necessarily French-speaking) votes in the 35 Flemish municipalities of Halle-Vilvoorde. And so they refused to compromise. For the second time in as many years, the Belgian state was painfully confronted with its own institutional limitations. BHV remained unsolved.

The escalation of events in both the DHL and the BHV dossiers took place against the background of yet another new radicalisation of regional standpoints. This regional radicalisation was officially endorsed by the governing Flemish liberal VLD at its party congress in November 2002, and was becoming increasingly prominent in the public statements of the party's leading figures, who now included a number of former members of the nationalist *Volksunie*. The liberals approved the following radical text at their congress, many elements of which would have been unthinkable just a decade earlier (my italics):

"The VLD wants better governance for Flanders, which can only be achieved through greater autonomy. *The centre of gravity must be switched towards the regions*, which must agree on the competencies to be left at national level. Flanders must have the necessary powers to deal with *public health, child benefit, employment policy* and *mobility policy*. Each institutional level must be granted *full fiscal autonomy* in order to cover its own expenditure. Matters which can be decided at a lower level should not be referred to a higher level. *Solidarity can never mean that the contributing party ultimately ends up with fewer resources than the receiving party.*" [144]

The same congress also agreed that the role of the king should be reduced to purely ceremonial matters or to matters of protocol.

It would be incorrect to assert that these policies were popular with all liberals, but there was nevertheless a clear consensus in favour of 'confederation', thanks largely to the insistence of *Jong VLD*, the youth wing.

King Albert II no doubt watched these developments with growing concern, particularly the arrival of the N-VA in the regional Flemish government as the partner of CD&V. In his Christmas address to the nation in 2005, the king referred to "a separatism which is rejected by the vast majority of our fellow citizens." In his New Year address to parliament he went even further. The answer to the nation's problems "lays not in turning inwards on ourselves, nor in the development of a species of sub-nationalism, nor in an open or disguised separatism." The Belgian political world regarded this statement as a thinly veiled criticism of CD&V and its cartel with the N-VA. After all, nobody could deny that the N-VA is indeed a supporter of disguised separatism. However, the cartel and its coalition partners had no intention of taking this criticism lying down. The Flemish Minister of Culture, Bert Anciaux, called the king's comments stupid and unfortunate, and Minister-President Yves Leterme dismissed the royal intervention in sharp terms.

King Albert's position was, of course, a difficult one. In the modern nation state the monarchy is, above all, a unifying factor. However, this is no longer the case in Belgium. Since the First World War, the Flemish nationalists have been largely anti-monarchist and after 1970 a number of other incidents led to an even greater decline in royalist feeling. In particular, King Boudewijn caused considerable ill-will through his approach to Voeren and the amnesty question.

Albert II tried to redress this negative balance by adopting a more cautious approach, but this was reckoning without the 'performance' of his son, Prince Philip, the heir to the throne. In 1999, the prince married a Walloon countess, Mathilde d'Udekem d'Acoz. This 'romantic' marriage to a charming and beautiful young woman certainly increased the popularity of the monarchy and of Prince Philip in Wallonia, much as the Swedish Princess Astrid had done for Leopold III in Flanders during the 1930s. For a short period after his marriage, even the Flemish press gave the prince some extra credit, but this soon changed. Much more than his father, Philip liked to portray himself as the guardian of Belgian unity. Unfortunately, he was (and is) not very good at it. His somewhat formal manner, combined with an imperfect knowledge of the Dutch language, led to a number of satirical and critical articles in the Flemish papers.

Prince Philip gives a speech following the award of an honorary doctorate at the Catholic University of Leuven, February 2002.

This was much less the case in Wallonia, where respect for the royal family (even in press circles) is that much greater.

This difference in approach reflects a growing difference in public opinion between Wallonia and Flanders, and is yet another symptom of how – and how far – the regions are growing apart. When the Catholic University of Leuven decided to award Prince Philip an honorary doctorate, this led to comments in Flanders which would have been unthinkable in Wallonia. Even so, Philip's poor reputation in Flanders is not simply based on scurrilous gossip and slander. It is undeniable that he occasionally makes ill-advised statements which are difficult to reconcile with the constitutional position of the monarch. For example, during a trade mission to China in December 2004, he told the reporter of a popular weekly magazine: "In our land there are people and parties, such as the Flemish Block, who are against Belgium, who want to destroy the country. These people will have to deal with me, and make no mistake: I can be really tough when I need to be. They won't just walk all over me!"[145] The prince was also rash enough to ask the reporter to publish these comments – which of course he did.

The publication caused uproar. No member of the royal family had ever made such a radical political statement on the subject of the regional question, except perhaps Leopold III in his Political Testament. The monarchy must be neutral, must stand above party politics. This means that the king – and, by extension, the crown prince – must not express their own personal opinions in public. The matter was discussed in the government, where the comments were far from complimentary. "If Philip thinks that he is Belgium's saviour, then Belgium really is finished," joked the chairman of the Flemish socialists. The cabinet decided that it was necessary to issue the prince with a mild reprimand, which Premier Verhofstadt did in a carefully-worded statement: "Although I can understand how the prince might feel little sympathy for parties which are in favour of splitting the country, his comments are not in keeping with his present and, above all, with his future constitutional role in our land. This role requires discretion and restraint as far as public statements are concerned, particularly with regard to political parties, even if those parties do not indeed have the future interests of our country at heart." [146]

Regrettably, similar problems occurred during a trade mission to South Africa in March 2006, resulting in the prince being given a new battering in the Flemish press, to which he reacted in his now typical manner.

Perhaps not surprisingly, this made him more popular in Wallonia. Viewed from a Belgian perspective, this is a disturbing development. The role of the monarchy is to hold the nation together. Unfortunately, the current heir to the throne seems to act as a catalyst for ever-increasing anti-monarchist feeling in Flanders, which is closely linked to the region's growing alienation from Belgium. In contrast, there is a corresponding increase in pro-royalist feeling in Wallonia, which is closely linked to that region's fear for the further splitting of the nation. This means that the monarchy is currently associated with just one side of the Belgian debate – the French-speaking side. This is undermining the royal family's position as an impartial institution which must stand above party (and regional) politics. The effects of this changing situation are already being felt. Since the introduction of the new municipality law in Flanders – one of the consequences of the Lambermont agreement – local councillors are no longer required to swear an oath of allegiance to the king. More symbolically significant, in a number of town halls in Flanders the 'traditional' photographs of the king and queen have been removed…

These events formed the backdrop to the landslide victory of the CD&V and N-VA cartel in the general election of June 2007. Yves Leterme – the former minister-president of Flanders – won a massive 800,000 personal votes and King Albert II had little option but to accept him as *formateur* for the new national administration. Leterme is a representative of the confederal wing of CD&V, which has steadily been gaining the upper hand in the party since 2001. In fact, the 2007 election result was a triumph for radicalism *tout court*. The cartel polled 1,230,000 votes (29.6% of the votes cast in Flanders). The separatist Flemish Interest Party (*Vlaams Belang*) was still good for 800,000 votes. Even the new (ephemeral) party *Lijst Dedecker* started by Jean-Marie Dedecker – a confirmed confederalist – managed to persuade 230,000 voters. Add to this the 790,000 votes polled by the liberal VLD, which has also been flirting with confederalism in recent years, and the inescapable conclusion is that more than

King Albert greets Minister Yves Leterme during the swearing-in ceremony for the Verhofstadt-III administration, 21 December 2007.

three-quarters of the Flemish electorate voted for a party which favours the further disintegration of the federal Belgian state.

The cartel of CD&V and N-VA felt that the results of the June 2007 election legitimised their demands for further far-reaching state reform. However, the two parties were unable to deliver what they had promised, because they were opposed by a united French-speaking front which refused point-blank to consider any meaningful reform proposals. This resulted in a failure to form a new national administration in the aftermath of the election. This undesirable situation – a democratic land without a government – persisted until the end of 2008. A new federal government finally took office at the beginning of 2009, but it, too, failed to force the required breakthrough in the field of state reform. Consequently, the government resigned in April 2010.

This stalemate was largely a consequence of an important change of course made by the French-speaking socialists, the PS. In the past, the PS had played an important contributory role in helping to push through state reform in socio-economic fields. In this respect, the party could almost be described as an 'ally' of the Flemish Movement, and it was certainly the trendsetting party as far as the reform process in Wallonia was concerned (in much the same manner that the Christian-democrats were the trendsetting party in Flanders). In the summer of 2007, it became apparent for the first time that the PS was now adopting a fundamentally different approach to the question of state reform. The Walloon socialists felt the same weight of mass public opinion as Yves Leterme – but in Wallonia this opinion was strongly *against* further institutional reform. Since 1991, the southern part of the country has been gradually awakening to the fact that Belgium may not remain a federalist state for ever. This has created a certain degree of fear in Wallonia, and fear is an excellent breeding ground for conservatism. As the leading political party in the region, the PS now reflected this conservatism in its dealings with Flanders at the negotiating table. In this respect, the fake television report of December 2006 about a unilateral Flemish declaration of independence was crucial in helping to shape Walloon consciousness. Confirmation of these doubts, if any were needed, came on the evening of 10 June 2007: the sight of a victorious Yves Leterme (CD&V) and Bart De Wever (N-VA), surrounded by their flag-waving supporters and singing the Flemish national anthem, was deeply disturbing to the French-speaking community in a way that few Flemings can understand.

From the point of view of the French-speaking political family, the reform of the federal state had been completed by the Lambermont agreements of 2000-2003. In one sense, they were correct, since further reforms would see a move away from the existing federalist state structure towards greater regional autonomy. This is a development which they fear – and perhaps with good reason. Wallonia is already much poorer than Flanders, and this evolution could effectively mean the loss of Flemish subsidies for Walloon deficits. As a result, all the French-speaking parties – PS, MR, Ecolo, CDH, FDF, etc. – are unwilling to compromise on what for them is a 'life-and-death' issue. As with DHL and BHV, Belgium is faced with a new national deadlock from which no escape seems possible. The Flemings want further state reform and the Walloons are determined less or more not to let them have it.

In this respect, the next great trail of strength between the regions was the national election of June 2010. The regional elections held in June 2009 had already suggested that there had been no decrease in radicalism, certainly at the Flemish level. The 2010 election emphasised more clearly than ever before the extent to which the country had become polarised into opposing camps. In Flanders, the N-VA polled 28.5% of the votes (cf. the combined total of 29.6% for the CD&V – N-VA cartel in the 2007 election). Most of the other parties (with the exception of the Greens) scored badly – including CD&V. In Wallonia, the PS attracted an impressive 37.6% of the votes, an increase of 7.9% in comparison with 2007. This result meant that the parties at the two extremes of the political spectrum were condemned to negotiate with each other, with the almost impossible objective of reaching further agreement on comprehensive state reform.

And so the merry-go-round continues. Where will it all lead? Does Belgium really have a future? Is the end of the nation in sight?

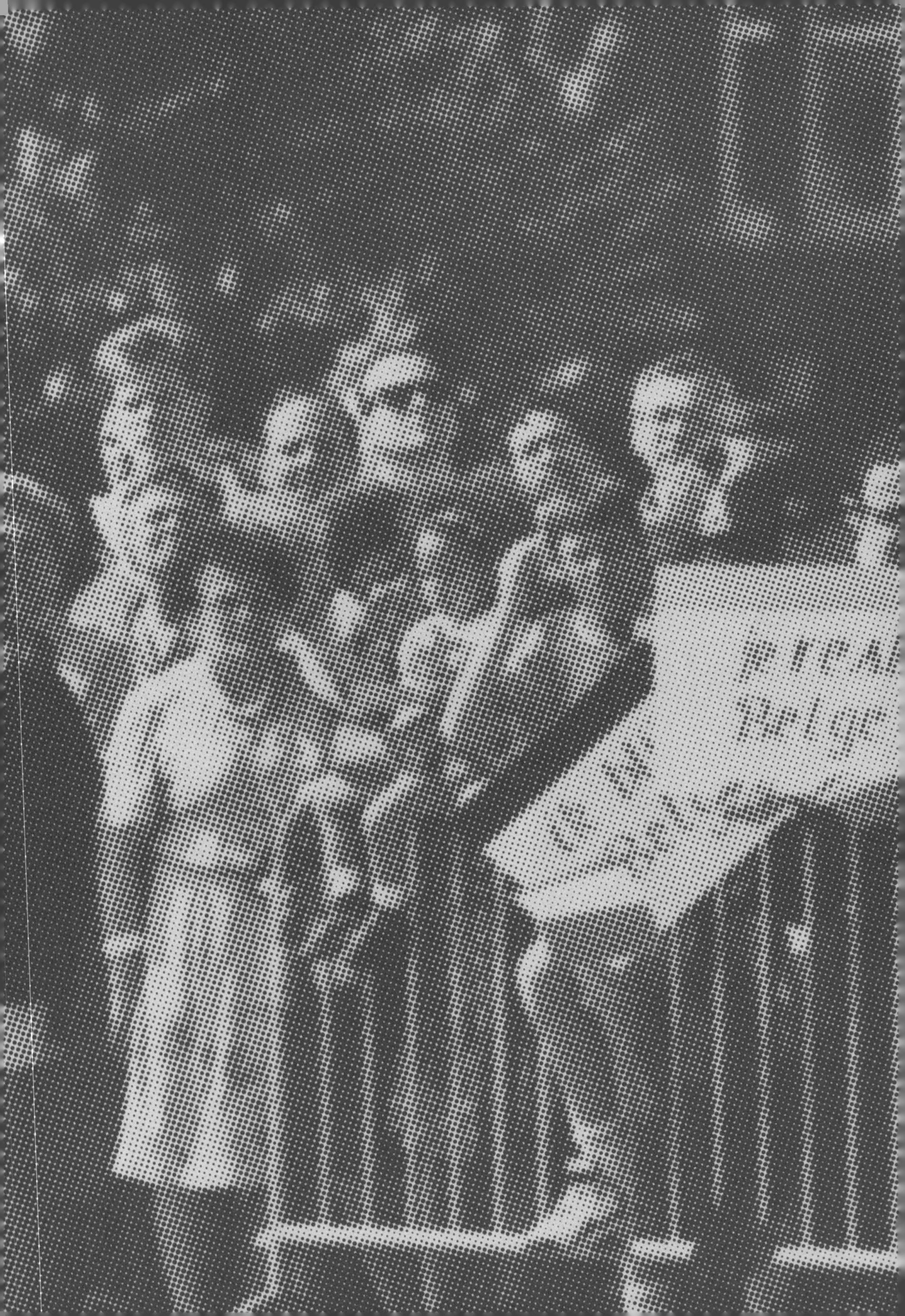

Conclusion and diagnosis

Belgium 1831-1893

In 1830 Belgium broke away from The Netherlands, to become an independent nation in its own right. The constitution of 1831 gave the new country a parliamentary monarchy which was 'modern' for its time. The king was responsible to his ministers, who in turn were responsible to a sovereign and nationally elected parliament. The state was conceived as a centralised, unitary whole: policy was drawn up by the national government, which had to work with the national legislature. Belgium was ruled from Brussels.

At this stage, the concepts of 'Flanders' and 'Wallonia' as political entities did not exist. However, the increasing use of the French language by a small, bilingual elite in the local administration of the towns and villages in Flanders after 1831 quickly provoked a counter-reaction in the shape of the so-called Flemish Movement, which made its first appearance in the 1840s. King Leopold I (1831-1865) was a supporter of this movement. This was related to his personal vision of Belgium as a neutral counterweight in the European balance of power. The preservation of the Dutch language in Flanders allowed Belgium to distance itself from France, potentially one of the country's most dangerous neighbours, certainly after 1848. Moreover, the new Flemish Movement was closely linked with Catholicism, which was particularly strong in Flanders, and the king saw the Catholic Church as one of the most important unifying factors in his kingdom. These views were largely the result of Leopold's German upbringing, which meant that the Francophile culture of the Belgian ruling class was alien to him. This would not necessarily be the case with his successors.

Leopold I not only gave his support to the 'literary' Flemish Movement of the early 1840s, but after 1848 he repeatedly (and explicitly) encouraged the movement's fledgling political wing, which wanted new laws to protect the Flemish language. The purpose of these laws would be to introduce a Dutch-speaking administration alongside the existing French-speaking one. Leopold was concerned by the increasing 'Frenchification' of Flanders. In this respect, he was probably responsible for the setting up of the Grievances Commission in 1856. Yet at this stage it all signified very little, and certainly posed no threat to the existence of the nation. The Flemish Movement was little more than a language pressure group, with no strong regional or national following.

The central premise of this book is that the unitary Belgian state could only continue to exist within the political framework created by the tax-based electoral system introduced by the constitution of 1831. This system placed voting power in the hands of the wealthy, largely French-speaking minority, and ensured that the 'electoral divide' within the country coincided with the 'language divide'. The emotional belief in 'Belgium' as a nation had been experienced by its people since long before the French Revolution of 1789. Indeed, this proto-nationalism was an unmistakable pre-condition for the Belgian Revolution of 1830. But it was only after the creation of an independent Belgium that the transformation from romantic national concept to modern nation state became possible, based on the active form of nationalism which was sweeping through Europe at this time. The institutional 'Frenchification' of Flanders after 1831 should be seen within this context, since it reflected the widely held view that a nation state should be governed in a single language.

Unfortunately, the constitution of 1831 also ensured that Belgium would be saddled with the fundamental weaknesses inherent in a democratic system. This system gives groupings smaller than the 'national' grouping the right to pursue their own interests. If these smaller groupings consider their objectives to be absolute, so that no compromise is possible, this must inevitably damage the minimal levels of cohesion which are essential for the existence of the nation state. The Indian political scientist Sunil Khilnani has described this as "the self-devouring capacity of modern democratic politics".[147] These 'non-national' interests create fault lines running through the population, which can lead to a kind of civil war within the national structure. This conflict often takes the form of a class struggle, or a social conflict, or a religious dispute. When the fault lines are territorial, it can even result in the division of the country into separate regions.

In the years immediately following 1830 there was in Belgium a political system without parties, which sought to achieve the broadest possible national consensus. However, the fault lines soon began to appear. These were created and encouraged by the majority electoral system, which effectively gave power to just two broad bands of opinion, which finally were reflected in two political parties: the Catholics and the liberals. The gap between these two parties became ever wider, particularly after 1857. Leopold I was concerned by this growing ideological conflict and feared that it might even lead to the break-up of his kingdom. In 1864, he wrote to his daughter Charlotte, the Empress of Mexico: "How can a little country like ours continue to exist, if it is always divided against itself? This is a serious problem".[148]

In the long run, it seemed as if the king would be proved right, since the ideological divide began to correspond more and more closely to the language divide. For example, in 1884 every member of parliament elected to the Lower House from Flanders was a Catholic. Nevertheless, we must be careful not to overstate the case. The liberal-Catholic split was not yet wholly synonymous with the Flanders-Wallonia split. Flanders might be uniformly Catholic, but Wallonia returned both Catholics *and* liberals to the national parliament.

Be this as it may, the 'language question' (as it was coming to be known) was rapidly gathering momentum. The language legislation passed in the years after 1873 encouraged the development of a Walloon Movement, which was even more radical than its Flemish counterpart. The new movement was particularly irritated by the fact that the new laws prevented the appointment of Walloon administrators in Flanders,

King Leopold II, circa 1905.

unless they were able to use Dutch. They regarded this as preferential treatment for the largely bilingual Flemings, whose knowledge of French meant that they were still able to 'steal' administrative positions in Wallonia. The Walloon Movement remained relatively small (it was largely confined to the administrative elite). Even so, the new king Leopold II felt that the Flemings must take due account of Walloon grievances, "if serious difficulties are to be avoided". In contrast to his father, Leopold I, the second Leopold never showed any public interest in the cause of Flemish language rights. In fact, his only serious 'contribution' was to ensure that his nephews, Boudewijn and Albert, were taught Dutch.

Yet once again, it is important to keep a proper sense of perspective. As the 19th century drew to a close, relations between Flanders and Wallonia were far from untroubled, but the tax-based election system ensured that these troubles could be kept within reasonable bounds. However, all this was about to change.

The power of institutional change: 1893 as a critical juncture

In terms of the reference framework worked out by the Czech professor Miroslaw Hroch, the Flemish nationalists of the 1830s and 1840s were in the first phase of a transition from a 'non-dominant ethnic group' to a 'national movement'. This phase involves the development of a specifically regional culture, based on the use of the local language in education, administration and economic life. The second phase of the transformation requires the creation of a complete social structure, including the development of a new regional elite. The final phase, according to Hroch, sees the granting of equal civil rights and a degree of autonomous self-government. In our opinion, the second phase of this transformation in Flanders was made possible by the reform of the electoral system in 1893.

This analysis places great importance on the role of crucial 'turning-points'– critical junctures – which can push a society or a people in a new direction. This, in turn, is based on the concept of 'path dependency', as developed and applied in the fields of social and economic science. Historians are sometimes reluctant to use this concept, since it can lead to an exaggeratedly 'determinist' analysis. Chance certainly plays a large part in the manner in which historical processes develop, and the complex actions of complex humans in complex situations are frequently influenced by unpredictable and irrational behaviour. Nevertheless, it is also true – as the American political scientist James Mahoney has pointed out – that collective events can sometimes be steered by what he calls "institutional or structural patterns that endure over time".[149] The key characteristic of these patterns is that they are irreversible: there must be no way back. Applying this to the history of Belgium, it is possible to argue that the democratisation of the franchise in 1893 gave the Flemish masses the necessary political power to collectively achieve the far-reaching advancement of the Dutch language in the social, economic and cultural life of Flanders. And it was an opportunity which the Flemish people – working 'bottom up' – seized with both hands.

Nationalism is a collective process. For this reason, the analysis in this book – following, amongst others, the social anthropologist Ernest Gellner – emphasises the importance of collective nationalist emotion. [150] This is the instinctive, irrational element in the nationalist equation. A chronological assessment of the growth of 'national awareness' in Flanders and Wallonia allows us to study this emotional component at close range. One of the most striking conclusions is that this emotional 'group happening' is constantly subjected to the renewing influence of its own internal dynamic, so that the emotional element becomes stronger and stronger, almost in a kind of permanent escalation. Viewed within the group-related context of a union or movement, this means that after 1893 the Flemish nationalists began a process of collective agitation, with ever increasing conviction and ever increasing success. An internal dynamic can indeed play a major role in the strengthening of particular institutional and structural patterns. The German social psychologist Harald Welzer used precisely this concept of an internal dynamic for his analysis of genocidal group behaviour. [151] He described genocide as a process of social transformation which is continuously 're-dynamised' from within. This process has a clear structure with a beginning, a middle and an end, each phase of which contains recurring ritual elements. With his study of this extreme form of nationalist behaviour, Welzer has offered a socio-psychological framework which can also be applied in the investigation of more 'ordinary' nationalist phenomena. This framework relates to the workings of a shared collective emotion, whose exponents, explicitly or not, continually stimulate each other to ever new heights of emotion, so that this internal dynamism, with its related nationalist symbols and rituals, eventually results in an ever more extreme position. Within the group, the emotional, irrational component of nationalism is experienced as being 'normal', but this is not how others see it. This explains why the modern-day Flemish nationalists understand each other perfectly – and why they are viewed with suspicion and incomprehension in other parts of Belgium and Europe.

Belgium is an interesting case study for an examination of path dependency and irreversibility in an institutional decision-making process. The language issue gradually began to rouse the Flemish masses during the 19th century, while simultaneously alarming the ruling Walloon elite. This basic development formed the foundations for everything which followed after 1893, when the mass of non French-speaking Flemings were empowered for the first time. The crucial turning point was the electoral reform of 1893, which for the first time empowered the mass of non-French-speaking Flemings. These masses gradually came to realise that the language barrier was also a social and economic barrier, and so they became convinced that all French influences had to be removed from their region. The political breakthrough of 1893 was therefore accompanied by a transformation in the nature of the Flemish Movement, from a 'soft', almost romantic attachment to the local Dutch language, into a 'hard', nationalist, political struggle for a monolingual Flanders. The first crack in the Belgian national fabric had appeared.

This crack only widened gradually, as a result of a succession of different events. The analysis in this book places an emphasis on the new institutional patterns which came into being after 1893. These patterns should be interpreted literally, since they relate to laws, to clear institutional options. This was a consequence of the democratised parliament. Legislation in both national languages (following the Equality Law of 1898) and the fact that Dutch was now spoken in parliament meant that the Walloons no longer had to take account of non-French-speakers in Flanders alone, but also at the national political level. The Equality Law also implied that in some circumstances Walloon administrators and magistrats might be required to use Dutch, and that in theory even ministers might in theory need to become bilingual. This was a rude awakening for the non-Dutch-speaking elites in Wallonia and Brussels.

These institutional changes in the organisation of the Belgian state soon developed a strong internal dynamic. The changes encountered strong Walloon resistance and a complete lack of understanding, with claims that it was impossible (and unthinkable) that the French-speaking elite should be required to speak "the inferior peasant dialect" spoken in Flanders. This principled rejection of the Dutch language provoked an equally principled response in Flanders: "If we have to learn French, you have to learn Dutch". This was the standard Flemish argument, although it was an argument which overlooked the very real shortcomings of the Dutch tongue as it was spoken and taught in Flanders. On the other side of the linguistic fence, the French-speakers used these shortcomings as an easy excuse for doing nothing to overcome their anti-Dutch aversion. Both sides were locked into a cycle of emotional nationalist reaction, in which there was no place for a pragmatic approach which might have created a liveable compromise for both communities – and for the future of the Belgian nation.

After 1893, government ministers quickly came to realise that the enfranchisement of millions of relatively uneducated Flemings had saddled the Belgian nation with a serious nationality problem. However, until 1914 it was possible to govern the country on the basis of a homogenous Catholic majority, based largely on electoral support from Flanders. Concerned for national unity, these Catholic administrations (probably with the blessing of King Leopold II) sought to achieve bilingualism throughout the country. In other words, they sided with the 'principled' Flemish position. Between 1897 and 1910 there were numerous legislative efforts to introduce a form of bilingualism in administrative matters, but with very little success.

Moreover, the governments' efforts became increasingly half-hearted, so that in reality their position was moving closer and closer to that of the French-speakers. People in Flanders had expected bilingualism, but all they got was a reinforcement of mono-lingualism in Wallonia.

And so the snowball of the language question rolled further and further downhill. If Wallonia rejected bilingualism and its intellectual elite refused to learn Dutch, then the Flemish were determined to respond by demanding administrative mono-lingualism for their own region, based on the principle of equality. But the situation was not equal, because the Flemish establishment was already bilingual, whereas the Walloon establishment was not. Flanders was not a single language region in its entirety, but this is what the Flemish Movement now wanted to achieve. By pursuing their new 'invented' identity of an exclusively Flemish Flanders, a section of the Flemish elite developed a new and more virulent stain of nationalism. Even though many of them could speak French, they now insisted on speaking in Dutch, even in their dealings with monolingual Walloons. To many people this just seemed like provocation, and it only served to strengthen the anger and incomprehension felt on the French-speaking side of the language frontier.

The democratisation of the franchise in 1893 not only caused an institutional earthquake in political circles, but also resulted in the linking of the language question to broader socio-economic problems, at least in Flanders. In other words, the electoral reforms generated not only institutional patterns in the strict sense of the word, but also broader structural patterns. This unleashed a series of powerful mechanisms, in which the importance of the invented concept of a 'national' Flanders can again be seen. Flanders was not a unified economic region, any more than Wallonia was. Nevertheless, the Flemish nationalists began to develop an economic analysis based largely on this assumption, using language rather than economic reality as their basic criteria. As a result, they created a picture of an economically homogeneous Flanders, with global statistics and structural models which (as might be expected) were very different from Wallonia. This picture was distorted (for example, there were much larger inter-regional variations within Flanders) but nobody really stopped to look closely at the details. The image was self-confirmatory and encouraged a policy which sought to develop Flanders as a homogenous economic region. A similar over-simplification was evident in Wallonia, where there was constant reference to "the region's decline", whereas in reality this was only confined to the provinces of Hainault and Liege.

The Flemish economic demands for an own territory "for the benefit of our own people", to use the words of the Flemish politician Lodewijk De Raet, were experienced by the Walloons as an extreme form of provocation. This feeling of alienation was further strengthened by the electoral dominance of the more populous Flanders, which resulted in an unbroken series of Catholic administrations between 1884 and

1914, with an essentially conservative programme. The result was the nation's first nationalist crisis in 1912. The Walloon establishment reacted to the developments of the previous 28 years by formulating their own strain of radical Walloon nationalism, which found expression in a growing demand for federal status. Inevitably, this inspired a similar response in Flanders and the years 1912-1914 witnessed the growth of a more militant form of nationalism north of the language frontier. All the necessary preconditions were now in place for the eventual disintegration of the Belgian state. All that was necessary was for someone or something to light the fuse. That 'something' was the First World War, which broke out in August 1914.

The pre-war context made possible what now followed. The First World War was not a critical juncture, but the German *Flamenpolitik* was a new, nation-related factor, which led to a sharp radicalisation of existing regional polarities. In the occupied territories, the Germans (logically enough in the circumstances) tried to detach Flemish public opinion from Belgium by pursuing a language and cultural policy favourable to Flanders. Even in the small unoccupied part of the country behind the River IJzer, the language question caused dissent amongst the ranks of the Belgian army, particularly with Flemish soldiers who were required to follow orders given in French. Once again, the approach to such issues was highly emotional, whereby nationalist language and nationalist forms were used to give expression to more important underlying social issues, which in the case of the army were often class-related. Be this as it may, the long-term consequences of the *Flamenpolitik* were considerable. It led to the further radicalisation of Flemish demands after 1918 and in the 1930s even pushed a section of the Flemish Movement in the direction of anti-parliamentarianism and fascism. It also introduced a strong anti-royalist element into Flemish national thinking.

King Albert I and the Flemish Movement

Between 1909 and 1923 the king maintained a very consistent line on 'regional' matters. He shared the widely-held opinion that Flanders was bilingual (even though this was only true of a small minority of the population in the higher echelons of society). Like his royal predecessors, he saw this as a differentiating element for the outside world and as a unifying element for his own people. Perhaps the limited bilingualism in Flanders was also a contributory factor in Albert's defence of regional recruiting for the army in 1913, a measure which could only be popular with the Flemings. Albert further supported the extension of monolingual Dutch education in Flanders, including university level. At the same time, the king taught and hoped that the Flemish establishment would never fully abandon the French language, and all that it stood for. To reinforce this hope, he insisted that the right to follow French-language education in Flanders from secondary level onwards must be maintained.

Conclusion and diagnosis

Inauguration du monument Frédéric de Mérode — Berchem le 27 Août 1905
L'arrivée de S. A. R. le Prince Albert à la gare de Berchem

Inauguration du monument Frédéric de Mérode — *Les sociétés défilant devant le monument*
Berchem le 27 Août 1905

Belgian nationalism grew rapidly during the 19th century, reaching its high water mark during the anniversary celebrations held to commemorate 75 years of the Belgian state in 1905. From this date onwards, Belgian national unity went into a gradual decline, from which it has never recovered. The unveiling of a statue to a 'Fallen Warrior of the 1830 Revolution' at Berchem (near Antwerp, in Flanders) in 1905 was clearly both a 'popular' and a 'Belgian' event. This type of postcard was largely intended to amuse the bilingual Flemish elite, which explains the use of the French language.

Although Albert believed in bilingualism as a kind of national cement, he did not share the view held in Flemish circles that Wallonia should also be made bilingual. He was afraid of the reaction that this might provoke. In this sense, he saw the Walloon Movement as an even bigger threat to national unity than the Flemish Movement. This is understandable within the context of his time, since the French still had dreams of annexing Wallonia, and some Walloons still had dreams of being annexed. In contrast, there was no such possibility of Flanders ever being reunited with The Netherlands. Even today, the Elysee Palace keeps a watchful eye on public opinion in Wallonia.

During the war of 1914-18, it was logical that the government-in-exile in Le Havre should take whatever measures it could to counteract pro-Flemish, 'activist' collaboration in the occupied territories. The king and his ministers were in agreement that Flemish agitation within the ranks of the army fighting on the River IJzer also needed to be stamped out. Even so, Albert expected that the limited bilingual provisions of the 1913 Army Act would now be implemented. As a pragmatic man, Albert was wise enough to see that the Flemings needed to be given something more. However, the king had little room for manoeuvre. Any support for the Flemish Movement would displease his French ally, would arouse the fury of his ministers and would irritate the largely French-speaking officer corps, which formed the backbone of his army. He personally opposed the idea of splitting the army into separate Flemish and Walloon regiments, but he did toy with the idea of separate units at company level. However, his ministerial council refused to consider the proposal. For the lack of anything more positive, between 1916 and 1918 the king constantly argued in favour of a conciliatory royal declaration about the future of Flanders after the war. Yet even this limited measure was rejected by his ministers, notwithstanding the fact that several of them were pro-Flemish Catholics.

The main stumbling block – certainly within the context of the war years – continued to be the inability of a large majority of the army cadre to speak Dutch. This was a situation which could only be improved in time (probably decades), following further pro-Dutch reforms of the education system. But how was the general staff to deal with the more immediate problem of an arrogant and superior French-speaking officer class, which was having difficulty in maintaining control over its increasingly rebellious Flemish soldiery, for whom it had little sympathy and no understanding? There was only one answer: repression of the Flemings.

The activities of the Military Security Service from July 1917 onwards are a dark chapter in the history of the Flemish national movement. These activities were characterised by prejudice and arbitrariness. Even so, most Flemish historians tend to forget that the purpose of these often misguided measures was to restore discipline in an army that was fighting a war of national survival. During the summer of 1916 and again in December 1917 there had been several demonstrations against the general staff and the general conduct of the war. Given the recent Russian example of where this type of behaviour might eventually lead, it is hardly surprising that the army top reacted with an iron fist rather than a velvet glove. It is to Albert's credit that he refused to allow the execution of any of his soldiers, even though this was common practice in the British and French armies, and notwithstanding the fact that it was actually suggested by his own ministers in March 1918.

This summary of King Albert's actions up to 1918 suggests that he was conciliatory onwards to the Flemish Movement. Nevertheless, after the Armistice he remained deaf to Flemish complaints about the socially discriminating prominence of the French language in Flemish life. In Albert's vision of Flanders, there was still place for two separate linguistic pillars, a French one and a Dutch one. This being said, he continued to be a pragmatist and was always prepared to adjust his views to changing circumstances. This was already apparent during the war years. For example, in February 1918 he again suggested to the general staff that the moment was ripe to experiment with "the bilingual system", although he pointed out that "there is still time to take more extreme measures", if the experiment should not have the desired effect. This realistic approach was also evident in the king's post-war approach to language matters. The Flemish question was not a major issue in the years immediately after the war. In part, this was due to an anti-Flemish backlash, caused by the unpatriotic behaviour of the small group of Flemish collaborators during the war years. This, too, was yet another area in which Albert demonstrated his practical, common sense approach. He was not in favour of principled declarations of the question of an amnesty for convicted 'activists', but he was happy to tolerate each case being considered individually.

By 1923, the king finally realised that his dream of a bilingual Flanders was no longer feasible. He now understood that the full introduction of Dutch as the sole language in the University of Ghent – a key Flemish demand – was only a matter of time. In keeping with his pragmatic political philosophy, he once again changed course and threw his weight behind the measure. Much the same was true of his approach towards Van Cauwelaert's Minimum Programme, which he supported when the Flemish question again became a 'live' issue at the end of the 1920s. In concrete terms, bilingual Flemings were no longer to have the right to insist on the use of French for administrative matters within their own region. Nevertheless, Albert continued to believe in the value of bilingualism as a form of national cement, and so he now switched his attention to bilingualism in the so-called central administrations. This was a policy which was guaranteed to irritate the Walloons more than the Flemings, and which failed completely.

During the 1930s, the Minimum Programme was finally achieved, first with the concurrence of King Albert and later with the concurrence of his successor, King Leopold III. In this manner, the traditional politicians hoped to hold the nation together. However, they were mistaken. On the contrary, the strategy of forcing through controversial aspects of language legislation on the strength of the Flemish majority (there were more Flemings and therefore they had more seats in parliament) had the potential to divide the two regions more deeply than ever before. The Walloons were indignant at such measures.

Flanders was also concerned with its own economic agenda during the inter-war period, and considered the possibility of "seizing the Belgian market place". Crucial to these considerations was a socio-economic analysis based on the idealised notions of 'Flanders 'and 'Wallonia' (on both sides of the language frontier) – an analysis which often ignored the real similarities and differences between the two regions. In this respect, the Walloon approach towards the child benefit issue in the 1930s reveals much about the growing strength of both Walloon and Flemish nationalism. The arguments on this sensitive matter completely overlooked the fact that there were areas in Flanders with relatively few children and areas in Wallonia with relatively many children. However, these statistics did not conform to the stereotypical image that both regions wished to portray – and so they were quietly glossed over.

The nationalist 'construction' of Flanders and Wallonia, based on a regionalised interpretation of both an emotional language conflict and a more reasoned socio-economic agenda, widened the cracks in the Belgian national fabric still further. This found expression in Flanders in a new blossoming of cultural life, centred around 'Flemish' organisations and associations, and also in a radicalisation of election results, which suggested that the people were now starting to push the politicians in a direction they did not want to go – or, at least, not that quickly. In this sense, the democratisation of 1893 continued to make itself felt. In keeping with this trend, in 1936 the Catholic party showed its first tentative support for greater federalism, and the socialist BWP was also moving in the same direction. A division of national political parties along linguistic lines could only help to speed up the disintegration of Belgium. However, the Second World War and its aftermath ensured that this issue was frozen for more than two decades.

The end of the "narrow-minded and egotistical minority": a balance

During the 1930s, Belgium finally removed all remaining administrative privileges (even in the field of education) for the French-speakers in Flanders – meaning the bilingual Flemings. Even the Walloon politicians had voted for these measures, in order to secure and maintain language homogeny in their own region. King Leopold III also had few problems with this monolingual policy, since in his Political Testament, written in the spring of 1944, he described the French-speaking Flemings as "a narrow-minded and egotistical minority, which refused to speak the language or participate in the life of the people." This somewhat un-kingly statement contained a good deal of truth. King Leopold accused this minority of using their knowledge of French to create a closed world in which the language barrier was used as an instrument to perpetuate social and economic inequality. The history of Europe in the 20th century offers numerous examples of social movements which finally managed to sweep away class barriers, resulting in new social measures to implement reforms in the field of social insurance, compulsory education, health care, etc. The pace of these changes varied from country to country, but the democratisation of the franchise was often the motive force. This was also the case in Belgium. The electoral reforms empowered the mass of ordinary Flemish people, and ensured the ultimate demise of the linguistic apartheid system in Flanders. In this respect, the removal of the language barrier made a significant contribution to the development of a welfare state which was available to all, allowing a fairer redistribution of material wealth and a better general level of education.

It goes without saying that individuals still had the right to speak French in Flanders, but in the years between 1929 and 1935 the politicians of both linguistic communities decided that the bilingual Flemings should no longer benefit from legal protection by the state. This consensus was only achieved gradually, largely because the majority of Flemish politicians came from this small bilingual milieu. This bilingualism was deep-rooted and was the basis for a French-Flemish culture of considerable sophistication. Would the removal of language facilities – particularly in the field of education – not put an end to this culture? Would it not weaken the position of the Flemings in the wider world, especially in the colonies? It was thinking of this kind which explains why support for Van Cauwelaert was initially so limited, even within his own pro-Flemish Catholic party. It also explains the vacillating attitude of Camille Huysmans and the Flemish socialists.

Nevertheless, the decision to remove the language facilities was taken and the old French culture in Flanders has indeed become a thing of the past. With a few notable exceptions, the French now spoken by the very few remaining bilingual Flemings is characterised by a lack of vocabulary and a flexible approach to grammar and syntax. It is also noticeable how frequently they switch from French to Dutch and back again. Their language is undergoing an evolution similar to that of the Arab or Turkish immigrants of the second or third generation in Belgium, and their limited social milieu only survives thanks to a subtle policy of marital alliances. This separate community comes together at parties or in social organisations. As we have already seen, the number of bilingual Flemings was never large, probably reaching a high point during the period 1900-1930. Nowadays, interest and numbers are declining each year, and within the next half century the last remnants of the bilingual community will probably have ceased to exist.

This evolution implies a certain loss. For most young Flemings, French is now a 'foreign' language, with which they are only moderately familiar. Their feeling for the Roman-French cultural world is non-existent: they have a much greater affinity for the cultural environment of the new world language – English. Moreover, Flanders has developed its own high quality regional culture which has close links with The Netherlands, creating a cultural network of some 20 million Dutch speakers. This will guarantee the existence of the Dutch language in Europe for many years to come.

The power of an institutional choice: 1970

Events during and after the Second World War had a major impact on the internal dynamic of the nationalist question. The growing Walloon identity which had already been evident before the war was further strengthened by the conflict. The existence of Wallonia as a single uniform socio-economic reality was emphasised ever more strongly after 1944, even though this concept was as questionable as the similar belief in a Flemish socio-economic entity. In this sense, for example, the socialist (and industrialised) provinces of Hainault and Liege have little in common with the rest of Wallonia. But as so often in nationalist scenarios, perception was more important than reality. People *believed* that there were two clearly identifiable socio-economic regions and the resulting analyses based on this perspective put a heavy strain on the unitary Belgian state.

In Flanders, the widespread collaboration of the war years led to the temporary abandonment of further demands for greater linguistic and cultural autonomy. However, at the end of the 1960s the language question reappeared on the political agenda with renewed vigour, as a consequence of the Voeren issue and the problems surrounding the French-speaking university in the Flemish city of Leuven. One of the first 'victims' of the renewed conflict was the national Christian-democratic party, which split into two regional wings – the CVP and the PSC – in 1969. Some commentators have suggested that this split occurred more by accident than by design, and it is certainly true that the two new parties maintained close informal contacts for many years to come. The same cannot be said, however, of the unitary socialist party, which was split in 1978. In this instance, the split was engineered by the French-speaking PS militants in Hainault and Liege, because they believed that the unitary Belgian state was no longer in a position to solve Wallonia's regional economic problems. The Flemish socialists were effectively cut adrift, faced with the discouraging prospect of being a left wing party in an essentially centre-right Flanders.

These 'desperado' tactics were only made possible by a new critical juncture in Belgian political history: the state reforms of 1970, with their notorious article 107 quater. These reforms pushed Belgium into granting a degree of autonomous regional self-government. In particular, the 'blank letter' of article 107 quater unintentionally constituted an open invitation to think seriously about further reform in the socio-economic sphere, under the motto of "everything is possible". This inevitably resulted in a further radicalisation of public opinion in both Flanders and Wallonia, and the 1974 election gave the new Tindemans administration a clear mandate to move in the direction of autonomous regions. In this manner, Belgium was launched on an irreversible process of the devolution of power away from the central government.

Belgium: an institutional *perpetuum mobile*

Throughout the past 80 years there must have been many occasions when governments and monarchs alike hoped that a single, all-embracing round of reform would solve the regional question once and for all. Perhaps the first such wish was expressed by Premier Jaspar as long ago as 1928, when he called together the nation's press after the 'shocking' Borms election, to announce that he intended to solve the nationality problem in its entirety before the new elections. As we now know, it was destined to take a little longer. King Boudewijn must have nurtured similar hopes, but from 1960 onwards he too was forced to accept the reality that a reform of the state structure, with less emphasis on its unitary aspects, was inevitable. Like Albert I before him, he was no longer able to close his eyes to the clearly expressed wishes of his people. This, of course, is the fate of all kings in a constitutional monarchy. It was certainly the fate of the Belgian kings during the 20th century. They were constantly required to push forward new institutional boundaries, often to the detriment of their own position or the position of their kingdom. King Boudewijn tried to draw the line at separatism and confederation, and a similar strategy has been pursued by Albert II. The few details which are available suggest that Boudewijn tried to steer or even force the process of state reform (between 1972-1980, and 1987-1988), in the expectation that the process could be completed. When he realised that this was not the case, he tried to apply the brake, but without success. The snowball continued to rumble downhill.

Has the Belgian monarchy had a significant impact on the regional question in broader terms? It is certainly true to say that on numerous occasions the impact of the monarchs' interventions was coloured by their inability to assess the strength of feeling aroused by the language question. During the inter-war years both Albert I and Leopold III believed that the Flemings would continue to learn French. This miscalculation probably explains why Albert, under the pressure of increasing Flemish radicalisation, changed course in the 1920s and eventually accepted that French language education in Flanders should no longer be supported by the state. If he had been able to see two or three generations into the future, when the full implications of this decision had become clear, he might have felt more strongly inclined to resist.

Having lost the education battle, King Albert next pinned his hopes on the preservation of bilingualism at director level in the central government departments.

His reasoning was that ambitious Walloons would make the effort to learn Dutch. Yet even if this had been true, it would only have affected a handful of administrators: hardly enough to form the strong 'national' cement that the king envisaged. As it was, the Walloon politicians rejected the idea of bilingualism for senior positions *a fortiori*: "Walloons cannot learn Dutch", they claimed, which meant that the Flemings would 'steal' all the best jobs. The Walloons stood firm and the king threatened to impose his royal veto. However, he eventually backed down, accepting a system of bilingual 'assistants', who would assist their monolingual colleagues. It made a mockery of the original proposal.

While it cannot be disputed that the monarchy has had some degree of political impact throughout the years and on occasion has even been able to influence the decision-making process (as in 1932 and 1988), the experience of Albert I with regard to the central administration tends to be the rule rather than the exception. The balance of power in a modern constitutional monarchy is such that it is always the king who has to give way. This is the price of democracy and, in Belgian terms, was an inevitable consequence of the electoral reforms of 1893. The king can advise his politicians, or warn them, or encourage them. He can exhort his people to be moderate, or to show solidarity, or to set a good example as citizens. But this is about all he can do. Even his role in the formation of new governments has been watered down to the point of irrelevance. Given the peculiarities of the Belgian situation, coalition forming has become a long and complex process. Moreover, it is a process in which the monarch is not actively involved, other than to appoint a *formateur* (who is usually the most obvious candidate for prime minister). It is therefore unthinkable that the king should try to influence the formation process after it has been completed, and usually with so much difficulty.

It should also be remembered that the monarchy was seriously weakened by the 'Royal Question' and the abdication of Leopold III in 1950. His son, King Boudewijn, had to be content with asking many, many questions of his ministers, but he was unable to prevent the progress of state reform, which was made more urgent by the growing radicalisation of election results. Typical in this respect are the state reforms of 1993. The disturbing election results of 1991 eventually led to the formation of a new administration under Jean-Luc Dehaene, a politician who Boudewijn disliked and distrusted, because of his inclinations towards a further devolution of powers to the regions. Dehaene confirmed the king's fears by pushing through a programme of reforms to which Boudewijn had already objected in 1988 under the previous Martens administration, including the regionalisation of the right to conclude treaties and the possibility to transfer elements of the so-called residual powers to the regions and communities. Dehaene even withdrew the earlier concession which had been made to the royal court, namely that the term 'government' should not be used when referring to the regional executives. Boudewijn had originally been converted to 'federalism' in

Conclusion and diagnosis

the 1970s, when he believed it offered a permanent solution to his nation's problems. He now saw with alarm that his government was moving beyond federalism, in the direction of what is now known in Belgium as 'confederalism' – but by this stage he was powerless to do anything about it.

Yet Boudewijn was by no means alone in being deceived on this point. Like many others, he saw state reform as a finite process, which, like many others, he believed had come to an end by the beginning of the 1990s. But this was not the case. The reforms of 1970-1993 had laid the basis for a new federal state structure, but many regional grievances remained unaddressed. This meant that further adjustments were necessary, if long-term political stability was to be restored. Perhaps fortunately, Boudewijn did not live to see the implementation of the Lambermont agreement during the period 2000-2003, which further divided up the remaining national competencies, including foreign trade. He would probably have been even more distressed by the declaration made by the new Flemish Christian-democrat party – CD&V – at its foundation conference in Kortrijk in 2001, which stated explicitly that Belgium must become a confederal state. Pursuing this line of thinking to its logical conclusion, in 2004 the CD&V entered into an electoral alliance with the Flemish nationalist N-VA. This cartel won a crushing victory in the national election of June 2007, on a programme which promised further far-reaching state reform.

King Boudewijn stands 'eye to eye' with King Leopold II during a visit to the National Bank of Belgium, Brussels, 7 June 1991.

However, the extent of this democratic victory and the level of radicalism on which it was based so alarmed the French-speaking parties that they formed a united front, which rejected point-blank any further amendment of the state structure. The resulting stalemate led to the single most important and longest institutional crisis since the formation of the nation in 1830. The inability of the politicians – divided along exclusively regional lines – to agree a programme of reform brought the political process in Belgium to a virtual standstill. King Albert II also failed to make any real impact on the situation. The institutional paralysis was complete.

It took almost 200 days to form even an interim administration, which was appointed for a period of just three months. This was little more than a temporary expedient, designed to allow a number of 'current' matters to be urgently dealt with. This interim cabinet was under the leadership of Guy Verhofstadt, the former liberal prime minister. Yet even this emergency administration had its own plans for further state reforms. In one sense, Verhofstadt III tried to turn the clock back: its proposals saw a further devolution of competencies to the regions, but combined with a strengthening of the federal government at the centre (much as King Boudewijn had recommended to Premier Martens in 1988). In an interview with the *De Standaard* newspaper on 9 January 2008, Prime Minister Verhofstadt was asked whether or not his proposals – which had already been shot down in flames by the French-speaking parties – represented the final stage in the reform of state. Verhofstadt replied: "The final agreement must lay the basis for one or two decades of calm. The previous state reforms also resulted in 20 years of relative stability. But a federal state is never complete. Even in Germany and Canada, new discussions flare up every 20 years or so. Federal countries are always on the lookout for new and more efficient means of organisation."

Perhaps there is something to be said for this. How stable are 'normal' countries? France is currently being ruled by its Fifth Republic in just over 200 years. Germany's reunification was only achieved as recently as 1989. Spanish union is as fragile as majolica porcelain and even Great Britain is coming apart at the seams. By comparison, Belgium – with its constitution dating from 1831 – is one of the grand old dames of Europe. But this should not blind us to the fact that this particular old dame has severe institutional problems. Not surprisingly, the political leaders of Europe are watching with argus eyes the continuing developments in this small country, which is so central to the future of the European ideal. It is a situation which requires a diagnosis.

Belgium – a diagnosis

The organisation of the Belgian state contains a number of fundamental weaknesses, which make the entire national edifice unsound and act as a permanent source of destabilisation.

Conclusion and diagnosis

First of all, the 'idea' of Belgium as an 'invented nation' has been steadily losing ground in recent years, particularly in Flanders. As a result, it is becoming increasingly difficult to talk of a common Belgian frame of reference – there is no longer any sense of a shared national past. For most Flemings nowadays, Wallonia is a foreign country, no different from France (where most of them go on holiday each year). As a result, there is no longer a feeling of common national consciousness which is a precondition for the existence of any nation state. This being said, the comment made by Denise Van Dam in her doctoral thesis of 1990 is still correct: the Walloons are more attached to Flanders than the Flemings to Wallonia. [152]

Whatever the truth of this matter, it is indisputable that 'Belgian-ness' belongs to a national past which is unlikely ever to return. The Flemings are Flemish, and the Walloons are Walloon. In recent years both regions have come to specialise in identity-creating slogans and statements which seem specifically designed to alienate the other regional community. Consider, for example, the following statement made in 2007 by Joelle Milquet, the leader of the French-speaking Christian-democrats. "We have a cultural problem. The French-speakers are Latins. They are closer to France. It is almost as if we have a double identity, Belgian and French. Much more so than the Dutch-speakers, who are more closely related to Germanic culture." [153] To which she added that the problem created by this contradiction is "unsolvable". It is clearly a discouraging sign for the future of a multi-cultural Europe when leading Belgian politicians regard the gap between Flanders and Wallonia as unbridgeable. And yet the pronouncements on both sides of the linguistic divide continue to emphasise the extent to which the two regions have grown apart. In 2007, the French-speaking socialist vice-premier Laurette Onklinckx described the Flemings as "the fungus which rots the wood of the house from the inside" [154] In the same year, the Flemish Christian-democrat Yves Leterme compared the French-speaking RTBF radio station with *Milles Collines*, the radio station of the genocidal regime in Rwanda. On another occasion Leterme said that each Fleming was "carrying a rucksack filled with stones", meaning the Walloons.[155] The true irony of the Belgian situation is perhaps best appreciated if we remember that Leterme has a Walloon father and that Onkelinckx *père* was once a Flemish worker, who 'emigrated' to Wallonia.

The gradual disappearance of a common feeling of national identity is closely linked to a second key factor: namely, the fact that the media in Belgium are strictly divided into two autonomous linguistic entities – a French-speaking one and a Dutch-speaking one, each confined to its own region. A Fleming will almost never read a Walloon paper, and a Walloon will almost never watch the Flemish television news: exceptions are very rare. A neutral person examining the Flemish and Walloon press would probably conclude that he is looking at news reports from two different countries. In particular, both medias seem keen to concentrate on stereotypical images of themselves and each other, which serve to reinforce and perpetuate the differences between them. This, too, used to be different. In the years around 1970, the news bulletins on both the French and Dutch-speaking radio services were very similar. In this sense, the regionalisation of the national media culture reflects the regionalisation of the nation's political structures.

A third undermining feature, which is also interwoven with the other two, is the splitting of the national political parties. In every other federal country, national politics is based on federally structured political parties, operating across internal regional borders. This is no longer the case in Belgium – a fact which also explains why Belgium has more political parties than any other country in the European Union. The French and Dutch-speaking branches of the main political families – socialists, liberals and Christian-democrats – all have fundamental differences of opinion on many key issues. This hampers the formation of strong governments at national level, since it is difficult to agree an effective programme which can command the support of sufficient parties to form a majority in parliament. This is reflected in the increasing length of time which is now necessary to form a new administration. In this respect, the crisis following the June 2007 election has broken all records: it now seems likely to last until at least 2011. Moreover, the failed coalition negotiations since 2007 have had more in common with international discussions between rival sovereign states than with internal discussions between potential partners in government. These negotiations were also important for what they revealed about the declining institutional role of the king during the government-forming process. In February 2008, the *De Standaard* newspaper – one of Belgium's most influential daily journals – published a three-page article on this 'role', which it later expanded to create a short book. The indiscretions in this book – unprecedented from a constitutional point of view – made it clear that a number of politicians, particularly on the Flemish side, no longer felt a need to protect the king, even in the middle of a national crisis. Quite the contrary: they were happy to 'reveal all'. This, too, is symptomatic of the decline of a Belgium-oriented political culture. It comes as no surprise that there is now much more talk than ever before about reducing the powers of the king, in reality if not in law, to simple matters of protocol. In fact, in 2010 this was the only point on which the feuding Flemish and Walloon negotiators were actually able to agree, probably inspired by the prospect of Prince Philip ascending to the Royal throne in the foreseeable future.

The fourth undermining factor – once again in contrast to all other major federal states – is the limited number of component units in the Belgian model. It is a bipolar federal system with just two units: Flanders and Wallonia (the small German-speaking region traditionally follows the Wallonian line). Writing in 1971, Minister Leo Tindemans put his finger on the problem: "I have no – I repeat, no – prejudice against the idea of a federal system. If it would lead to the better organisation of our country, with fewer disputes and with no loss of prosperity, then we would be mad not to adopt it. But the greatest specialists in the world, many of whom I have consulted, all say that federalism with just two partners – the only kind of federalism which is acceptable to the Flemings – is a contradiction in terms. Federalism with two, they tell me, is not really federalism at all: it is the juxtaposition of two peoples who are moving in different directions." [156] These words proved to be prophetically accurate. The radically different profiles of Flanders and Wallonia mean that the two regions are constantly being compared with each other. This leads automatically to the conclusion that one region is 'stronger' than the other; or to put it in fiscal terms, that one region is financing the other. The financial transfers between Flanders and Wallonia are an annually recurring theme in the press, and one that has a profound effect on public opinion. A study by the National Bank in 2008 estimated that the transfer in favour of Wallonia amounts to some 5.8 billion euros per annum. Moreover, at least 5 billion euros of this negative balance is accounted for by higher fiscal receipts: Flanders is one of the richest regions in Europe, while Wallonia is considerably poorer. As far as expenditure is concerned, money is transferred to Wallonia in order to meet its higher unemployment benefit costs, whereas Flanders receives funding from Wallonia to cover its greater expenditure on pensions (since the average age in Flanders is significantly higher than in Wallonia). These transfers are nearly always discussed in global terms from the perspective of the Flanders-Wallonia divide. This trend is particularly evident in Flanders, where there is a widespread belief that the Flemings are 'paying' for the Walloons. Inter-regional transfers within Flanders tend to be glossed over, because they fail to conform to this stereotyped picture. Much the same is true of the various positive transfers from Wallonia to Flanders. In this respect, it is interesting to note that the National Bank study of 2008 predicted a rapid shrinking of the level of transfers out of Flanders, as a result of the continuing ageing of its population.

However, we can also approach our diagnostic problem from another angle: what are the factors that are still holding Belgium together?

The first factor is public opinion itself. Although Flanders and Wallonia are growing ever further apart, poll after poll continue to show that a clear majority are against separatism, even amongst the Flemings. But like most polls, the phrasing of the question is crucial. "Are you against separatism?" is a very different question to "Are you in favour of continuing financial transfers to Wallonia?" And the answers would be very different, too.

The second factor – in spite of everything - is the monarchy. Under King Albert II monarchist feeling is still strongest amongst the French-speakers, but there also seems to be a consensus in Flanders that the king should be retained. However, the monarchy has lost whatever influence it once had in the process of state reform. Its chief remaining function as a bulwark against separatism is simply 'being there'. Anti-royalist feeling is a clear part of the separatist movement and a key issue will be the performance of Crown Prince Philip, when he finally ascends to the throne. Will he have a positive impact on the consensus in Flanders?

Thirdly, there are still a number of key government departments which have preserved their 'national' status, thereby creating a unifying effect. But even these departments are coming under increasing 'regional' pressure. The most important of the national departments is undoubtedly Social Insurance. This department acts as a framework for the system of fiscal and financial solidarity in Belgium. However, the framework is slowly beginning to crack. There are two major problems. On the one hand, there is the huge scale of the transfers between Flanders and Wallonia. The current simplistic transfer debate being conducted in the Flemish media and by Flemish politicians is helping to create a political culture which regards the abandonment of this "one-sided charity" as both reasonable and desirable. On the other hand, there is an urgent need to control the spiralling overall cost of social insurance. This requires maximum optimisation of the available resources, but this is not easy given the very different socio-economic profiles of Flanders and Wallonia.

Similar problems also exist in other departments. In theory, Justice is perhaps the most national of all the national departments. But in practice, it is perfectly feasible to split the department along regional lines, as the example of several leading federal states clearly shows. There are growing calls in Flanders for a similar split, given the very differing approaches to issues such as penal policy and juvenile crime in the Dutch and French-speaking communities.

The trade unions are a fourth factor working in favour of unity. In contrast to the political parties, the most important unions have not been split along regional lines. Their position on further state reform tends to be contra, rather than pro or neutral, because they remain firmly attached to the principle of national solidarity, particularly in the field of social insurance. Their stance on this matter cannot be easily ignored by the politicians.

The fifth and final factor in the pro-Belgium cocktail is Brussels. If anything, Brussels is rather like a child in a marriage which has gone wrong: it does not make things right, but it helps to keep the partners together. In this respect, the Flemish Movement has shown – and continues to show – a good deal of goodwill towards Brussels and its special position. They have long turned a blind eye to the fact that the requirement for full bilingualism in Brussels-19 is still a problem in the police force, the hospitals and the town halls. They are also at pains not to over-emphasise the success of Dutch-language education in the capital in recent years, which is partly the result of the large numbers of poor foreigners in the French-speaking schools. This pragmatic, almost emotion-free Flemish approach towards Brussels is remarkably 'un-nationalist' and is in stark contrast to the Movement's approach towards Wallonia. Notwithstanding the growing numbers and growing influence of French-speakers in the Brussels agglomeration, political Flanders apparently does not want "to let Brussels go". The Flemish government, the Flemish parliament and most Flemish regional administrations are all based in the city. It is also worth noting that the Dutch-speakers in Brussels are institutionally well integrated into Flanders, in a manner which cannot be said for the French-speakers and Wallonia. The only thing which really holds French-speaking Brussels and Wallonia together is the language question, but this nevertheless continues to be a powerful and emotive bond. Nor should the importance of Brussels as a source of employment for Flanders be under-estimated. Hundreds of thousands of Flemings commute each day to the nation's capital, and its economic benefits are felt far beyond the borders of Brussels-19.

The important role played by Brussels in holding the Belgian state together once again became evident following the June 2010 elections. The polarisation resulting from this election was so great that the Flemish and Walloon negotiators were forced to seriously consider – perhaps for the very first time – the possible division of the country into two separate states. Realistically, this can only mean the break-away of Flanders from Wallonia and Brussels-19, who together would form a new political entity, which would be seen internationally as a continuation of the 'old' Belgium in a new form. However, when they stopped to think about the possible implications of such a development, many Flemings quickly came to the conclusion that Brussels is vital for the future of Flanders, particularly as an economic centre and a place of employment. In short, Flanders without Brussels would find it very hard to 'go it alone'.

In addition, there is also an important technical issue relating to social insurance in Brussels. The inhabitants of Brussels do not have a Flemish or Walloon sub-nationality. So what would happen to them if the nation splits? A social insurance status based on the language of the 'head of the household' seems unthinkable, since the operation of two parallel systems in the same city, offering radically different benefits, could only lead to uncontrollable social discontent. Might a separate social insurance system for Brussels alone offer a potential solution? Not really, since the agglomeration is not capable of financing such a system, and the idea of joint Flemish-Walloon 'guardianship' over such a system is equally unrealistic. A transfer of the city en bloc to Wallonia is likewise out of the question, since the region would also be unable to afford it. In short, any realistic division of the Belgian state would automatically lead to the impoverishment of Brussels. This in turn might lead to the very real possibility that the hundreds of thousands of poor immigrants who live in the capital – many of them from Muslim and African countries – would seek to move across the new 'border' into Flanders, placing a huge added burden on an economy which is already struggling to cope with a continuous influx of refugees from all over the world.

The bilingual Brussels agglomeration, with its 1.1 million inhabitants, is therefore the single largest stumbling block to a full partition of the Belgian state – a fact which the separatist minority in Flanders still seems keen to ignore. But if Brussels helps to keep Flanders and Wallonia together, it is nevertheless also a source of continued conflict. The Flemings might be prepared to show understanding for the situation in

Brussels-19, but it is a different matter in the Brussels 'rand'. Here reasoned behaviour is often hard to find. This is especially true with regard to the dispute surrounding the splitting of the Brussels-Halle-Vilvoorde electoral district. The long-standing BHV problem is often incomprehensible to outsiders, but in reality it is a continuation of the age-old language question, combined with a more modern battle for precious voters.

Much the same is true of the other linguistic problems in the 'rand', which are potentially even more difficult to solve than BHV. In this instance, the problems relate to the Flemish municipalities which border on the bilingual Brussels-19 agglomeration, many of which have been subject to increasing 'Frenchification' in recent years, as a result of the migration of French-speaking inhabitants from the capital. These French-speakers have full language facilities in six 'rand' municipalities: this means that they can obtain French documents at the town hall, that their children can be educated in French and that the street names in their locality are indicated in both languages. But this is no longer enough. They are granted all these benefits as an 'exception' and not as an absolute 'right'. And it is this 'exceptional' status which irritates them. In practical terms, the language problems in the 'rand' are almost insignificant, but this is not the point. What matters is the principle, not the practice. And on this particular matter of principle no compromise seems possible. In this sense, the 'rand' has replaced Voeren as the battleground on which Dutch-speakers and French-speakers from throughout Belgium fight out their deep-rooted regional antagonisms.

Similar problems also occur in the Flemish municipalities which share a common boundary with Brussels-19 and which have Dutch as their sole official administrative language. These municipalities have no 'right' to offer language facilities, but they are often confronted with French-speaking 'immigrants' from Brussels. In practice, however, these newcomers have a strong influence on the communities in which they live. They converse in French, they shop in French, they socialise in French. Perhaps even more crucially, their relative 'wealth' means that they are gradually forcing out the poorer, indigenous Flemish population (because their capital is pushing up house prices). Consequently, there is a real possibility that French-speakers will increasingly form a majority in these traditionally Dutch-speaking districts. In this respect, the language question in the 'rand' is similar to the language question on the IJzer front between 1914 and 1918: it also contains a strong social dimension. The key question is whether or not the principled, emotional and historically-coloured unwillingness of the French-speakers to accept the official local language – in this case, Dutch – is a reasonable and acceptable approach.

This, indeed, is the crux of the matter: how do you define the official language of a particular country or region? In our modern world, the efficiency of the state can be significantly increased if a country can be administered in a single language. The existence of a second administrative language automatically means that at senior hierarchical levels a knowledge of both languages is indispensable. In terms of its origins, the USA is also multi-national, but it has a single official language: English.

Of course, reasonable efforts have been made to assist the non-English-speakers (translation services in government buildings, bilingual street signs, etc.) but there is no formal 'right' to provide official documents in their own language. In this respect, the current situation in Belgium and Europe – with their important Turkish and Arabic-speaking minorities – is not dissimilar to that of the United States. The possibility of official administrative facilities for these 'immigrant' languages is unrealistic, unnecessary and undesirable. On the contrary, the learning of the national language by the newcomers is regarded as an essential aspect of their integration and social emancipation.

This being said, many municipal authorities in Flanders adopt a pragmatic approach to the multi-lingualism of their immigrant population, providing translators where necessary and translating basic government documents into a number of different languages. In the City of Antwerp, for example, the local council has arranged the use of translators in the municipal schools to facilitate organised contact between parents and teachers. However, this kind of 'tolerant' approach is more difficult to achieve around Brussels, in areas where the majority of the 'immigrants' are 'rich' French-speaking Belgians. Their situation is very different from that of immigrants from, say, Africa or Asia. They understand Dutch – the language is taught as a compulsory subject throughout the Belgian French-speaking education network – but they do not wish to use it. Instead, they wish the language of 'their' municipality to be changed to French, simply because they and large numbers of their fellow French-speakers have moved there. In other words, it is a principled, political demand which must be viewed within the framework of the regional conflict between Flanders and Wallonia.

Perhaps with this in mind, Flanders has still not ratified the 1995 European Framework Treaty for the Protection of National Minorities. The fear that it may give French-speakers new language rights, in order to force through the official use of French in Flanders, seems unfounded. French is already taught as a compulsory subject in all Flemish secondary schools. Similarly, Belgium has already accorded language rights to its historical linguistic minorities, by offering language facilities in the few 'mixed' regions along the age-old language frontier between Flanders and Wallonia. Flanders has even offered language facilities in six municipalities in the Brussels 'rand', notwithstanding all the problems which this has created. Moreover, it needs to be emphasised that these concessions were part of a national agreement negotiated in 1962-1963, as a result of which the French-speakers agreed to a permanent setting of the administrative-linguistic boundaries between Flanders, Wallonia and Brussels. In this sense, the recent influx of French-speakers into the 'rand' and other cities in Flemish Brabant is irrelevant. The boundaries between states cannot be continuously adjusted to reflect the movements of peoples. In these circumstances, it is the people who must adjust – and not the states, although the states must do all in their power to make the cultural and linguistic integration of 'immigrants' as easy as possible.

The end of Belgium? New critical junctures

State reform in Belgium is rather like a giant snowball, which continues to role unstoppably downhill. How is this unstable situation likely to develop, given the historically-charged internal dynamic of the nationality question?

A first scenario might involve the maintenance of the existing status-quo, with minimal adjustments to settle the current issues. This is the preferred option of the French-speaking community. From their perspective, the state reforms which took place between 1970 and 2000 represent a completed process. The main task is now to preserve the 'balance' which this process established between the regions and the federal government. Consequently, a further devolution of powers to the regions must be accompanied by a strengthening of the federal structure, so that this all-important balance is not lost. This essentially means a perpetuation of so-called unionist federalism.

Within the framework of these aims – balance and status quo – it has been suggested that the country's national and regional elections should take place simultaneously. This would reduce the frequency of inter-regional debate, but it would not prevent the formation of regionally-based coalitions. In recent generations, Flanders has always voted centre-right, while Wallonia has always voted centre-left. Simultaneous elections would do little to alter these traditional voting patterns, and these patterns are a core element in the differences between the two regions – and so they will remain.

It has also been suggested that certain regional powers should be re-federalised. Supporters of this option speak in terms of 'nation-forming' powers. In particular, they argue that the central level should be strengthened by the introduction of a new federal electoral district for the Lower House, which would elect 15 of the current 150 members of parliament. In reality, this is just a backstairs attempt to circumvent the regional differences which eventually led to the break-up of the old 'Belgian' party political system. National politicians instead of national parties? Could it really work? Would the 15 nationally elected MPs (9 Dutch-speaking and 6 French-speaking) really adopt a pro-Belgian line in inter regional disputes? Would they remain firm in the face of pressure from their own regional parties? And how would Flemish voters react when faced with the pro-Belgian (and therefore potentially pro-French) stance of their supposedly 'Flemish' representatives to the national parliament?

Given the institutional and historical weaknesses inherent in the Belgian system, the maintenance of the status quo is not a feasible option. The French-speakers are also coming to realise this, and in July 2009 even King Albert II appealed for further, far-reaching state reform. This was yet further confirmation that the monarchy needs to be pragmatic in its approach to what it sees as unavoidable political developments. For these developments are indeed unavoidable, a fact which is closely related to the underlying realities of the situation. In this respect, the institutional mechanisms contained within the so-called 'completed' state reforms of the period 1993-2000 appear in retrospect to constitute a new critical juncture. As a result of these reforms, it became possible to form different political coalitions at national and regional levels. This is what has happened in practice since 2004. Consequently, it is now possible for a party to be part of the government at national level, but to be in opposition at regional level – and vice versa. This means that parties which are coalition partners at one level may turn out to be each other's fiercest critics at the other level. The absence of overarching national political parties ensures that there is no central direction in national political life. This places the individual parties in a difficult situation: they need to decide which level of government is most important to them – the national or the regional. The tendency toward immobility at national government level in recent years has persuaded many parties to place their priority on the regional level. This combination of circumstances – no national parties and different coalitions at different government levels – helps to explain, for example, an incident which occurred during the interim Verhofstadt III federal administration in 2008. As a possible solution for the administration's budgetary difficulties, Budget Minister Leterme suggested that the regions might be prepared to take over a larger responsibility for the pensions of their own personnel. The Flemish government replied that it would not pay a eurocent, unless the federal government made firm commitments in respect of further state reforms. The stalemate seems almost complete.

In these circumstances, the most likely scenario is the further dismantling of the federal state and the creation of a new 'confederal' model *à la belge*. The biggest stumbling block in this respect is the remaining national departments and their financing. Economic analyses – including a report by the IMF in 2008 – show an institutional imbalance between the funding of central government and the funding of the regions. The regions can calmly continue to spend the money which the federal government is obliged to give them by law, whilst that same federal government is experiencing major problems to finance its own key national departments, such as Social Insurance and Justice.

The most obvious solution for this institutional anomaly is the introduction of greater accountability, not only for expenditure, but also for income. This could be achieved by granting greater fiscal autonomy to the regions, linked to a system of bonuses for the regions which perform well. Greater accountability could also offer a way out of the current social insurance impasse. A non-emotional assessment of the situation by social and economic experts suggests that 'social federalism' offers the most hopeful long-term possibilities. This implies new levels of accountability, decentralisation and co-ordination, which in turn should result in a better, fairer and more transparent resource distribution system. A basic scenario might involve the retention of a nationally financed social insurance system, but with the option to allocate certain global budgets to the regions, which will then be responsible for their internal distribution and use. Employment policy is another area where there seems to be scope for further reform. Statistics show conclusively that the average age of the unemployed is significantly higher in Flanders than in Wallonia. These different problems obviously require different solutions, which a regionalised approach could ensure. This would also be in keeping with the basic premise of federalism, which states that policy-making powers should be entrusted to the institutional level which can put them to most effective use.

On the positive side, it must also be said that the crisis of June 2007 showed that Belgium is a modern, well-organised welfare state with a strong economy, which can operate for long periods on automatic pilot. Nevertheless, the country is currently incapable of developing and implementing the new policies which are necessary to meet new needs and tackle new problems (ageing of the population, immigration, the environment, etc.). The words of King Albert I, written to Minister Van de Vyvere in 1930, still ring true: "I hope, as you do, that the future will bring a certain relaxation of tension, as far as the language question is concerned. This remains, of course, our gravest problem." [157] Could King Albert have been serious when he made these comments? Just the year before, the world economy had spiralled into freefall, following the Wall Street Crash. In Germany, the radical NSDAP had begun its dramatic rise to power. Given this background, were regional disputes over 'national' rights and language facilities really the most serious challenges facing the Belgian nation in 1930? From an institutional point of view, they undoubtedly were. Because without a proper settlement of the national question, it is impossible for governments in Belgium to take meaningful action on other, more fundamental matters. This was proved again during the 1980s, when measures to fight a new economic depression could only be taken *after* a programme of state reforms dealing with regional issues had been agreed. And this continues to be the case in 2010. It will only be possible to meet the new challenges of our modern society if the Belgian regions can first reach agreement on their own more parochial differences. Because it is these differences which set the ground rules for political negotiations in Belgium. It is also these differences which determine the financial and policy frameworks. In this sense, the nationality question is indeed still the "gravest problem" in Belgium.

Endnotes

Endnotes

The endnotes only refer to direct quotations. For other matters, please refer to the chapter by chapter bibliography at the end of the book.

1. Quoted by L. Picard, *Geschiedenis van de Vlaamsche en Groot-Nederlandsche beweging*, vol. 1, Antwerp, 1937, p. 271.
2. P.J. Bemelmans, *Receuil administratif contenant les arrêtés, règlements (....) relatifs à l'administration de l'armée*, vol. 5, Brussels, 1833, p. 315-316.
3. F. Prims, *Karel Theodoor le Bon, 1777-1834*, Antwerp, 1935, p. 133-144.
4. H. Conscience, *Geschiedenis mijner jeugd*, s.d., p. 267 and 268.
5. Quoted by H.J. Elias, *Geschiedenis van de Vlaamse gedachte*, vol. 2, Antwerp, 1971, p. 139.
6. *Denkwurdigkeiten aus den Papieren des Freiherrn Chr. Fr. von Stockmar*, Braunschweig, 1872, p. 366.
7. *Kölnische Zeitung*, circa 26 July 1847 (see Th. Coopman & J. Broeckaert, *Bibliographie van den Vlaamschen Taalstrijd*, Ghent, 1904-1914, no. 1327).
8. Cfr. *L'Indépendance belge*, 9 September 1847 (Th. Coopman & J. Broeckaert, *Bibliographie van den Vlaamschen Taalstrijd*, no. 1353).
9. The quotes are to be found in G. Deneckere, *Sire, het volk mort. Sociaal protest in België (1831-1918)*, Ghent, 1997, p. 131 and 151.
10. Cf. *Annales Parlementaires de Belgique, Chambre des Représentants*, 27 June 1849, p. 1705-1708, and 28 June 1849, p. 1711-1714.
11. Th. Coopman & J. Broeckaert, *Bibliographie*, no.1652.
12. The appeal of the Central Committee from 15 March 1853 in Th. Coopman & J. Broeckaert, *Bibliographie*, no. 1946; see also *L'Indépendance belge*, 10 April 1853.
13. Letter from Leopold I to Queen Victoria, 13 February 1854, Brussels, Royal Archives, 'correspondence Victoria', vol. 12.
14. *Journal d'Anvers et de la Province*, 4/5 September 1853.
15. L. de Lichtervelde, *Léopold Ier*, p. 276-277. From *Gazette van Ghent*.
16. Letters from Prince Leopold to Goffinet, 6 and 11 September 1856, with the reactions of Goffinet, Brussels, Royal Archives, Fonds Goffinet, *in dato*.
17. Quoted in *120 jaar geleden: de eerste 11 juli-viering in Brugge*, http://lvb.net.
18. Quoted in *De taalstrijd: hier en elders*, Antwerp, 1884-1903, vol. 7 (1890), p. 178.
19. Reception held on 29 February 1892: *De taalstrijd: hier en elders*, vol. 9 (1892), p. 62-65, quotation on p. 64.
20. Brussels, Royal Archives, *Secrétariat des Commandements du Roi*, nr. 261/1.
21. M.-R. Thielemans & E. Vandewoude, *Le Roi Albert, au travers de ses lettres inédites,1882-1916*, Brussels, 1982, p. 258.
22. Letter from King Albert to Jules Bosmans, 30 November 1899, in M.-R. Thielemans & E. Vandewoude, *Le Roi Albert, au travers de ses lettres inédites*, p. 257-258; J. Velaers, *Albert I koning in tijden van oorlog en crisis*, Tielt, 2009, p. 44.
23. The petitions: Brussels, Royal Archives, *Secrétariat des Commandements du Roi*, nr. 261/1.

24 Courts in Ghent, Bruges and Antwerp. Cfr. H. Van Goethem, *De taaltoestanden in het Vlaams-Belgisch gerecht*, p. 216.
25 Letter from the *Zuid-Vlaamsche Sprekersbond* to Joris Helleputte, 1892, quoted by T. Raeymaekers, *De politieke strijd om de Gelijkheidswet*, Masters thesis, unedited, State University of Ghent (Rijksuniversiteit Gent), History Department, 1997-98, p. 20.
26 Cfr. P. Pierson, 'Increasing returns, path dependence, and the structure of politics', *American Political Science Review*, 2000, p. 251-267; J. Mahoney, *The Legacies of Liberalism: Path Dependence and Political Regimes in Central America*, Baltimore-London, 2001; J. Mahoney & D. Rueschemeyer (eds.), *Comparative Historical Analysis in the Social Sciences*, Cambridge-New York, 2003, in particular the analysis made by Ira Katznelson (p. 81-112).
27 For example F. Sabetti, 'Path dependency and civic culture: some lessons from Italy about interpreting social experiments', *Politics and Society*, 1996, p. 19-44.
28 Quoted by M. Van Ginderachter, *Het rode vaderland. De vergeten geschiedenis van de communautaire spanningen in het Belgische socialisme voor WOI*, Tielt, 2005, p. 177.
29 Quoted by T. Raeymaekers, *De politieke strijd om de Gelijkheidswet*, p. 70.
30 Quoted by T. Raeymaekers, *De politieke strijd om de Gelijkheidswet*, p. 75.
31 *Annales Parlementaires de Belgique, Chambre des Représentants*, 28 January 1897, p. 234-236; T. Raeymaekers, *De politieke strijd om de Gelijkheidswet*, p. 82.
32 In *Mercure de France*, April 1897, p. 101. Cfr. W. Houtman, *Vlaamse & Waalse documenten over Federalisme*, s.l., 1954, p. 54; R. de Nolf, *Federalisme in België*, p. 108-109.
33 For example, the political programme put forward by Émile Jennissen (a liberal from Liege) in 1911, concerning an administrative partition of the country : 'Aucun texte ou document émanant du pouvoir central ne sera publié en flamand en Wallonie et le bilinguisme des timbres, cartes, Indicateur [Railway Guide] etc... disparaîtra, afin de chasser l'inscription flamande de nous.' In W. Houtman, *Vlaamse & Waalse documenten over federalisme*, p. 26.
34 Cf. Ph. Destatte, *L'identité wallonne. Essai sur l'affirmation politique de la Wallonie aux XIX en XXèmes siècles*, Charleroi, 1997, p. 64-65.
35 Antwerp, Letterenhuis, Juliaan De Vriendt Files, V9086/B.
36 *Annales Parlementaires de Belgique, Chambre des Représentants*, 16 March 1898, p. 861 and 17 March 1898, p. 882. T. Raeymaekers, *De politieke strijd om de Gelijkheidswet*, p. 127 and p. 129.
37 J. Erk, 'Sub-state nationalism and the left-right divide: critical junctures in the formation of nationalist labour movements in Belgium', *Nations and Nationalism*, 2005, p. 551-570.
38 O. Boehme, *Greep naar de markt*, p. 941-942 and *passim*.
39 J. Destrée, *Lettre au roi sur la séparation de la Wallonie et de la Flandre,* Brussels, 1912, p. 20.
40 Cf . Ph. Destatte, *L'identité wallonne*, p. 69.
41 H. Van Velthoven, *De Vlaamse kwestie*, p. 222.
42 Quoted by R. de Nolf, *Federalisme in België*, p. 119.
43 R. de Nolf, *Federalisme in België*, p. 127-133.

44 *Hooger Leven*, 31 January 1914.
45 A. Duchesne, 'L'armée et la politique militaire belges de 1871 à 1920 jugées par les attachés militaires de France à Bruxelles', *Revue Belge de Philologie et d'Histoire*, 1961-62, p. 1115.
46 Draft text in: Brussels, Royal Archives, Cabinet King Albert I, nr. 283.
47 M.-R. Thielemans & E. Vandewoude, *Le Roi Albert, au travers de ses lettres inédites*, p. 433-435.
48 *De Nieuwe Gazet*, 16 August 1912.
49 M.-R. Thielemans & E. Vandewoude, *Le Roi Albert, au travers de ses lettres inédites*, p. 69 and p. 435-436.
50 M.-R. Thielemans, *Albert Ier. Carnets et correspondance de guerre 1914-1918*, Paris, 1991, p. 29.
51 King Albert, quoted by M.-R. Thielemans, *Albert Ier. Carnets*, p. 123-126.
52 S. De Schaepdrijver, *De Groote Oorlog*, p. 151-154; see also L. Wils, *Flamenpolitik en activisme*, p. 45-55.
53 M.-R. Thielemans & E. Vandewoude, *Le Roi Albert, au travers de ses lettres inédites*, p. 591-592. See also S. De Schaepdrijver, *De Groote Oorlog*, p. 155-156.
54 Letter of 22 July 1916, quoted by D. Vanacker, *De Frontbeweging*, p. 72.
55 L. Schepens, *Koning Albert, Charles de Broqueville en de Vlaamse beweging*, p. 58; L. Wils, *Frans Van Cauwelaert en de barst van België*, p. 166-167.
56 Quoted by D. Vanacker, *De Frontbeweging*, p. 69.
57 'Parler au Roi : 8. Ecole (flamand et français)'. Annotation by Broqueville, 14 February 1916, Brussels, Central State Archives, de Broqueville Files, nr. 372.
58 In V. Janssens, *Burggraaf Aloys van de Vyvere in de geschiedenis van zijn tijd (1871-1961)*, Tielt, 1982, p. 86.
59 Brussels, Royal Archives, Military House King Albert I (Galet), nr. 6/1.
60 M.-R. Thielemans, *Albert Ier. Carnets*, p. 278.
61 M.-R. Thielemans, *Albert Ier. Carnets*, p. 282.
62 L. Schepens, *Koning Albert, Charles de Broqueville en de Vlaamse beweging*, p. 282.
63 M.-R. Thielemans, *Albert Ier. Carnets*, p. 286.
64 L. Schepens, *Koning Albert, Charles de Broqueville en de Vlaamse beweging*, p. 119.
65 Quoted by L. Wils, *Frans Van Cauwelaert en de barst van België*, p. 196.
66 L. Wils, *Frans Van Cauwelaert en de barst van België*, p. 200.
67 L. Schepens, *Koning Albert, Charles de Broqueville en de Vlaamse beweging*, p. 114-117 and L. Wils, *Frans Van Cauwelaert en de barst van België*, p. 199-200; D. Vanacker, *De Frontbeweging*, p. 131.
68 D. Vanacker, *De Frontbeweging*, p. 194-196; the quotation is on p. 194.
69 A. Duchesne, 'L'armée et la politique militaire belges de 1871 à 1920', *Revue Belge de Philologie et d'Histoire*, 1961-62, p. 1210.
70 M.E. Belpaire, *Gestalten in 't Verleden*, Bruges, 1947, p. 272, 281, 300.
71 L. Wils, *Frans Van Cauwelaert en de barst van België*, p. 213-214.
72 Quoted by M.-R. Thielemans, *Albert Ier. Carnets*, p. 122.

73 Quoted by R. Boijen, *De taalwetgeving in het Belgische leger*, p. 76.
74 D. Vanacker, *De Frontbeweging*, p. 172-173.
75 D. Vanacker, *De Frontbeweging*, p. 199-201.
76 Quoted by L. Wils, *Frans Van Cauwelaert en de barst van België*, p. 227.
77 Quoted by L. Wils, *Frans Van Cauwelaert en de barst van België*, p. 227-228.
78 R. Boijen, *De taalwetgeving in het Belgische leger*, p. 86, report dated 13 August; A. Duchesne, 'L'armée et la politique militaire belges', op.cit., p. 127; D. Vanacker, *De Frontbeweging*, p. 225; M.-R. Thielemans, *Carnets et correspondance*, p. 123 (by mistake the quotations are dated 13 March).
79 Quotes by D. Vanacker, *De Frontbeweging*, p. 220.
80 M.E. Belpaire, *Gestalten*, p. 301.
81 R. Boijen, *De taalwetgeving in het Belgische leger*, p. 87.
82 D. Vanacker, *De Frontbeweging*, p. 225-228; also the quotations.
83 Cfr. D. Vanacker, *De Frontbeweging*, p.230.
84 Quoted by D. Vanacker, *De Frontbeweging*, p. 46
85 Quoted by D. Vanacker, *De Frontbeweging*, p. 287.
86 Quoted by D. Vanacker, *De Frontbeweging*, p. 45.
87 Quoted by D. Vanacker, *De Frontbeweging*, p. 46.
88 Quoted by D. Vanacker, *De Frontbeweging*, p. 283.
89 Quoted by D. Vanacker, *De Frontbeweging*, p. 284.
90 Cfr. D. Vanacker, *De Frontbeweging*, p. 229-230, 241; R. Boijen, *De taalwetgeving in het Belgische leger*, p. 87-88; L. Schepens, *Koning Albert, Charles de Broqueville en de Vlaamse beweging*, p. 127-134.
91 Minutes of the Cabinet Council, Brussels, Central State Archives, de Broqueville Files, nr. 382; R. Boijen, *De taalwetgeving in het Belgische leger*, p. 91.
92 Letter dated 17 October 1917, Antwerp, Letterenhuis, Alfons Van de Perre Files; D. Vanacker, *De Frontbeweging*, p. 243.
93 M.-R. Thielemans, *Albert Ier. Carnets*, p. 124 and p. 125.
94 Quoted by L. Schepens, *Koning Albert, Charles de Broqueville en de Vlaamse beweging*, p. 167.
95 *In extenso* in M.-R. Thielemans, *Albert Ier. Carnets*, p. 453-454. Cf. also the letter from King Albert to Prosper Poullet, 25 June 1929, in J. Velaers, *Albert I*, p. 940.
96 *Annales parlementaires de Belgique, Chambres Réunis*, 22 November 1918, p. 4-5.
97 *Annales parlementaires de Belgique. Chambre des Représentants*, 28 November 1918, p. 11.
98 J. Velaers, *Albert I*, p. 838.
99 Note by M.-L Gérard to King Albert, Brussels, Royal Archives, quoted by G. Deneckere, 'Lode Wils en Koning Albert I', *Wetenschappelijke Tijdingen op het gebied van de geschiedenis van de Vlaamse Beweging*, 1996, p. 176-195, in annex.
100 L. Wils, *Frans Van Cauwelaert en de barst van België*, p. 63.
101 Quoted by L. Wils, *Burgemeester Van Cauwelaert 1923-1932*, p. 18.
102 Cfr. J. De Volder, *Benoît XV et la Belgique durant la Grande Guerre*, Brussels-Rome 1996, p. 191. Jan De Volder provided me with the Italian text.

103 M.-R. Thielemans, 'La chute du gouvernement d'union nationale et la formation du Cabinet Theunis, 1921', *Revue Belge de Philologie et d'Histoire*, 1979, p. 372.
104 J. Velaers, *Albert I*, p.877-893.
105 *Albert, un roi, une époque*, Brussels, 1975, p. 75. See also J. Velaers, *Albert I*, p. 893: in a letter to the Walloon P. Berryer, Albert did not mention the word '*provisoire*'.
106 Letter from Theunis to King Albert, 21 December 1923, in R. Boijen, *De taalwetgeving in het Belgische leger*, p. 166; see also the answer from the king, the same day, in J. Velaers, *Albert I*, p. 912.
107 M.-R. Thielemans, 'Le Roi Albert et Georges Theunis, premier ministre', in *Actes du colloque Roi Albert. Handelingen van het colloquium Koning Albert*, Brussels, 1976, p. 325-326; the quotation is on p. 326.
108 Quoted by G. Deneckere, 'Oudstrijders op de vuist in Brussel. Het amnestieconflict tijdens het interbellum', *Belgisch Tijdschrift voor Nieuwste Geschiedenis*, 1994-1995, p. 281.
109 M. Cordemans, *Edmond Rubbens: een levensverhaal*, Ghent, 1965, p. 243.
110 V. Janssens, *Burggraaf Aloys van de Vyvere*, p. 225.
111 In G. Deneckere, *Turbulentie*, p. 207 and 230.
112 Quoted by A. von Busekist, *La Belgique. Politique des langues et la construction de l'État de 1780 à nos jours*, Louvain-la-Neuve, 1998, p. 238.
113 Cfr. H. Van Goethem, *100 jaar Vlaams rechtsleven*, p. 114-116.
114 Brussels, Royal Archives, Louis Wodon Files, 1/2 (draft). Cfr. J. Velaers, *Op de grens*, p. 451-452.
115 *Nieuw Vlaanderen*, 31 August 1935.
116 G. Deneckere, 'Oudstrijders op de vuist in Brussel', op.cit., p. 289.
117 G. Deneckere, 'Oudstrijders op de vuist in Brussel', op.cit., p. 302.
118 Dutch text in *De Morgenpost*, 3 July 1937.
119 O. Boehme, *Greep naar de markt*, p. 481. See also the quotations of Troclet.
120 O. Boehme, *Greep naar de markt*, p. 484.
121 With regard to the Political Testament: J. Velaers & H. Van Goethem, *Leopold III. De Koning, het Land, de Oorlog*, p. 830-847.
122 Quoted by H. Van Goethem, 'Prins Karel, regent van België', in *De democratie heruitgevonden*, p. 108. See also V. Dujardin, *Pierre Harmel*, p. 257-277 on King Boudewijn in the fifties.
123 G. Eyskens, *De memoires*, p. 471-479.
124 King Boudewijn's official speeches to the nation are published in *Koning Boudewijn, 35 jaar dialoog met de Natie. Een keuze uit de koninklijke toespraken van 1951 tot 1986*, Tielt, 1986; and also *Koninklijke toespraken*, 2 vol., T. Luykx & E. De Bens (eds.), Brussels, 1973-1982.
125 Cfr. G. Eyskens, *De Memoires*, Tielt, 1993, p. 701-708.
126 L. Tindemans, *De memoires. Gedreven door een overtuiging*, Tielt, 2002, p. 32-33.
127 G. Eyskens, *De Memoires*, p. 724.
128 *Documents Parlementaires de Belgique, Sénat*, 1969-70, no. 391, p. 14. Cfr. J. Clement, *Taalvrijheid, bestuurstaal en minderheidsrechten*, p. 666.

129 Quoted by J. Clement, *Taalvrijheid, bestuurstaal en minderheidsrechten*, p. 667.
130 *Annales Parlementaires de Belgique, Sénat*, 7 July 1971, p. 2368.
131 J. Clement, *Taalvrijheid, bestuurstaal en minderheidsrechten*, p. 668.
132 G. Eyskens, *De Memoires*, p. 854 and p. 856.
133 G. Eyskens, *De Memoires*, p. 950. See also G. Eyskens, *Het laatste gesprek: herinneringen aan veertig jaar politiek leven*, J. Smits (ed.), Kapellen, 1988, p. 194.
134 L. Tindemans, *De memoires*, p. 223.
135 W. Martens, *De memoires*, p. 771-772. Cfr. also J.-L. Dehaene, *Er is nog leven na de 16*, Leuven, 2002, p. 88-90.
136 L. Tindemans, *De memoires*, p. 368, p. 380, p. 382 and p. 384.
137 W. Martens, *De memoires*, p. 153.
138 W. Martens, *De memoires*, p. 321.
139 H. De Ridder, *Sire, geef me honderd dagen*, Leuven, 1989, p. 86.
140 W. Martens, *De memoires*, p. 459.
141 D. Ilegems and J. Willems, *De kroon ontbloot*, p. 30.
142 Chr. Laporte, *Albert II. De biografie*, Tielt, 2003, p. 168-174.
143 Royal address by King Albert II, December 2004.
144 *De Burgerkrant*, October 2002, p. 19.
145 *Story Magazine*, 1 December 2004.
146 B. Leyts, B. Balfoort and M. Van den Wijngaert, *Kroonprins Filip*, p. 187-188.
147 S. Khilnani, 'The development of civil society', in *Civil Society. History and Possibilities*, S. Kaviraj and S. Khilnani (eds.), Cambridge, 2001, p. 11-32.
148 Letter from Leopold I to Princess Charlotte, Brussels, Royal Archives, 'Empress Charlotte of Mexico', correspondence from Leopold to Charlotte 1864-1865, 15.
149 J. Mahoney, *The Legacies of Liberalism: Path Dependence and Political Regimes in Central America*, Baltimorte, 2001, p. 6.
150 E. Gellner, *Nations and nationalism*, Oxford, 1983.
151 H. Welzer, *Täter. Wie auch normalen Menschen Massenmörder werden*, Frankfurt am Main, 2005.
152 D. Van Dam, *Blijven we buren in België? Vlamingen en Walen over Vlamingen en Walen*, Leuven, 1996, p. 108.
153 In 2007, quoted by L. Beyer de Ryke, *La Belgique en sursis*, Paris, 2008, p. 35-36.
154 Onkelinckx said: *'Vous savez ce que sont les Flamands? Des mérules, ces champignons qui se nourrissent de bois et rongent la maison de l'intérieur jusqu'à la rendre inhabitable.'* Quoted by L. Beyer de Ryke, *La Belgique en sursis*, Paris, 2008, p. 37.
155 In an interview given to the RTBF on 12 December 2007 and to the VRT on 5 September 2006.
156 *Annales Parlementaires de Belgique, Sénat*, 7 July 1971, p. 2368.
157 V. Janssens, *Burggraaf Aloys van de Vyvere*, p. 225.

Bibliography

Albert, un roi, une époque, Brussels, 1975.

Anderson, B., *Imagined communities. Reflections on the origin and spread of nationalism*, London, 1983.

Boehme, O., *Greep naar de markt. De sociaaleconomische agenda van de Vlaamse Beweging en haar ideologische versplintering tijdens het interbellum*, Tielt, 2008.

Bouva, L., *'Pour les Flamands la même chose'. Hoe de taalgrens ook een sociale grens was*, Ghent, 1994.

Buckinx, H., *Ruim 40 jaar koninklijke toespraken door Koning Boudewijn. Een inhoudsanalyse*, Antwerp, 1994.

Clement, J., *Taalvrijheid, bestuurstaal en minderheidsrechten. Het Belgische model*, Antwerp, 2003.

Comparative Historical Analysis in the Social sciences, J. Mahoney and D. Rueschenmeyers (eds.), Cambridge-New York, 2003.

Coolsaet, R., *België en zijn buitenlandse politiek 1830-1990*, Leuven, 1998.

Coopman Th. and Broeckaert J., *Bibliographie van den Vlaamschen Taalstrijd*, 10 vol., Ghent, 1904-1914.

Deneckere, G., 'Lode Wils en Koning Albert I', *Wetenschappelijke tijdingen op het gebied van de geschiedenis van de Vlaamse Beweging*, 1996, p. 181-196.

De Nolf, R., *Federalisme in België als grondwettelijk vraagstuk*, Antwerp, 1968.

De Ridder, H., *De strijd om de 16*, Tielt, 1993.

De Ridder, H., *Sire, geef me honderd dagen*, Leuven, 1989.

De Schaepdrijver, S., *De Groote Oorlog*, Amsterdam-Antwerp, 1997.

Destatte, Ph., *L'identité wallonne. Essai sur l'affirmation politique de la Wallonie aux XIX en XXèmes siècles*, Charleroi, 1997.

De Wever, B., *Greep naar de macht. Vlaams-nationalisme en Nieuwe Orde, het VNV, 1933-1945*, Tielt, 1994.

Dubois, S., *L'invention de la Belgique. Génèse d'un État-Nation 1648-1830*, Brussels, 2005.

Emmery, R., *Prins Karel. Leven in de schaduw van Leopold III*, Antwerp, 2007.

Erk, J., 'Sub-state nationalism and the left-right divide: critical junctures in the formation of nationalist labour movements in Belgium', *Nations and Nationalism*, 2005, p. 551-570.

Eyskens, G., *De Memoires*, Tielt, 1993.

Eyskens, G., *Het laatste gesprek. Herinneringen aan veertig jaar politiek leven*, J. Smits (ed.), Kapellen, 1988.

Gellner, E., *Nations and nationalism*, Oxford, 1983.

Gerard, E., *De katholieke partij in crisis: partijpolitiek leven in België (1918-1940)*, Leuven 1985.

Haag, H., *Le comte Charles de Broqueville, Ministre d'État, et les luttes pour le pouvoir*, 2 vol., Brussels-Louvain-la Neuve, 1990.

Houtman, W., *Vlaamse & Waalse documenten over Federalisme*, Schepdaal, 1963.

Hunin, J., *Het enfant terrible Camille Huysmans 1871-1968*, Amsterdam-Leuven, 1999.

Ilegems, D. and Willems, J., *De kroon ontbloot. Over de macht van Boudewijn*, Leuven, 1991.

Janssens, V., *Burggraaf Aloys van de Vyvere in de geschiedenis van zijn tijd*, Tielt 1982.

Kesteloot, Ch., *Au nom de la Wallonie et de Bruxelles français. Aux origines du FDF*, Brussels, 2004.

Khilnani, S., 'The development of civil society', in *Civil Society. History and Possibilities*, S. Kaviraj and S. Khilnani (eds.), Cambridge, 2001, p. 11-32.

Koning Boudewijn 35 jaar Dialoog met de Natie. Een keuze uit de koninklijke toespraken van 1951 tot 1986, Tielt, 1986.

Koninklijke toespraken, 2 vol., T. Luykx and E. De Bens (eds.), Brussels, 1973-1982.

Laporte, Chr., *Albert II, premier Roi fédéral*, Brussels, 2004.

Leyts, B., Balfoort, B., and Van den Wijngaert, M., *Kroonprins Filip*, Antwerp-Amsterdam, 2007.

Mahoney, J., *The Legacies of Liberalism: Path Dependence and Political Regimes in central America*, Baltimore-London, 2001.

Martens, W., *De memoires. Luctor et emergo*, Tielt, 2006.

Molitor, A., *La fonction royale en Belgique*, Brussels, 1979.

Nationalisme in België. Identiteiten in beweging 1780-2000, K. Deprez and L. Vos (eds.), Antwerp, 1999.

Nieuwe Encyclopedie van de Vlaamse Beweging, 3 vol., Tielt, 1998.

Pierson, P. 'Increasing returns, path dependence, and the structure of politics', *American Political Science Review*, 2000, p. 251-267.

Reynebeau, M., *Een geschiedenis van België*, Tielt, 2003.

Sabetti, F., 'Path dependency and civic culture: some lessons from Italy about interpreting social experiments', *Politics and Society*, 1996, p. 19-44.

Stengers, J., *L'action du Roi en Belgique depuis 1831. Pouvoir et influence,* Parijs-Louvain-la-Neuve, 1992.

Thielemans, M.-R., *Albert Ier. Carnets et correspondance de guerre 1914-1918*, Parijs, 1991.

Thielemans, M.-R. and Vandewoude, E., *Le Roi Albert, au travers de ses lettre inédites, 1882-1916*, Brussels, 1982.

Tindemans, L., *De memoires. Gedreven door een overtuiging*, Tielt, 2002.

Vanacker, D., *De Frontbeweging: de Vlaamse strijd aan de IJzer*, Koksijde, 2000.

Vanacker, D., *Het aktivistisch avontuur*, Ghent, 1991.

Van Dam, D., *Blijven we buren in België? Vlamingen en Walen over Vlamingen en Walen*, Leuven, 1996

Van Ginderachter, M., *Het rode vaderland. De vergeten geschiedenis van de communautaire spanningen in het Belgische socialisme voor WOI*, Tielt, 2005.

Van Ginderachter, M., *Le chant du coq. Nation et nationalisme en Wallonie depuis 1880*, Ghent, 2005.
Van Goethem, H., *De monarchie en het 'einde van België, Een communautaire geschiedenis van Leopold I tot Albert II*, Tielt, 2008.
Van Goethem, H., *De taaltoestanden in het Vlaams-Belgisch gerecht, 1795-1935*, Brussels, 1990.
Van Velthoven, H., *De Vlaamse kwestie 1830-1914. Macht en onmacht van de vlaamsgezinden*, Kortrijk 1982.
Van Ypersele, L., *Le roi Albert. Histoire d'un mythe*, Ottignies-Louvain-la-Neuve, 1995.
Velaers, J., *Albert I. Koning in tijden van oorlog en crisis*, Tielt, 2009.
Velaers, J., 'De staatshervorming: van een unitaire naar een federale staat', in W. Dewachter e.a. (eds.), *Tussen Staat en Maatschappij 1945-1995. Christen-democratie in België*, Tielt, 1995, p. 378-412.
Velaers, J. and Van Goethem, H., *Leopold III. De Koning, het Land, de Oorlog*, Tielt, 1994.
Von Busekist, A., *La Belgique: politique des langues et construction de l'État de 1780 à nos jours*, Louvain-la-Neuve, 1998.
Waar België voor staat. Een toekomstvisie, G. Buelens, J. Goossens and D. Van Reybrouck (eds.), Antwerp-Amsterdam, 2007.
Wils, L., *Burgemeester Van Cauwelaert 1923-1932. Schepper van de vernederlandsing van Vlaanderen*, Antwerp, 2005.
Wils, L., *Flamenpolitik en activisme*, Leuven 1974.
Wils, L., *Van Clovis tot Di Rupo. De lange weg van de naties in de Lage Landen*, Antwerp, 2005.
Witte, E. and Van Velthoven, H., *Language and politics: the Belgian case study in a historical perspective*, Brussels, 1999.